For All Life

For All Life

Toward a Universal Declaration of a Global Ethic

An Interrreligious Dialogue

Edited by Leonard Swidler

WHITE CLOUD PRESS
ASHLAND, OREGON

01 00 99   5 4 3 2 1

First edition March 1999

Cover design by Impact Graphics
Printed in Canada

Library of Congress Cataloging-in-Publication Data

For all life : toward a universal declaration of a global ethic :
an interreligious dialogue / edited by Leonard Swidler. -- 1st ed.
    p. cm.
  Includes bibliographical references.
  ISBN 1-883991-22-6
  1. Religious ethics. I. Swidler, Leonard J.
  BJ1188 .F67 1998
  291.5 -- ddc21
                            98-42631
                            CIP

Table of Contents

TOWARD A UNIVERSAL DECLARATION OF A GLOBAL ETHIC

LEONARD SWIDLER

Humans TEND TO GROUP themselves in communities with similar understandings of the meaning of life and how to act accordingly. For the most part, in past history such large communities, called cultures or civilizations, have tended on the one hand to live unto themselves, and on the other to dominate and, if possible, absorb the other cultures they encountered. For example, Christendom, Islam, China.

I. The Meaning of Religion (Ideology)

At the heart of each culture is what is traditionally called a Religion, that is: "An explanation of the ultimate meaning of life, and how to live accordingly." Normally all religions contain the four "C's": Creed, Code, Cult, Community-structure, and are based on the notion of the Transcendent.

Creed refers to the cognitive aspect of a religion; it is everything that goes into the "explanation" of the ultimate meaning of life.

Code of behavior or ethics includes all the rules and customs of action that somehow follow from one aspect or another of the *Creed*.

Cult means all the ritual activities that relate the follower to one aspect or other of the Transcendent, either directly or indirectly, prayer being an example of the former and certain formal behavior toward representatives of the Transcendent, like priests, of the latter.

Community-structure refers to the relationships among the followers; this can vary widely, from a very egalitarian relationship, as among Quakers, through a "republican" structure like Presbyterians have, to a monarchical one, as with some Hasidic Jews vis-a-vis their "Rebbe."

The *Transcendent*, as the roots of the word indicate, means "that which goes beyond" the every-day, the ordinary, the surface experience of reality. It can refer to spirits, gods, a Personal God, an Impersonal God, Emptiness, etc.

Especially in modern times there have developed "explanations of the ultimate meaning of life, and how to live accordingly" which are not based on a notion of the Transcendent, e.g., secular humanism, Marxism. Although in every respect these "explanations" function as religions traditionally have in human life, because the idea of the Transcendent, however it is understood, plays such a central role in religion, but not in these "explanations," for the sake of accuracy it is best to give these "explanations" not based on notion of the Transcendent a separate name; the name often used is: *Ideology.* Much, though not all, of the following will, *mutatis mutandis*, also apply to Ideology even when the term is not used.

II. From the Age of Monologue to the Age of Dialogue

1. A Radically New Age

Those scholars who earlier in the twentieth century with a great show of scholarship and historical/sociological analysis predicted the impending demise of Western Civilization were "dead wrong." After World War I, in 1922, Oswald Spengler wrote his widely acclaimed book, *The Decline of the West*.[1] After the beginning of World War II Pitirim A. Sorokin published in 1941 his likewise popular book, *The Crisis of Our Age*.[2] Given the massive, world-wide scale of the unprecedented destruction and horror of the world's first global war, 1914-18, and the even vastly greater of the second global conflict, 1939-45, the pessimistic predictions of these scholars and the great following they found are not ununderstandable.

In fact, however, those vast world conflagrations were manifestations of the dark side of the unique breakthrough in the history of humankind in the modern development of Christendom-become-Western Civilization, now becoming Global Civilization. Never before had there been world wars; likewise, never before had there been world political organizations (League of Nations, United Nations). Never before did humanity possess the real possibility of destroying all human life—whether through nuclear or ecological catastrophe. These unique negative realities/potentialities were possible, however, only because of the correspondingly unique accomplishments of Christendom/Western/Global Civilization—the like of which the world has never before seen. On the negative side, from now on it will always be true that humankind could self-destruct. Still, there are solid empirical grounds for reasonable hope that the inherent, infinity-directed life force of humankind will nevertheless prevail over the parallel death force.

The prophets of doom were correct, however, in their understanding that humanity is entering into a radically new age. Earlier in this century the nay-sayers usually spoke of the doom of only Western Civilization (e.g., Spengler, Sorokin), but after the advent of nuclear power and the Cold War, the new generation of pessimists—as said, not without warrant: *corruptio optimae pessima*—warned of *global* disaster. This emerging awareness of global disaster is a clear, albeit negative, sign that something profoundly, radically new is entering onto the stage of human history.

There have, of course, also recently been a number of more positive signs that we humans are entering a radically new age. In the 1960s there was much talk of "The Age of Aquarius," and there still is today the continuing fad of "New Age" consciousness. Some may be put off from the idea of an emerging radically new age because they perceive such talk to be simply that of fringe groups. I would argue, however, that the presence of "the crazies" around the edge of any idea or movement, far from being a sign of the invalidity of that idea or movement, is on the contrary a confirmation precisely of its validity, at least in its core concern. I would further argue that if people are involved with a movement which does not eventually develop its "crazies," its extremists, the movement is not touching the core of humankind's concerns—they should get out of the movement, they are wasting their time!

Moreover, there have likewise recently been a number of very serious scholarly analyses pointing to the emergence of a radically new age in human history. Two of them will be dealt with in some detail. The first is the concept of the "Paradigm-Shift," particularly as expounded by Hans Küng.[3] The second is the notion of the "Second Axial Period," as articulated by Ewert Cousins.[4] Then, including these two, but setting them in a still larger context, I shall lay out my own analysis, which I see as the movement of humankind out of a multi-millennia long "Age of Monologue" into the newly inbreaking "Age of Dialogue," indeed, an inbreaking "Age of Global Dialogue."

Of course there is a great deal of continuity in human life throughout the shift from one major "Paradigm" to another, from one "Period" to another, from one "Age" to another. Nevertheless, even more striking than this continuity is the ensuing break, albeit largely on a different level than the continuity. This relationship of continuity and break in human history is analogous to the transition of water from solid to fluid to gas with the increase in temperature. With water there is throughout on the chemical level the continuity of H_2O. However, for those who have to deal with the water, it makes a fantastic difference whether the H_2O is ice, water, or steam! In the case of the major changes in humankind, the physical base remains the same, but on the level of consciousness the change is massive. And here too it makes a fantastic difference whether we are dealing with humans whose consciousness is formed within one paradigm or within another, whose consciousness is Pre-Axial, Axial-I or Axial-II, whose consciousness is Monologic or Dialogic.

2. A Major Paradigm-Shift

Thomas Kuhn revolutionized our understanding of the development of scientific thinking with his notion of paradigm shifts. He painstakingly showed that fundamental "paradigms" or "exemplary models" are the large thought frames within which we place and interpret all observed data and that scientific advancement inevitably brings about eventual paradigm shifts—from geocentricism to heliocentrism, for example, or from Newtonian to Einsteinian physics—which are always vigorously resisted at first, as was the thought of Galileo, but finally prevail.[5] This insight, however, is valid not only for the development of thought in the natural sciences, but also applicable to all major disciplines of human thought, including religious thought. For example, the move from the Semitic thought world of Jesus and his followers into the Hellenistic world of early Christianity and then into the Byzantine and Medieval Western Christian worlds, and further, generated a number of greater and lesser paradigm shifts in European religion and culture over the centuries.

3. The Modern Major Paradigm-shift

Since the eighteenth century European Enlightenment, Christendom-now-become-Western Civilization has been undergoing a major paradigm shift, especially in how we humans understand our process of understanding and what meaning and status we attribute to "truth," that is, to our statements about reality—in other words, to our epistemology. This new epistemological paradigm is increasingly determining how we perceive, conceive, think about, and subsequently decide and act on things.

It is difficult to overestimate the importance of the role in religion, in the "ultimate understanding of reality and how to live accordingly," played by the conceptual paradigm or model one has of reality. The paradigm within which we perceive reality not only profoundly affects our theoretical understanding of reality, but also has immense practical consequences. For example, in Western medicine the body is usually conceived of as a highly nuanced, living machine, and therefore if one part wears out, the obvious thing to do is to replace the worn part—hence, organ transplants originated in Western, but not in Oriental, medicine.

However, in Oriental, Chinese, medicine, the body is conceived of as a finely balanced harmony: "pressure" exerted on one part of the body is assumed to have an opposite effect in some other part of the body—hence, acupuncture originated in Oriental, but not in Western, medicine.[6] Our conceptual paradigms have concrete consequences.

Furthermore, obviously some particular paradigms or models for perceiving reality will fit the data better than others, and they will then be preferred—e.g., the shift from the geocentric to the heliocentric model in astronomy. But sometimes differing models will *each* in their own ways "fit" the data more or less adequately, as in the example of Western and Oriental medicines. The differing models are then viewed as complementary. Clearly it would be foolish to limit one's perception of reality to only one of the complementary paradigms.

Let me turn now to the post-Enlightenment epistemological Paradigm-Shift. Whereas the Western notion of truth was largely absolute,
static, and monologic or exclusive up to the past century, it has since
become deabsolutized, dynamic and dialogic—in a word, it has become "relational."[7] This "new" view of truth came about in at least six
different, but closely related, ways. In brief they are:

a. Historicism: Truth is deabsolutized by the perception that reality is always described in terms of the circumstances of the
   time in which it is expressed.
b. Intentionality: Seeking the truth with the intention of acting
   accordingly deabsolutizes the statement.
c. Sociology of knowledge: Truth is deabsolutized in terms of
   geography, culture, and social standing.
d. Limits of language: Truth as the meaning of something, and
   especially as talk about the transcendent, is deabsolutized by
   the nature of human language.
e. Hermeneutics: All truth, all knowledge, is seen as interpreted
   truth, knowledge, and hence is deabsolutized by the observer
   who is always also interpreter.
f. Dialogue: The knower engages reality in a dialogue in a language the knower provides, thereby deabsolutizing all statements about reality.[8]

In sum, our understanding of truth and reality has been undergoing a radical shift. This new paradigm which is being born under-
stands all statements about reality, especially about the meaning of
things, to be historical, intentional, perspectival, partial, interpretive
and dialogic. What is common to all these qualities is the notion of
relationality, that is, that all expressions or understandings of reality
are in some fundamental way related to the speaker or knower. It is
while bearing this paradigm shift in mind that we proceed with our
analysis.

Before the nineteenth century in Europe, truth (that is, *a statement about
reality*) was conceived in quite an absolute, static, exclusivistic either-or
manner. If something was true at one time, it was always true; not only
empirical facts but also the meaning of things or the oughtness that
was said to flow from them were thought of in this way. At bottom, the

notion of truth was based exclusively on the Aristotelian principle of contradiction: a thing could not be true and not true in the same way at the same time. Truth was defined by way of exclusion; A was A because it could be shown not to be not-A. Truth was thus understood to be absolute, static, exclusivistically either-or. This is a *classicist* or *absolutist* view of truth.

a. Historicism:

In the nineteenth century many scholars came to perceive all statements about the truth of the meaning of something as partially the products of their historical circumstances. Those concrete circumstances helped determine the fact that the statement under study was even called forth, that it was couched in particular intellectual categories (for example, abstract Platonic, or concrete legal, language), particular literary forms (for example, mythic or metaphysical language), and particular psychological settings (such as a polemic response to a specific attack). These scholars argued that only if the truth statements were placed in their historical situation, their historical *Sitz im Leben*, could they be properly understood. The understanding of the text could be found only in context. To express that same original meaning in a later *Sitz im Leben* one would require a proportionately different statement. Thus, all statements about the meaning of things were now seen to be deabsolutized in terms of time.

This is a *historical* view of truth. Clearly at its heart is a notion of *relationality*: any statement about the truth of the meaning of something has to be understood in relationship to its historical context.

b. Intentionality:

Later thinkers like Max Scheler added a corollary to this historicizing of knowledge; it concerned not the past but the future. Such scholars also saw truth as having an element of intentionality at its base, as being oriented ultimately toward action, or praxis. They argued that we perceive certain things as questions to be answered and set goals to pursue specific knowledge because we wish to do something about those matters; we intend to live according to the truth and meaning that we hope to discern in the answers to the questions we pose, in the knowledge we decide to seek. The truth of the meaning of things was thus seen as deabsolutized by the action-oriented intentionality of the thinker-speaker.

This is an *intentional* or *praxis* view of truth, and it too is basically *relational*: a statement has to be understood in relationship to the action-oriented intention of the speaker.

c. The sociology of knowledge:
Just as statements of truth about the meaning of things were seen by some thinkers to be historically deabsolutized in time, so too, starting in this century with scholars like Karl Mannheim, such statements began to be seen as deabsolutized by such things as the culture, class and gender of the thinker-speaker, regardless of time. All reality was said to be perceived from the perspective of the perceiver's own world view. Any statement of the truth of the meaning of something was seen to be perspectival, "standpoint-bound" (*standortgebunden*), as Karl Mannheim put it, and thus deabsolutized.

This is a *perspectival* view of truth and is likewise *relational*: all statements are fundamentally related to the standpoint of the speaker.

d. The limitations of language:
Following Ludwig Wittgenstein and others, many thinkers have come to see that any statement about the truth of things can be at most only a partial description of the reality it is trying to describe. Although reality can be seen from an almost limitless number of perspectives, human language can express things from only one perspective at one time. If this is now seen to be true of what we call "scientific truths," it is so much the more true of statements about the truth of the meaning of things. The very fact of dealing with the truth of the "meaning" of something indicates that the knower is essentially involved and hence reflects the perspectival character of all such statements.

A statement may be true, of course—it may accurately describe the extramental reality it refers to—but it will always be cast in particular categories, language, concerns, etc., of a particular "standpoint," and in that sense will be limited, deabsolutized.

This also is a *perspectival* view of truth, and therefore also *relational*.

This limited and limiting, as well as liberating, quality of language is especially clear in talk of the transcendent. The transcendent is by definition that which goes beyond our experience. Any statements about the transcendent must thus be deabsolutized and limited far beyond the perspectival character seen in ordinary statements.

e. Hermeneutics:

Hans-Georg Gadamer and Paul Riceour recently led the way in developing the science of hermeneutics, which, by arguing that all knowledge of a text is at the same time an *interpretation* of the text, further deabsolutizes claims about the "true" meaning of the text. But this basic insight goes beyond knowledge of texts and applies to all knowledge. In all knowledge *I* come to know something; the object comes into me in a certain way, namely, through the lens that I use to perceive it. As St. Thomas Aquinas stated: "Things known are in the knower according to the mode of the knower—*cognita sunt in cognoscente secundum modum cognoscentis.*"[9]

This is an *interpretive* view of truth. It is clear that *relationality* pervades this hermeneutical, interpretative, view of truth.

f. Dialogue:

A further development of this basic insight is that I learn not by being merely passively open or receptive to, but by being in dialogue with, extramental reality. I not only "hear" or receive reality, but I also—and, I think, first of all—"speak" to reality. I ask it questions, I stimulate it to speak back to me, to answer my questions. In the process I give reality the specific categories and language in which to respond to me. The "answers" that I receive back from reality will always be in the language, the thought categories, of the questions I put to it. It can "speak" to me, can really communicate with my mind, only in a language and categories that I understand.

When the speaking, the responding, grows less and less understandable to me, if the answers I receive are sometimes confused and unsatisfying, then I probably need to learn to speak a more appropriate language when I put questions to reality. If, for example, I ask the question, "How far is yellow?" of course I will receive a non-sense answer. Or if I ask questions about living things in mechanical categories, I will receive confusing and unsatisfying answers.

This is a *dialogic* view of truth, whose very name reflects its *relationality*.

With this new and irreversible understanding of the meaning of truth, the critical thinker has undergone a radical Copernican turn. Just as the vigorously resisted shift in astronomy from geocentrism to heliocentrism revolutionized that science, the paradigm shift in the understanding of truth statements has revolutionized all the humanities, including theology-ideology. The macro-paradigm with which critical thinkers operate today is characterized by historical, social, linguistic, hermeneutical, praxis and dialogic—*relational*—consciousness. This paradigm shift is far advanced among thinkers and doers; but as in the case of Copernicus, and even more dramatically of Galileo, there are still many resisters in positions of great institutional power.

With the deabsolutized view of the truth of the meaning of things we come face to face with the specter of relativism, the opposite pole of absolutism. Unlike *relationality*, a neutral term which merely denotes the quality of being in relationship, *relativism*, like so many "isms," is a basically negative term. If it can no longer be claimed that any statement of the truth of the meaning of things is absolute, totally objective, because the claim does not square with our experience of reality, it is equally impossible to claim that every statement of the truth of the meaning of things is completely relative, totally subjective, for that also does not square with our experience of reality, and of course would logically lead to an atomizing isolation which would stop all discourse, all statements to others.

Our perception, and hence description, of reality is like our view of an object in the center of a circle of viewers. My view and description of the object, or reality, will be true, but it will not include what someone on the other side of the circle perceives and describes, which will also be true. So, neither of our perceptions and descriptions of reality is total, complete—"absolute" in that sense—or "objective" in the sense of not in any way being dependent on a "subject" or viewer. At the same time, however, it is also obvious that there is an "objective," doubtless "true" aspect to each perception and description, even though each is relational to the perceiver-"subject."

But if we can no longer hold to an absolutist view of the truth of he meaning of things, we must take certain steps so as not to be logically forced into the silence of total relativism. First, besides striving to be as accurate and fair as possible in gathering and assessing information and submitting it to the critiques of our peers and other thinkers and scholars, we need also to dredge out, state clearly, and analyze our own pre-suppositions—a constant, ongoing task. Even in this of course we will be operating from a particular "standpoint."

Therefore, we need, secondly, to complement our constantly critiqued statements with statements from different "stand-points." That is, we need to engage in dialogue with those who have differing cultural, philosophical, social, religious viewpoints so as to strive toward an ever fuller perception of the truth of the meaning of things. If we do not engage in such dialogue we will not only be trapped within the perspective of our own "standpoint," but will now also be unaware of our lack. We will no longer with integrity be able to remain deliberately turned in on ourselves. Our search for the truth of the meaning of things makes it a necessity for us as human beings to engage in dialogue. Knowingly to refuse dialogue today could be an act of fundamental human irresponsibility—in Judeo-Christian terms, a sin.

4. The Second Axial Period[10]

It was the German philosopher Karl Jaspers who almost a half-century ago in his book *The Origin and Goal of History*[11] pointed to the "axial" quality of the transformation of consciousness that occurred in the ancient world. He called the period from 800-200 B.C.E. the "Axial Period" because "it gave birth to everything which, since then, man has been able to be." It is here in this period "that we meet with the most deepcut dividing line in history. Man, as we know him today, came into being. For short, we may style this the `Axial Period.'"[12] Although the leaders who effected this change were philosophers and religious teachers, the change was so radical that it affected all aspects of culture, for it transformed consciousness itself. It was within the horizons of this form of consciousness that the great civilizations of Asia, the Middle East, and Europe developed. Although within these horizons many developments occurred through the subsequent centuries, the horizons themselves did not change. It was this form of consciousness which spread to other regions through migration and explorations, thus becoming the dominant, though not exclusive, form of consciousness in the world. To this day, whether we have been born and raised in the culture of China, India, Europe, or the Americas, we bear the structure of consciousness that was shaped in this Axial Period.

What is this structure of consciousness and how does it differ from pre-Axial consciousness? Prior to the Axial Period the dominant form of consciousness was cosmic, collective, tribal, mythic, and ritualistic. This is the characteristic form of consciousness of primal peoples. It is true that between these traditional cultures and the Axial Period there emerged great empires in Egypt, China, and Mesopotamia, but they did not yet produce the full consciousness of the Axial Period.

The consciousness of the tribal cultures was intimately related to the cosmos and to the fertility cycles of nature. Thus there was established a rich and creative harmony between primal peoples and the world of nature, a harmony which was explored, expressed, and celebrated in myth and ritual. Just as they felt themselves part of nature, so they experienced themselves as part of the tribe. It was precisely the web of interrelationships within the tribe that sustained them psychologically, energizing all aspects of their lives. To be separated from the tribe threatened them with death, not only physical but psychological as well. However, their relation to the collectivity often did not extend beyond their own tribe, for they often looked upon other tribes as hostile. Yet within their tribe they felt organically related to their group as a whole, to the life cycles of birth and death and to nature and the cosmos.

The Axial Period ushered in a radically new form of consciousness. Whereas primal consciousness was tribal, Axial consciousness was individual. "Know thyself" became the watchword of Greece; the Upanishads identified the *atman*, the transcendent center of the self; Gautama charted the way of individual enlightenment; Confucius laid out the individual's ethical path; the Jewish prophets awakened individual moral responsibility for powerless persons. This sense of individual identity, as distinct from the tribe and from nature, is the most characteristic mark of Axial consciousness.

From this flow other characteristics: consciousness which is self-reflective, analytic, and which can be applied to nature in the form of scientific theories, to society in the form of social critique, to knowledge in the form of philosophy, to religion in the form of mapping an individual spiritual journey. This self-reflective, analytic, critical consciousness stood in sharp contrast to primal mythic and ritualistic consciousness. When self-reflective *logos* emerged in the Axial Period, it tended to oppose the traditional *mythos*. Of course, mythic and ritualistic forms of consciousness survive in the post-Axial Period even to this day, but they are often submerged, surfacing chiefly in dreams, literature, and art.

Following the lead of Ewert Cousins, if we shift our gaze from the first millennium B.C.E. to the eve of the twenty-first century, we can discern another transformation of consciousness, which is so profound and far-reaching that he calls it the "Second Axial Period."[13] Like the first, it is happening simultaneously around the earth, and like the first it will shape the horizon of consciousness for future centuries. Not surprisingly, too, it will have great significance for world religions, which were constituted in the First Axial Period. However, the new form of consciousness is different from that of the First Axial Period. Then it was individual consciousness, now it is global consciousness.

This global consciousness which is generated on a "horizontal" level through the world-wide meeting of cultures and religions, is only one of the global characteristics of the Second Axial Period. The consciousness of this period is global in another sense, namely, in rediscovering its roots in the earth. At the very moment when the various cultures and religions are meeting each other and creating a new global community, our life on the planet is being threatened. The very tools which we have used to bring about this convergence—industrialization and technology—are undercutting the biological support system that sustains life on our planet. The future of consciousness, even life on the earth, is shrouded in a cloud of uncertainty.

Cousins is not suggesting a romantic attempt to live in the past, rather that the evolution of consciousness proceeds by way of recapitulation. Having developed self-reflective, analytic, critical consciousness in the First Axial Period, we must now, while retaining these values, reappropriate and integrate into that consciousness the collective and cosmic dimensions of the pre-Axial consciousness. We must recapture the unity of tribal consciousness by seeing humanity as a single tribe.

Further, we must see this single tribe related organically to the total cosmos. This means that the consciousness of the twenty-first century will be global from two perspectives: (1) from a horizontal perspective, cultures and religions must meet each other on the surface of the globe, entering into creative encounters that will produce a complexified collective consciousness; (2) from a vertical perspective, they must plunge their roots deep into the earth in order to provide a stable and secure base for future development. This new global consciousness must be organically ecological, supported by structures that will insure justice and peace. The voices of the oppressed must be heard and heeded: the poor, women, racial and ethnic minorities. These groups, along with the earth itself, can be looked upon as the prophets and teachers of the Second Axial Period. This emerging twofold global consciousness is not only a creative possibility to enhance the twenty-first century; it is an absolute necessity if we are to survive.

5. Globalization

Since the 16th-century European "Age of Discovery," the earth has tended more and more to become, as Wendell Wilkie put it in 1940, "One World." This increasingly happened in the form of "Christendom" dominating and colonizing the rest of the world. In the 19th century, however, "Christendom" became less and less "Christian" and more and more the "secular West," shaped by a secular ideology, or ideologies, alternative to Christianity. Still, the religious and ideological cultures of the West, even as they struggled with each other, dealt with other cultures and their religions in the customary manner of ignoring them or attempting to dominate, and even absorb, them—though it became increasingly obvious that the latter was not likely to happen.

As the 20th century drew to a close, however, all of those ways of relating become increasingly impossible to sustain. For example: What happened in other cultures quickly led young men and women of the West to die on the volcanic ash of Iwo Jima or the desert sands of Kuwait. But more than that, the "West" could no longer escape what was done in the "First World," such as the production of acid rain, in the "Second World," such as the Chernobyl nuclear accident, or in the "Third World," such as the mass destruction of the Amazon rain forest, "the world's lungs."

At the same time the world has been slowly, painfully emerging from the millennia-long Age of Monologue into the Age of Dialogue. As noted above, until beginning a century or so ago, each religion, and then ideology—each culture—tended to be very certain that it alone had the complete "explanation of the ultimate meaning of life, and how to live accordingly." Then through the series of revolutions in understanding, which began in the West but ultimately spread more and more throughout the whole world, the limitedness of all statements about the meaning of things began to dawn on isolated thinkers, and then increasingly on the middle and even grass-roots levels of humankind: The epistemological revolutions of historicism, pragmatism, sociology of knowledge, language analysis, hermeneutics, and finally dialogue.

Now that it is more and more understood that the Muslim, Christian, secularist, Buddhist, etc. perception of the meaning of things is necessarily limited, the Muslim, Christian, secularist, etc. increasingly feels no longer driven to replace, or at least dominate, all other religions, ideologies, cultures, and may even be drawn to enter into dialogue with them, so as to expand, deepen, enrich each of their necessarily limited perceptions of the meaning of things. Thus, often with squinting, blurry eyes, humankind is emerging from the relative darkness of the "Age of Monologue" into the dawning "Age of Dialogue"— dialogue understood as a conversation with someone who differs from us *primarily* so *we* can learn, because of course since we now growingly realize that our understanding of the meaning of reality is necessarily limited, we might learn more about reality's meaning through someone else's perception of it.

6. The Age of Global Dialogue

Ewert Cousins has basically affirmed everything Hans Küng has described as the newly emerging contemporary paradigm-shift, but Cousins sees the present shift as much more profound than simply another in a series of major paradigm-shifts of human history. He sees the current transformation as a shift of the magnitude of the First Axial Period which will similarly reshape human consciousness. I, too, want to basically affirm what Küng sees as the emerging contemporary Major Paradigm-Shift, as well as with Cousins that this shift is so profound as to match in magnitude the transformation of human consciousness of the Axial Period, so that it should be referred to as a Second Axial Period.

More than that, however, I am persuaded that what humankind is entering into now is not just the latest in a long series of major paradigm-shifts, as Hans Küng has so carefully and clearly analyzed. I am also persuaded that it is even more than the massive move into the consciousness transforming Second Axial Period, as Ewert Cousins has so thoroughly demonstrated. Beyond these two radical shifts, though of course including both of them, humankind is emerging out of the "from-the beginning-till-now" millennia-long "Age of Monologue" into the newly dawning "Age of Dialogue."

The turn toward dialogue is, in my judgment, *the most fundamental, the most radical and utterly transformative* of the key elements of the newly emerging paradigm, which Hans Küng has so penetratingly outlined, and which Ewert Cousins also perceptively discerns as one of the central constituents of the Second Axial Age. However, that shift from monologue to dialogue constitutes such a radical reversal in human consciousness, is so utterly new in the history of humankind *from the beginning*, that it must be designated as literally "revolutionary," that is, it turns everything absolutely around. In brief: Dialogue is *a whole new way of thinking* in human history.

To sum up and reiterate: In the latter part of the twentieth century humankind is undergoing a Macro-Paradigm-Shift (Hans Küng). More than that, at this time humankind is moving into a transformative shift in consciousness of the magnitude of the Axial Period (800-200 B.C.E.) so that we must speak of the emerging of the Second Axial Period (Ewert Cousins). Even more profound, however, now at the edge of the Third Millennium humankind is slipping out of the shadowy Age of Monologue, where it has been since its beginning, into the dawn of the Age of Dialogue (Leonard Swidler). Into this new Age of Dialogue, Küng's Macro Paradigm Shift and Cousins' Second Axial Period are sublated (*aufgehoben*, in Hegel's terminology), that is, taken up and transformed. Moreover, as Ewert Cousins has already detailed, humankind's consciousness is becoming increasingly global. Hence, our dialogue partners necessarily must also be increasingly global. In this new Age of Dialogue dialogue on a global basis is now not only a possibility, it is a necessity. As I noted in the title of a recent book—humankind is faced with ultimately with two choices: Dialogue or Death![14]

III. The Need for a Global Ethic

When the fact of the epistemological revolutions leading to the growing necessity of interreligious, interideological, intercultural dialogue is coupled with the fact of all humankind's interdependency—such that any significant part of humanity could precipitate the whole of the globe into a social, economic, nuclear, environmental or other catastrophe—there arises the pressing need to focus the energy of these dialogues on not only how humans perceive and understand the world and its meaning, but also on how they should act in relationship to themselves, to other persons, and to nature, within the context of reality's undergirding, pervasive, overarching source, energy and goal, however understood. In brief, humankind increasingly desperately needs to engage in a dialogue on the development of, not a Buddhist ethic, a Christian ethic, a Marxist ethic, etc., but of a global ethic—and I believe a key instrument in that direction will be the shaping of a *Universal Declaration of a Global Ethic.*

I say ethic in the singular rather than ethics in the plural, because what is needed is not a full blown global ethics in great detail—indeed, such would not even be possible—but a global consensus on the fundamental attitude toward good and evil and the basic and middle principles to put it into action. Clearly, also, this ethic must be global. It will not be sufficient to have a common ethic for Westerners or Africans or Asians, etc. The destruction, for example, of the ozone layer or the loosing of a destructive gene mutation by any one group will be disastrous for all.

I say also that this *Universal Declaration of a Global Ethic* must be arrived at by consensus through dialogue. Attempts at the imposition of a unitary ethics by various kinds of force have been had aplenty, and they have inevitably fallen miserably short of globality. The most recent failures can be seen in the widespread collapse of communism, and in an inverse way in the resounding rejection of secularism by resurgent Islamism.

That the need for a global ethic is most urgent is becoming increasingly apparent to all; humankind no longer has the luxury of letting such an ethic slowly and haphazardly grow by itself, as it willy nilly will gradually happen. It is vital that there be a conscious focusing of energy on such a development. Immediate action is necessary:

1. Every scholarly institution, whether related to a religion or ideology or not, needs to press its experts of the widest variety of disciplines to use their creativity among themselves and in conjunction with scholars from other institutions, both religiously related and not, in formulating a Global Ethic.
2. Every major religion and ethical group needs to commission its expert scholars to focus their research and reflection on articulating a Global Ethic from the perspective of their reli-

gion or ethical group—in dialogue with all other religions and ethical groups.

3. Collaborative "Working Groups," of scholars in the field of ethics which are very deliberately interreligious, interideological need to be formed specifically to tackle this momentous task, and those which already exist need to focus their energies on it.

4. Beyond that there needs to be a major permanent Global Ethic Research Center, which will have some of the best experts from the world's major religions and ethical groups in residence, perhaps for years at a stretch, pursuing precisely this topic in its multiple ramifications.

When the *Universal Declaration of a Global Ethic* is finally drafted—after multiple consultation, revision and eventual acceptance by the full range of religious and ethical institutions—it will then serve as a minimal ethical standard for humankind to live up to, much as the United Nation's 1948 *Universal Declaration of Human Rights.* Through the former, the moral force of the world's religious and ethical institutions can be brought to bear especially on those issues which are not very susceptible to the legal and political force of the latter. Such an undertaking by the Religions and Ideologies of the world would be different from, but complementary to, the work of the United Nations.

After the initial period, which doubtless would last several years, the "Global Ethic Research Center" could serve as an authoritative religious and ideological scholarly locus to which always-new specific problems of a global ethic could be submitted for evaluation, analysis and response. The weightiness of the responses would be "substantive," not "formal." That is, its solutions would carry weight because of their inherent persuasiveness coming from their intellectual and spiritual insight and wisdom.

IV. Principles of a Universal Declaration of a Global Ethic

Let me first offer some suggestions of the general notions that I believe ought to shape a Universal Declaration of a Global Ethic, and then offer a tentative draft constructed in their light:

1. *The Declaration should use language and images that are acceptable to all major religions and ethical groups; hence, its language*

*ought to be "humanity-based," rather than from authoritative re-
ligious books; it should be from "below," not from "above."*

2. *Therefore, it should be anthropo-centric, indeed more, it must be
anthropo-cosmo-centric, for we can not be fully human except
within the context of the whole of reality.*

3. *The affirmations should be dynamic in form in the sense that they
will be susceptible to being sublated (aufgehoben), that is, they
might properly be reinterpreted by being taken up into a larger
framework.*

4. *The Declaration needs to set inviolable minimums, but also open-
ended maximums to be striven for; but maximums may not be
required, for it might violate the freedom-minimums of some persons.*

5. *It could well start with—though not limit itself to—elements of
the so-called "Golden Rule": Treat others as we would be treated.*

Excursus: the "Golden Rule"

A glimpse of just how pervasive the "Golden Rule" is, albeit in various
forms and expressions, in the world's religions and ideologies, great
and small, can be garnered from this partial listing:

a. Perhaps the oldest recorded version—which is cast in a positive form—stems from Zoroaster (628-551 B.C.E.): "That which
is good for all and any one, for whomsoever—that is good for
me . . . what I hold good for self, I should for all. Only Law
Universal is true Law" (*Gathas*, 43.1).

b. Confucius (551-479 B.C.E.), when asked "Is there one word
which may serve as a rule of practice for all one's life?" said:
"Do not to others what you do not want done to yourself"
(*Analects*, 12.2 & 15.23). Confucius also stated in a variant
version: "What I do not wish others to do to me, that also I
wish not to do to them" (*Analects*, 5.11).

c. The founder of Jainism was Vardhamana, known as Mahavira
("Great Hero—540-468 B.C.E.); the various scriptures of
Jainism, however, derived from a later period: "A man should
wander about treating all creatures as he himself would be
treated" (*Sutrakri-tanga* 1.11.33). "One who you think should
be hit is none else but you. . . . Therefore, neither does he
cause violence to others nor does he make others do so"
(*Acarangasutra* 5.101-2).

d. The founder of Buddhism was Siddhartha Gautama, known as the Buddha ("Enlightened One"—563-483 B.C.E.); the various scriptures of Buddhism also derived from a later period: "Comparing oneself to others in such terms as 'Just as I am so are they, just as they are so am I,' he should neither kill nor cause others to kill" *Sutta Nipata* 705). "Here am I fond of my life, not wanting to die, fond of pleasure and averse from pain. Suppose someone should rob me of my life. . . . If I in turn should rob of his life one fond of his life. . . . How could I inflict that upon another?" (*Samyutta Nikaya* v.353).

e. The Hindu epic poem, the 3rd-century B.C.E. Mahabharata, states that its "Golden Rule," which is expressed in both positive and negative form, is the summary of all Hindu teaching, "the whole Dharma": "Vyasa says: Do not to others what you do not wish done to yourself; and wish for others too what you desire and long for for yourself—this is the whole of Dharma; heed it well" (*Mahabharata*, Anusasana Parva 113.8).

f. In the biblical book of Leviticus (composed in the fifth century B.C.E., though some of its material may be more ancient) the Hebrew version of the "Golden Rule" is stated positively: "You shall love your neighbor as yourself" (Lev. 19: 18).

g. The deuterocanonical biblical Tobit was written around the year 200 B.C.E. and contains a negative version—as most are— of the "Golden Rule": "Never do to anyone else anything that you would not want someone to do to you" (Tobit 4:15).

h. The major founder of Rabbinic Judaism, Hillel, who lived about a generation before Jesus, though he may also have been his teacher, taught that the "Golden Rule"— his version being both positive and negative — was the heart of the Torah; "all the rest was commentary": "Do not do to others what you would not have done to yourself" (*Btalmud*, Shabbath 31a).

i. Following in this Jewish tradition, Jesus stated the "Golden Rule" in a positive form, saying that it summed up the whole Torah and prophets: "Do for others just what you want them to do for you" (Luke 6:31); "Do for others what you want them to do for you: this is the meaning of the Law of Moses [*Torah*] and of the teachings of the prophets" (Matthew 7:12).

j. In the seventh century of the Common Era Mohammed is said
    to have claimed that the "Golden Rule" is the "noblest Reli-
    gion": "Noblest Religion is this — that you should like for
    others what you like for yourself; and what you feel painful
    for yourself, hold that as painful for all others too." Again:
    "No man is a true believer unless he desires for his brother
    that which he desires for himself."[15]

k. The "Golden Rule" is likewise found in some non-literate re-
    ligions: "One going to take a pointed stick to pinch a baby
    bird should first try it on himself to feel how it hurts"[16]

l. The eighteenth-century Western philosopher Immanuel Kant
    provided a "rational" version of the "Golden Rule" in his fa-
    mous "Categorical Imperative," or "Law of Universal Fairness":
    "Act on maxims which can at the same time have for their
    object themselves as universal laws of nature. . . . Treat hu-
    manity in every case as an end, never as a means only."[17]

m. The late nineteenth-century founder of Baha'ism, Baha'ullah,
    wrote: "He should not wish for others that which he doth not
    wish for himself, nor promise that which he doth not fulfill."[18]

n. In 1915 a new version of Buddhism, Won Buddhism, was
    founded in Korea by the Great Master Sotaesan. In the teach-
    ings he left behind are found variants of the "Golden Rule":
    "Be right yourself before you correct others. Instruct yourself
    first before you teach others. Do favors for others before you
    seek favors from them." "Ordinary people may appear smart
    in doing things only for themselves, but they are really suffer-
    ing a loss. Buddhas and *Bodhisattvas* may appear to be stupid
    in doing things only for others, but eventually they benefit
    themselves."[19]

It is clear that the core of the world's major Religions, the "Golden
Rule," "does not attempt the futile and impossible task of abolishing
and annihilating the authentic ego. On the contrary, it tends to make
concern for the authentic ego the *measure* of altruism. 'Do not foster
the *ego* more than the *alter*; care for the *alter* as much as for the *ego*.' To
abolish egoism is to abolish altruism also; and *vice versa*."[20]

Authentic egoism and authentic altruism then are not in conflict
with each other; the former necessarily moves to the latter, even possi-

bly "giving one's life for one's friend." This, however, is the last and highest stage of human development. It is the stage of the (w)holy person, the saint, the arahat, the bodhisattva, the sage. Such a stage cannot be the *foundation* of human society; it must be the *goal* of it. The foundation of human society must be first authentic self-love, which includes moving outward to loving others.

Not recognizing this foundation of authentic self-love is the fundamental flaw of those idealistic systems, such as communism, that try to build a society on the *foundation* of altruism. A human and humanizing society should *lead* toward (w)holiness, toward altruism, but it cannot be built on the assumption that its citizens are (w)holy and altruistic to start with. Such an altruism must grow out of an ever developing authentic self-love; it cannot be assumed, and surely it cannot be forced (as has been tried for decades—with disastrous dehumanizing results).

---

6. *As humans ineluctably seek ever more knowledge, truth, so too they seek to draw what they perceive as the good to themselves (that is, they love). Usually this self is expanded to include the family, and then friends. It needs to continue its natural expansion to the community, nation, world and cosmos, and the source and goal of all reality.*

7. *But this human love necessarily must start with self-love, for one can love one's "neighbor" only AS one loves oneself; but since one becomes human only by inter-human mutuality, loving others fulfills one's own humanity, and hence is also the greatest act of authentic self-love.*

8. *Another aspect of the "Golden Rule" is that humans are always to be treated as ends, never as mere means, i.e., as subjects, never as mere objects.*

9. *Yet another implication of the "Golden Rule" is that those who cannot protect themselves ought to be protected by those who can.*

10. *A further ring of the expanding circles of the "Golden Rule" is that non-human beings are also to be reverenced and treated with respect because of their being.*

11. It is important that not only basic but also middle ethical principles be spelled out in this Declaration. Although most of the middle ethical principles that need to be articulated in this Declaration are already embedded in juridical form in the United Nations' 1948 Universal Declaration of Human Rights, it is vital that the religions and ethical traditions expressly state and approve them. Then the world, including both adherents and outsiders of the various religions and ethical traditions, will know what ethical standards all are committing themselves to.

12. If a Universal Declaration of a Global Ethic is to be meaningful and effective, however, its framers must resist the temptation to pack too many details and special interests into it. It can function best as a kind of "constitutional" set of basic and middle ethical principles from which more detailed applications can be constantly be drawn.

V. A Plan of Action

Such general suggestions need to be discussed, confirmed, rejected, modified, supplemented. Beyond that, it is vital that all the disciplines contribute what from their perspectives ought to be included in the Declaration, how that should be formulated, what is to be avoided—and this is beginning to happen. The year 1993 was the 100th anniversary of the 1893 World Parliament of Religions which took place in Chicago and marked the beginning of what became world-wide interreligious dialogue. As a consequence, a number of international conferences took place and in the center of them was the launching and developing of a *Universal Declaration of a Global Ethic.*

The first was held in New Delhi, India in February, 1993; the second in August of the same year in Bangalore, India and the third that year in September in Chicago. For that huge (over 6,000 participants) September 1993 Chicago Parliament of the World's Religions Professor Hans Küng drafted a document entitled "Declaration Toward a Global Ethic," which the Parliament adopted.[21]

Beyond that, the text given below, after having been commissioned by the January 1992 meeting in Atlanta, Georgia of the International Scholars' Annual Trialogue-ISAT (Jewish-Christian-Muslim), was drafted by Professor Leonard Swidler and submitted to and analyzed at the January, 1993 meeting of ISAT in Graz, Austria; it was focused on during the spring 1993 semester graduate seminar Leonard Swidler held at Temple University entitled: "Global Ethics-Human Rights-World Religions"; it was also a major focus of the First International Conference on Universalism in August, 1993, in Warsaw; a Consultation of the American Academy of Religion in November, 1993, in Washington D.C. was devoted to the topic; the sixth International Scholars' Annual Trialogue in January, 1994, concentrated for a second year on the Universal Declaration; in May, 1994, it was the subject of a conference sponsored by the International Association of Asian Philosophy and Religion—IAAPR in Seoul, Korea; the World Conference on Religion and Peace—WCRP in part focused on it in its fall, 1994 World Assembly in Rome/Riva del Garda, Italy; and on June 20-21, 1995, it was the subject of a conference in San Francisco in honor of the Fiftieth Anniversary of the Founding of the United Nations, entitled: "Celebrating the Spirit: Towards a Global Ethic."

In March, 1997, the Philosophy and Ethics Division of UNESCO held in Paris the first meeting of its newly established committee to work toward a "Universal Ethic." Its second meeting was held December, 1997 in Naples in conjunction with the Instituto Italiano degli Studii Filosofici. Both the above two Drafts (as well as the one described next) were submitted to this UNESCO committee.

More recently Professor Küng drafted a third text (also contained in this volume), this time within the context of the InterAction Council, entitled "A Universal Declaration of Human Responsibilities." The InterAction Council is a committee made up of former heads of states, chaired by retired Chancellor Helmut Schmidt of Germany. All three of these texts have been subjected to numerous consultations and comments by scholars and thinkers from multiple philosophical, religious and other backgrounds.

It is vital that we study this matter seriously, but we also need to act. We must not dally, for the changes in the world are mounting not only in arithmetic but in geometric fashion. We must hurry with our global ethical guiding light to "get ahead of the curve," lest Samuel Huntington's grim prediction of the "Clash of Civilizations" and worse, comes true. On the other hand, a document merely handed down from above will lack the "ownership" of those who it is to influence and guide.

In this matter we can learn from the methodology employed by the Earth Charter Project headquartered in Costa Rica and chaired by Professor Steven Rockefeller. They did indeed initially "prime the pump" with textual input from leading scholars and thinkers, but have then put their bread out on the water of a vast network of Non-Governmental Organizations (NGOs), religious, secular, political and semi-political organizations and individuals, urging them to bring insights and formulations up from below, which the headquarters is then synthesizing.

To summarize: It is imperative that various religious and ethical communities, ethnic groups and geographical regions work on discussing and drafting their own versions of a "Universal Declaration of a Global Ethic," that is, *what they consider their own basic ethical principles, which they at the same time believe people of all other religious and ethical traditions could also affirm.* The three already existing drafts should certainly be made use of in this process. But all communities and regions need to make their own contributions to the final Declaration, and in the process of wrestling with the issue and forging the wording, they will make the concern for a global ethic their own, and will thus better be able to mediate it to their "constituents" and enhance the likelihood of the Declaration in fact being adhered to in practice.

What needs to be stressed is that such a project cannot be carried out only by the scholars and leaders of the world's religious and ethical communities, though obviously the vigorous participation of these elements is vital. The ideas and sensitivities must also come from the grassroots.

Moreover, it is also at the grassroots, as well at the levels of scholars and leaders, that, first, consciousnesses must be raised on the desperate need for the conscious development of a Global Ethic, and then once drafted and accepted, the conviction of its validity must be gained. The most carefully thought out and sensitively crafted Declaration will be of no use if those who are to adhere to it do not believe in it. A Global Ethic must work on all three levels: scholars, leaders, grassroots. Otherwise it will not work at all. Hence, I urge:

- first, all religious, ethical, ethnic and geographical communities and organizations (either alone or in concert with others, but always in a dialogic spirit)—and most especially the myriad

NGOs of the world—need to move seriously but quickly to the drawing up of their own Draft of a "Universal Declaration of a Global Ethic";

- second, these groups need to strategize on how to maneuver their Drafts to gain the greatest influence in all the theaters each operates in: the UN, other NGOs, scholarly groups, religious groups, the vast world of the internet, myriads of grassroots organizations—in short, wherever aroused imaginations will lead;

- third, each group should send their Draft of a "Universal Declaration of a Global Ethic" to the *Center for Global Ethics* (Professor Leonard Swidler, *Journal of Ecumenical Studies*, Temple University, Philadelphia, PA 19122; FAX: 215-204-4569; E-mail: dialogue@vm.temple.edu), which will serve first as a collection and distribution center, and when the time is appropriate, a facilitator in the process of synthesizing a final Draft and devising in as democratic manner as possible a process of world-wide adoption.

In sum, having studied, listened and thought, I challenge us all to take up this vital task and act!

Footnotes

[1] Oswald Spengler, *Der Untergang des Abendlandes* (Munich: Beck, 1922-23), 2 vols.

[2] Pitirim A. Sorokin, *The Crisis of Our Age* (New York: Dutton, 1941).

[3] See among others, Hans Küng, *Theologie im Aufbruch* (Munich: Piper Verlag, 1987), esp. pp. 153 ff.

[4] See especially Ewert Cousins, "Judaism-Christianity-Islam: Facing Modernity Together, *Journal of Ecumenical Studies*, 30:3-4 (Summer-Fall, 1993), pp. 417-425.

[5] Thomas Kuhn, *The Structure of Scientific Revolutions* (Chicago: University of Chicago Press, 2nd ed., 1970).

[6] I am grateful for this exemplary comparison to Henry Rosemont, who I met when he was the Fulbright Professor of Philosophy at Fudan University, Shanghai, 1982-84.

[7] Already two millennia and more ago some Hindu and Buddhist thinkers held a nonabsolutistic epistemology, but that fact had no significant im-

pact on the West; because of the relative cultural eclipse of those civilizations in the modern period and the dominance of the Western scientific worldview, these ancient nonabsolutistic epistemologies have until now played no significant role in the emerging global society—though in the context of dialogue, they should in the future.

Since the middle of the nineteenth century Eastern thought has become increasingly better known in the West, and proportionately influential. This knowledge and influence appears to be increasing geometrically in recent decades. It is even beginning to move into the hardest of our so-called hard sciences, nuclear physics, as evidenced by the popular book of the theoretical physicist Fritjof Capra, *The Tao of Physics* (Boulder, CO: Shambhala, 2nd ed., 1983).

[8] For a full discussion of these epistemological issues and related matters, see my *After the Absolute: The Dialogical Future of Religious Reflection.* Minneapolis: Fortress Press, 1990

[9] Thomas Aquinas, *Summa Theologiae*, II-II, Q. 1, a. 2.

[10] I am in this section especially indebted to Ewert Cousins' essay "Judaism-Christianity-Islam: Facing Modernity Together, *Journal of Ecumenical Studies*, 30:3-4 (Summer-Fall, 1993), pp. 417-425.

[11] Karl Jaspers, *Vom Ursprung und Ziel der Geschichte* (Zurich: Artemis, 1949), pp. 19-43.

[12] Ibid., p. 19; trans. Michael Bullock, *The Origin and Goal of History* (New Haven: Yale University Press, 1953), p. 1. For the ongoing academic discussion of Jaspers' position on the Axial Period, see *Wisdom, Revelation, and Doubt: Perspectives on the First Millennium B.C., Daedalus* (Spring, 1975); and *The Origins and Diversity of Axial Age Civilizations*, ed. S.N. Eisenstadt (New York: State University of New York Press, 1989).

[13] For a more comprehensive treatment of Cousins' concept of the Second Axial Period, see his book *Christ of the 21st Century* (Rockport, MA: Element, 1992).

[14] Leonard Swidler et alii, *Death or Dialogue* (Philadelphia: Trinity Press International, 1990).

[15] Hadith: Muslim, chapter on iman, 71-2; Ibn Madja, Introduction, 9; Al-Darimi, chapter on riqaq; Hambal 3, 1976. The first quotation is cited in Bhagavan Das, *The Essential Unity of All Religions* (1934), p. 298.

[16] A Yoruba Proverb (Nigeria), cited in Andrew Wilson, ed., *World Scripture* (New York: Paragon House, 1991), p. 114

[17] Immanuel Kant, *Critique of Practical Reason*, A 54; and *Groundwork of the Metaphysics of Ethics*, BA 66f.

[18] *Gleanings from the Writings of Baha'u'llah*, trans. by Shoghi Effendi (Wilmette, IL: Baha'i Publishing Trust, 2d ed., 1976).

[19] *The Scripture of Won Buddhism* (Iri, Korea: Won Kwang Publishing Co., rev. ed. 1988), pp. 309f.

[20] Bhagavan Das, *The Essential Unity of All Religions* (1934), p. 303.

[21] Hans Küng and Karl-Josef Kuschel, eds., *A Global Ethic* (New York: Continuum, 1993).

Universal Declaration
of a Global Ethic

I. Rationale

We WOMEN AND MEN from various ethical and religious traditions commit ourselves to the following Universal Declaration of a Global Ethic. We speak here not of *ethics* in the plural, which implies rather great detail, but of *ethic* in the singular, i.e., the fundamental attitude toward good and evil, and the basic and middle principles needed to put it into action.

We make this commitment not despite our differences but arising out of our distinct perspectives, recognizing nevertheless in our diverse ethical and religious traditions common convictions that lead us to speak out *against* all forms of inhumanity and *for* humaneness in our treatment of ourselves, one another and the world around us. We find in each of our traditions:

a) grounds in support of universal human rights,
b) a call to work for justice and peace, and
c) concern for conservation of the earth.

We confirm and applaud the positive human values that are, at times painfully slowly, but nevertheless increasingly, being accepted and advocated in our world: freedom, equality, democracy, recognition of interdependence, commitment to justice and human rights. We also believe that conditions in our world encourage, indeed require, us to look beyond what divides us and to speak as one on matters that are crucial for the survival of and respect for the earth. Therefore we advocate movement toward a global order that reflects the best values found in our myriad traditions.

We are convinced that a just global order can be built only upon a global ethic which clearly states universally-recognized norms and principles, and that such an ethic presumes a readiness and intention on the part of people to act justly—that is, a movement of the heart. Secondly, a global ethic requires a thoughtful presentation of principles that are held up to open investigation and critique—a movement of the head.

Each of our traditions holds commitments beyond what is expressed here, but we find that within our ethical and religious traditions the world community is in the process of discovering elements of a fundamental minimal consensus on ethics which is convincing to all women and men of good will, religious and nonreligious alike, and which will provide us with a moral framework within which we can relate to ourselves, each other and the world in a just and respectful manner.

In order to build a humanity-wide consensus we find it is essential to develop and use a language that is humanity-based, though each religious and ethical tradition also has its own language for what is expressed in this Declaration.

Furthermore, none of our traditions, ethical or religious, is satisfied with minimums, vital as they are; rather, because humans are endlessly self-transcending, our traditions also provide maximums to be striven for. Consequently, this Declaration does the same. The maximums, however, clearly are ideals to be striven for, and therefore cannot be required, lest the essential freedoms and rights of some thereby be violated.

II. Presuppositions

As a Universal Declaration of a Global Ethic, which we believe must undergird any affirmation of human rights and respect for the earth, this document affirms and supports the rights and corresponding responsibilities enumerated in the 1948 Universal Declaration of Human Rights of the United Nations. In conjunction with that first United Nations Declaration we believe there are five general presuppositions which are indispensable for a global ethic:

a) Every human possesses inalienable and inviolable dignity; individuals, states, and other social entities are obliged to respect and protect the dignity of each person.

b) No person or social entity exists beyond the scope of morality; everyone—individuals and social organizations—is obliged to do good and avoid evil.

c) Humans are endowed with reason and conscience—the great challenge of being human is to act conscientiously; communities, states and other social organizations are obliged to protect and foster these capabilities.

d) Communities, states and other social organizations which contribute to the good of humans and the world have a right to exist and flourish; this right should be respected by all.

e) Humans are a part of nature, not apart from nature; ethical concerns extend beyond humanity to the rest of the earth, and indeed the cosmos. In brief: this Declaration, in reflection of reality, is not just anthropo-centric, but cosmo-anthropo-centric.

III. Fundamental Rule

We propose the Golden Rule, which for thousands of years has been affirmed in many religious and ethical traditions, as a fundamental principle upon which to base a global ethic: "What you do not wish done to yourself, do not do to others," or in positive terms, "What you wish done to yourself, do to others." This rule should be valid not only for one's own family, friends, community and nation, but also for all other individuals, families, communities, nations, the entire world, the cosmos.

IV. Basic Principles

1. Because freedom is of the essence of being human, every person is free to exercise and develop every capacity, so long as it does not infringe on the rights of other persons or express a lack of due respect for things living or non-living. In addition, human freedom should be ex-

ercised in such a way as to enhance both the freedom of all humans and due respect for all things, living and non-living.

2. Because of their inherent equal dignity, all humans should always be treated as ends, never as mere means. In addition, all humans in every encounter with others should strive to enhance to the fullest the intrinsic dignity of all involved.

3. Although humans have greater intrinsic value than non-humans, all such things, living and non-living, do possess intrinsic value simply because of their existence and, as such, are to be treated with due respect. In addition, all humans in every encounter with non-humans, living and non-living, should strive to respect them to the fullest of their intrinsic value.

4. As humans necessarily seek ever more truth, so too they seek to unite themselves, that is, their "selves," with what they perceive as the good: in brief, they love. Usually this "self" is expanded/transcended to include their own family and friends, seeking the good for them. In addition, as with the Golden Rule, this loving/loved "self" needs to continue its natural expansion/transcendence to embrace the community, nation, world, and cosmos.

5. Thus true human love is authentic self-love and other-love co-relatively linked in such a way that ultimately it is drawn to become all-inclusive. This expansive and inclusive nature of love should be recognized as an active principle in personal and global interaction.

6. Those who hold responsibility for others are obliged to help those for whom they hold responsibility. In addition, the Golden Rule implies: If we were in serious difficulty wherein we could not help ourselves, we would want those who could help us to do so, even if they held no responsibility for us; therefore we should help others in serious difficulty who cannot help themselves, even though we hold no responsibility for them.

7. Because all humans are equally entitled to hold their religion or belief—i.e., their explanation of the ultimate meaning of life and how to live accordingly—as true, every human's religion or belief should be granted its due freedom and respect.

8. In addition, dialogue—i.e., conversation whose *primary* aim is to learn from the other—is a necessary means whereby women and men learn to respect the other, ceaselessly to expand and deepen their own explanation of the meaning of life, and to develop an ever broadening consensus whereby men and women can live together on this globe in an authentically human manner.

V. Middle Principles

The following "Middle Ethical Principles" are in fact those which underlie the 1948 United Nations Universal Declaration of Human Rights, formally approved by almost every nation in the world.

1. Legal Rights/Responsibilities:
Because all humans have an inherent equal dignity, all should be treated equally before the law and provided with its equal protection.

At the same time, all individuals and communities should follow all just laws, obeying not only the letter but most especially the spirit.

2. Rights/Responsibilities Concerning Conscience and Religion or Belief:
Because humans are thinking, and therefore essentially free-deciding beings, all have the right to freedom of thought, speech, conscience and religion or belief.

At the same time, all humans should exercise their rights of freedom of thought, speech, conscience and religion or belief in ways that will respect themselves and all others and strive to produce maximum benefit, broadly understood, for both themselves and their fellow humans.

3. Rights/Responsibilities Concerning Speech and Information:
Because humans are thinking beings with the ability to perceive reality and express it, all individuals and communities have both the right and the responsibility, as far as possible, to learn the truth and express it honestly.

At the same time everyone should avoid cover-ups, distortions, manipulations of others and inappropriate intrusions into personal privacy; this freedom and responsibility is especially true of the mass media, artists, scientists, politicians and religious leaders.

4. *Rights/Responsibilities Concerning Participation in All Decision-making Affecting Oneself or Those forWhom One is Responsible:*
Because humans are free-deciding beings, all adults have the right to a voice, direct or indirect, in all decisions that affect them, including a meaningful participation in choosing their leaders and holding them accountable, as well as the right of equal access to all leadership positions for which their talents qualify them.

At the same time, all humans should strive to exercise their right, and obligation, to participate in self-governance as to produce maximum benefit, widely understood, for both themselves and their fellow humans.

5. *Rights/Responsibilities Concerning the Relationship between Women and Men:*
Because women and men are inherently equal and all men and women have an equal right to the full development of all their talents as well as the freedom to marry, with equal rights for all women and men in living out or dissolving marriage.

At the same time, all men and women should act toward each other outside of and within marriage in ways that will respect the intrinsic dignity, equality, freedom and responsibilities of themselves and others.

6. *Rights/Responsibilities Concerning Property:*
Because humans are free, bodily and social in nature, all individual humans and communities have the right to own property of various sorts.

At the same time, society should be so organized that property will be dealt with respectfully, striving to produce maximum benefit not only for the owners but also for their fellow humans, as well as for the world at large.

7. *Rights/Responsibilities Concerning Work and Leisure:*
Because to lead an authentic human life all humans should normally have both meaningful work and recreative leisure, individuals and communities should strive to organize society so as to provide these two dimensions of an authentic human life both for themselves and all the members of their communities.

At the same time, all individuals have an obligation to work appropriately for their recompense, and, with all communities, to strive for ever more creative work and re-creative leisure for themselves, their communities, and other individuals and communities.

8. Rights/Responsibilities Concerning Children and Education:
Children are first of all not responsible for their coming into existence or for their socialization and education; their parents are. Where for whatever reason they fail, the wider community, relatives and civil community, have an obligation to provide the most humane care possible, physical, mental, moral/spiritual and social, for children.

Because humans can become authentically human only through education in the broad sense, and today increasingly can flourish only with extensive education in the formal sense, all individuals and communities should strive to provide an education for all children and adult women and men which is directed to the full development of the human person, respect for human rights and fundamental freedoms, the promotion of understanding, dialogue and friendship among all humans—regardless of racial, ethnic, religious, belief, sexual or other differences—and respect for the earth.

At the same time, all individuals and communities have the obligation to contribute appropriately to providing the means necessary for this education for themselves and their communities, and beyond that to strive to provide the same for all humans.

9. Rights/Responsibilities Concerning Peace:
Because peace, as both the absence of violence and the presence of justice for all humans, is the necessary condition for the complete development of the full humanity of all humans, individually and communally, all individuals and communities should strive constantly to further the growth of peace on all levels, personal, interpersonal, local, regional, national and international, granting that

    a)   the necessary basis of peace is justice for all concerned;
    b)   violence is to be vigorously avoided, being resorted to only when its absence would cause a greater evil;
    c)   when peace is ruptured, all efforts should be bent to its rapid restoration—on the necessary basis of justice for all.

At the same time, it should be recognized that peace, like liberty, is a positive value which should be constantly cultivated, and therefore all individuals and communities should make the necessary prior efforts not only to avoid its break-down but also to strengthen its steady development and growth.

10. Rights/Responsibilities Concerning the Preservation of the Environment:
Because things, living and non-living, have an intrinsic value simply because of their existence, and also because humans cannot develop fully as humans, or even survive, if the environment is severely damaged, all individuals and communities should respect the ecosphere within which "we all live, move and have our being," and act so that

a) nothing, living or non-living, will be destroyed in its natural form except when used for some greater good, as, for example, the use of plants/animals for food;

b) if at all possible, only replaceable material will be destroyed in its natural form.

At the same time, all individuals and communities should constantly be vigilant to protect our fragile universe, particularly from the exploding human population and increasing technological possibilities which threaten it in an ever expanding fashion.

June 14, 1995 Revision

Send revisions to: Prof. Leonard Swidler, Religion Department, Temple University, Philadelphia, PA 19122, USA; FAX: 215-204-4569; E-mail: DIALOGUE@VM.TEMPLE.EDU

Explanatory Remarks Concerning a "Declaration of the Religions for a Global Ethic"

THE COUNCIL FOR A PARLIAMENt of the World's Religions in Chicago commissioned Professor Hans Küng of the University of Tübingen to develop a draft of a "Declaration of the Religions for a Global Ethic" to be submitted to the September 1993 Parliament of the World's Religions. Professor Küng was able to deal with the problems of such a Declaration throughout the entire summer semester (1992) in an interdisciplinary colloquium with participants from various religions and continents and produced an initial draft which was sent to various colleagues and friends for correction. The first draft received broad agreement from all those to whom it was sent. At the same time dozens of formal as well as material suggestions for correction were submitted, which were taken into account in producing a revised draft.

The following were the principles which have guided Professor Küng:

1. The document would in the first place be a Declaration of the *religions*, which could later be followed by a general Declaration (as for example within the framework of UNESCO).

2. In a "Declaration for a World Ethic" the focus cannot be on the *juridical* level of laws, codified rights and appealable paragraphs (e.g., Human Rights), or on the *political* level of concrete suggested solutions (e.g., in reference to the debt crisis of the Third World), but rather only the ETHICAL level: the level of binding values, *irrevocable standards* and *interior fundamental attitudes*. These three levels of course are related to each other.

3. Such a Declaration must be *capable of producing a consensus.* Hence, statements must be avoided which *a priori* would be rejected by one of the great religions, and as a consequence disputed moral questions (like abortion or euthanasia) had to be excluded.

This Declaration was signed by most of the nearly two hundred "delegates" of the world's religions who attended the "Parliament of the World's Religions" held on the centenary of the first "World Parliament of Religions" in Chicago in 1893. The 1993 "Parliament of the World's Religions" (attended by 6,500 persons) was held in Chicago August 28—September 4, 1993, and this Declaration was solemnly proclaimed on September 4, 1993.

The Parliament of the World's Religions Declaration of a Global Ethic[†]

The Principles of a Global Ethic

OUR WORLD IS EXPERIENCING a *fundamental crisis*: a crisis in global economy, global ecology, and global politics. The lack of a grand vision, the tangle of unresolved problems, political paralysis, mediocre political leadership with little insight or foresight, and in general too little sense for the commonweal are seen everywhere. Too many old answers to new challenges.

Hundreds of millions of human beings on our planet increasingly suffer from unemployment, poverty, hunger, and the destruction of their families. Hope for a lasting peace among nations slips away from us. There are tensions between the sexes and generations. Children die, kill, and are killed. More and more countries are shaken by corruption in politics and business. It is increasingly difficult to live together peacefully in our cities because of social, racial, and ethnic conflicts, the abuse of drugs, organized crime, and even anarchy. Even neighbors often live in fear of one another. Out planet contiues to be ruthlessly plundered. A collapse of the ecosystem threatens us.

[†] Not *ethics*, which implies rather great detail, but *ethic in the singular*, i.e., the fundamental attitude toward good and evil, and the principles to put it into action.

Time and again we see leaders and members of *religions* incite aggression, fanaticism, hate, and xenophobia—even inspire and legitimate violent and bloody conflicts. Religion often is misused for purely power-political goals, including war. We are filled with disgust.

We condemn these blights and declare that they need not be. An ethic already exists within the religious teachings of the world which can counter the global distress. Of course this ethic provides no direct solution for all the immense problems of the world, but it does supply the moral foundation for a better individual and global order: *a vision which can lead women and men away from despair, and society away from chaos.*

We are persons who have committed ourselves to the precepts and practices of the world's religions. We confirm that there is already a consensus among the religions which can be the basis for a global ethic—a minimal *fundamental consensus* concerning binding *values* irrevocable *standards*, and fundamental *moral attitudes*.

I. No Better Global Order Without a Global Ethic

We men and women of various religions and regions of this earth address here all people, religious and non-religious, for we share the following convictions:

- that we *all have a responsibility for a better global order*;
- that involvement for the sake of human rights, freedom, justice, peace and the preservation of the earth is reasonable and necessary;
- that our different religious and cultural traditions must not prevent our common involvement in opposing all forms of inhumanity and working for greater humaneness;
- that the principles expressed in this Declaration can be affirmed by all humans with ethical convictions, religiously grounded or not.
- that we as religious women and men who base our lives on an Ultimate Reality and draw spiritual power and hope therefrom in trust, in prayer or meditation, in word or silence have, however, a very special responsibility for the welfare of all humanity.

After two world wars, the collapse of fascism, nazism, communism and colonialism and the end of the cold war, humanity has entered a new phase of its history. Humanity today possesses sufficient economic, cultural and spiritual resources to introduce a better global order. But new *ethnic, national, social and religious tensions* threaten the peaceful building of a better world. Our time has experienced greater technological progress than ever existed before, and yet we are faced with the fact that world-wide poverty, hunger, death of children, unemployment, misery and the destruction of nature have not abated but rather to some extent increased. Many peoples are threatened with economic ruin, social disarray, political marginalization and national collapse.

In such a critical situation humanity needs not only political programs and actions, but also a *vision of a peaceful living together* of peoples, ethnic and ethical groupings, and religions; it needs hopes, goals, ideals, standards. But these have slipped from the hands of people all over the world. Do not the religions, however, despite their frequent historical failures, bear a responsibility precisely to demonstrate that such hopes, ideals and standards can be grounded, guarded and lived? This is especially true in the modern state: Precisely because it guarantees freedom of conscience and religion it needs binding values, convictions and norms which are valid for all humans regardless of their social origin, skin color, language or religion.

We are convinced of the fundamental unity of the human family. Therefore, we recall to mind the 1948 Universal Declaration of Human Rights of the United Nations. What it formally proclaimed on the level of *rights* we wish to confirm and deepen here from the perspective of an *ethic*: The full realization of the intrinsic dignity of the human person, of inalienable freedom, of the equality in principle of all humans, and the necessary solidarity of all humans with each other.

On the basis of personal life experiences and the burdensome history of our planet we have learned

- that a better global order cannot be created or, indeed, enforced with laws, prescriptions and conventions alone;
- that the realization of justice in our societies depends on the insight and readiness to act justly;

- that action in favor of rights presumes a consciousness of duty, and that therefore both the head and heart of women and men must be addressed;
- that rights without morality cannot long endure, and that *there will be no better global order without a global ethic.*

By a *global ethic* we do *not* mean a *single unified religion* beyond all existing religions, and certainly not the domination of one religion over all others. By global ethic we mean a *fundamental consensus on binding values, unconditional standards and personal attitudes.* Without such a basic consensus in ethic, every community sooner or later will be threatened by chaos or dictatorship.

II. A Fundamental Demand: Every Human Being Must Be Treated Humanely

However, because we all are fallible men and women with limitations and defects, and because we are aware of the reality of evil, we feel compelled, for the sake of human welfare, to express in this Declaration our convictions about what the fundamental elements of a global ethic should be—for individuals as well as for communities and organizations, for states as well as for religions themselves. For we trust that our often millennia-old religious and ethical traditions contain sufficient elements of an *ethic* which are convincing to and practicable for *all women and men of good will*, religious and non-religious, and which can thus form a common moral foundation for a humane life together on our earth.

At the same time we are aware that our various religions and ethical traditions often offer very different bases for what is helpful and what is unhelpful for men and women, what is right and what is wrong, what is good and what is evil. We do not wish to gloss over or ignore the serious differences among the individual religions. However, they should not hinder us from proclaiming publicly *those things which we already hold in common now*, to which we jointly feel obliged, each on the basis of our own religious or ethical grounds.

We are conscious that religions cannot solve the economic, political and social problems of this earth. However, they can indeed provide what obviously cannot be attained by economic plans, political programs or legal regulations alone: *They can effect a change in the in-*

ner orientation, the whole mentality, the "hearts," of people and move them to a "conversion" from a false path to a new orientation for life. Religions, however, are able to provide people a horizon of meaning for their lives, ultimate standards and a spiritual home. Of course religions can act credibly only when they eliminate those conflicts which spring from the religions themselves and dismantle mutual hostile images and prejudices, fear and mistrust.

We all know that now as before all over the world *women and men are treated inhumanely*: They are robbed of their freedom and their opportunities; their human rights are trampled under foot; their human dignity is disregarded. But might does not make right! In the face of all inhumanity our religions and ethical convictions demand that *every human being must be treated humanely!*

That means that every human being—without distinction of sex, age, race, skin color, language, religion, political view, or national or social origin—possesses an inalienable and *untouchable dignity*. And everyone, individuals as well as the state, is therefore obliged to honor this dignity and guarantee its effective protection. Humans must always be the subjects of rights, must be ends, never mere means, never objects of commercialization and industrialization in economics, politics and media, in research institutes and industrial undertakings. Also in our age no human being, no social class, no influential interest group, no power cartel and likewise no state stands "beyond good and evil." No, all men and women, as beings with reason and conscience, are obliged to behave in a genuinely human, not inhuman, fashion, to *do good and avoid evil!*

To clarify what this means concretely is the intention of our Declaration. We wish to recall that ethical norms should be not bonds and chains but helps and supports for humans so that they may always find and realize anew their life's direction, values, orientation and meaning.

For an authentically human attitude we especially call to mind that Golden Rule which is found and has been maintained in many religions and ethical traditions for thousands of years: *What you do not wish done to yourself, do not do to others*. Or positively: *What you wish done to yourself, do to others!* This should be the irrevocable, unconditional norm for all areas of life, for family and communities, for races, nations and religions. Self-determination and self-realization are thoroughly legitimate—so long as they are not separated from human self-responsibility and global-responsibility, from responsibility for fellow humans and nature. Every form of egoism, however, every self-seeking, whether individual or collective, whether in the form of class thinking, racism, nationalism or sexism, is to be rejected. For these prevent humans from being authentically human.

The Golden Rule implies very concrete standards to which we humans should and wish to hold firm when they concern the welfare of either individuals or humanity as a whole. There are above all *four ancient guidelines* for human behavior which are found in most of the religions of this world. They should be called to mind with a view to a better world order.

III. Four Irrevocable Directives

1. Toward a Culture of Non-violence and Respect for Life

a) Numberless women and men of all regions and religions strive to lead a life that is not determined by egoism but by commitment to their fellow humans and the world around them. And yet there exists in today's world endless hatred, envy, jealousy and violence not only between individuals but also between social and ethnic groups, between classes, races, nations and religions. The tendency toward the use of violence and organized crime, equipped with new technical possibilities, has reached global proportions. Many places are still ruled by terror, and large as well as small dictators oppress their own people. Even in some democracies prisoners are tortured, men and women are mutilated, hostages killed.

b) But in the great ancient religious and ethical traditions of humankind we find the teaching: *You shall not kill!* Or in positive terms: *Have respect for life!* Concretely that means that no one has the right to torture, injure, and certainly not to kill, any other human being. And no people, no race, no religion has the right to hate, to discriminate, and certainly not to exile or to liquidate a "foreign" minority which is different in behavior, different in belief.

c) Therefore young people should learn already at home and in school that violence may not be a means of settling differences with others. Only thus can a *culture of non-violence* be created. All people have a right to life, bodily integrity and the development of personality insofar as they do not injure the rights of others. Of course wherever there are humans there will be conflicts. Such conflicts, however, are to be resolved without violence. This is true for states as well as for individuals, for political power-holders should always commit themselves first of all to non-violent solutions within the framework of an international order of peace—which itself has need of protection and defence against perpetrators of violence. Armament is a mistaken path; disarmament is a commandment of the hour. There is no survival for humanity without peace!

A human person is infinitely precious and must be unconditionally protected. But likewise the lives of animals and plants which inhabit this planet with us deserve protection, preservation and care. As human beings we also have responsibility for the air, water and soil-precisely with a view to future generations. The dominance of humanity over nature and the cosmos is not to be propagated, but rather living in harmony with nature and the cosmos is to be cultivated. We speak for a *respect* for life, *for all life*.

d) To be authentically human in the spirit of our great religions and ethical traditions means that in public as well as private life we must not be ruthless and brutal but rather concerned for others and ready to help. Every people, every race, every religion must show tolerance, respect, indeed, high appreciation for every other. Minorities—whether they be racial, ethnic or religious—need our protection and our support.

2. Toward a Culture of Solidarity and a Just Economic Order

a) Numberless humans in all regions and religions strive even today to live a life in solidarity with one another and a life in work and authentic fulfillment of their vocation. Nevertheless there is in today's world endless hunger, deficiency and need for which not only individuals but even more unjust structures bear responsibility. Millions of men and women are without work, millions are exploited, are forced to the edge of society with possibilities for the future destroyed by poorly paid work. In many lands the gap between the poor and the rich, between the powerful and the powerless is monstrous. In a world in which state socialism as well as profit capitalism have hollowed out many ethical and spiritual values through a purely economic-political view of things, a greed for unlimited profit and a grasping for plunder without end could spread, as well as a materialistic mentality of claims which steadily demands more of the state without obliging oneself to contribute more. The cancerous social evil of corruption has grown in the developing as well as the developed countries.

b) However, in the great ancient religious and ethical traditions of humankind we find the teaching: *You shall not steal!* Or in positive terms: *Deal honestly!* And, in fact, no humans have the right to rob or dispossess—in any manner—other humans or the commonweal. Conversely, no humans have the right to use their possessions without concern for the needs of society. Where extreme poverty reigns, theft will time and again occur for the sake of survival, if indeed complete helplessness and overwhelming despair have not set in. And where power and wealth is accumulated ruthlessly, feelings of envy, resentment, and yes, deadly hate inevitably will well up in the disadvantaged. This leads all too easily to a diabolic circle of violence and counter-violence. There is no global peace without a global order in justice!

c) Therefore young people should learn already at home and in school that property, be it ever so small, carries with it an obligation and that its use should at the same time serve the commonweal. Only thus can a *just economic order* be built up. But if the plight of the poorest billions of humans, particularly women and children, is to be improved, the structures of the world economy must be fundamentally altered. Individual good deeds and assistance projects, indispensable as they are, are not sufficient. The participation of all states and the authority of international organizations are needed to arrive at a just arrangement.

Certainly conflicts of interest are unavoidable, and even the developing nations have need of a national searching of conscience. Yet a solution for the debt crisis and the poverty of the second and third worlds which can be supported by all sides must be sought. In any case, in the developed countries a distinction must be made between a justified and an unjustified consumerism, between a socially beneficial and a non-beneficial use of property, between a reasonable and an unreasonable use of natural resources, between a profit-only and a socially beneficial and ecologically oriented market economy. It is universally valid: Wherever those ruling threaten to repress those ruled, institutions threaten persons, might oppresses right, resistance—whenever possible, non-violent—is in place.

d) To be authentically human in the spirit of our great religions and ethical traditions in today's world means the following:

- Instead of misusing economic and political power in ruthless battles for domination, we must utilize them for service to humanity: In a spirit of compassion with those who suffer and with special care for the poor, handicapped, aged, refugees, the lonely.
- Instead of thinking only of power and unlimited power-politics in the unavoidable competitive struggles, a mutual respect, a reasonable balance of interests, an attempt at mediation and consideration should prevail.
- Instead of an unquenchable greed for money, prestige and consumption, once again a sense of moderation and modesty should reign! For in greed humans lose their "soul," their inner freedom, and thus that which makes them human.

3. Toward a Culture of Tolerance and a Life in Truthfulness

a) Numberless humans of all regions and religions strive to live a life of honesty and truthfulness. And yet there exist in the world today endless lies and deceit, swindling and hypocrisy, ideology and demagoguery:

- Politicians and business people who use lies as a way to success;
- Mass media which spread ideological propaganda instead of accurate reporting, disinformation instead of information;
- Scientists and researchers who give themselves over to morally questionable ideological or political programs or to economic interest groups, and who attempt to justify research and experiments which violate fundamental ethical values;
- Representatives of religions who dismiss members of other religions as of little value and who preach fanaticism and intolerance instead of respect, understanding and tolerance.

b) However, in the great ancient religious and ethical traditions of humankind we find the teaching: *You shall not lie!* Or in positive terms: *Speak the truth!* In fact, no woman or man, no institution, no state or church or religious community has the right to speak untruth to other humans. This is especially true for

- The mass media, to whom the right of freedom of the press and freedom of reporting for the sake of truth is assured and to whom the office of guardian is thus granted: They do not stand above morality, but remain duty bound to human dignity, human rights and fundamental values; they are duty bound to objectivity, fairness and the preservation of personal dignity and have no right to intrude into the private human sphere, to manipulate public opinion, or distort reality.
- Artists and scientists, to whom artistic and academic freedom is assured: They are not dispensed from general ethical standards and must serve the truth in sincerity.
- Politicians who, if they lie in the faces of their people, have frittered away their credibility and do not deserve to be re-elected.
- Finally, representatives of religion: When they stir up prejudice, hatred and enmity towards those of different belief they deserve no adherents.

c) Therefore young people should learn already at home and in school to think, speak and act in *truthfulness*. All humans have a right to the truth. They have a right to necessary information and education in order to be able to make decisions that will be formative for their lives. Without an ethical fundamental orientation they will hardly be able to distinguish the important from the unimportant in the daily flood of information today. Ethical standards will help them to discern when facts are twisted, interests are veiled, tendencies are played up and opinions absolutized.

d) To be authentically human in the spirit of our great religions and ethical traditions in today's world means the following:

- Instead of dishonesty, dissembling and opportunistic adaptation to life, cultivate the spirit of truthfulness also in the daily relationships between fellow humans.

- Instead of spreading ideological or partisan half-truths, seek the truth ever anew in incorruptible sincerity.
- Instead of confusing freedom with arbitrariness and pluralism with indifference, hold truth high.
- Instead of chasing after opportunism, serve in trustworthiness and constancy the truth once found.

4. Toward a Culture of Equal Rights and Partnership Between Men and Women

a) Numberless humans of all regions and religions strive to live their lives in the spirit of partnership between man and woman, of responsible action in the area of love, sexuality and family. Nevertheless, all over the world there are condemnable forms of patriarchy, of domination of one sex over the other, of exploitation of women, of sexual misuse of children as well as forced prostitution. The social differences on this earth not infrequently lead to the taking up of prostitution as a means of survival, particularly by women of less developed countries.

b) However, in the great ancient religious and ethical traditions of humankind we find the teaching: *You shall not commit sexual immorality!* Or in positive terms: *Respect and love one another!* Concretely that means: No one has the right to degrade others to mere sex objects, to lead them to or hold them in sexual dependency. Sexual exploitation is to be condemned as one of the worst forms of human degradation. Wherever—even in the name of a religious conviction—the domination of one sex over the other is preached and sexual exploitation is tolerated, wherever prostitution is fostered or children are misused, there resistance is commanded.

c) Therefore young women and men should learn already at home and in school that sexuality is fundamentally not a negative-destructive or exploitative but a creative force. Its function as a life-affirming shaper of community can be brought to bear all the more as it is lived out with responsibility for one's own happiness and that of one's partner. The relationship between men and women does indeed have a sexual dimension, but human fulfillment is not identical with sexual happiness. Sexuality should be an expression and reinforcement of a love relationship lived as partners. Conversely, however, some religious traditions know the ideal of a voluntary renunciation of the full use of sexuality; this renunciation can also be an expression of identity and meaningful fulfillment.

The socially institutionalized form of marriage, which despite all its cultural and religious variety is characterized by love, loyalty and permanence, aims at, and should guarantee, security and mutual support to the husband, wife and children, and secure their rights. It is in marriage that the relationship between a woman and a man should be characterized not by a patronizing behavior or exploitation, but by love, partnership and trustworthiness. All lands and cultures should develop economic and social relationships which will make possible marriage and family worthy of human beings, especially for older people. Parents should not exploit children, nor children parents; rather their relationship should reflect mutual respect, appreciation and concern.

d) To be authentically human in the spirit of our great religious and ethical traditions in today's world means the following:

- Instead of patriarchal domination or degradation, which are the expression of violence and engender counter-violence, mutual respect, partnership, understanding and tolerance.
- Instead of any form of sexual possessive lust or sexual misuse, mutual concern, tolerance, readiness for reconciliation, love. Only what has already been lived on the level of personal and familial relationships can be practiced on the level of nations and religions.

IV. A Transformation of Consciousness

All historical experience demonstrates the following: Our earth cannot be changed unless in the not too distant future an alteration *in the consciousness* of individuals is achieved. This has already been seen in areas such as war and peace or economy and ecology. And it is precisely for this alteration in inner orientation, in the entire mentality, in the "heart," that the religions bear responsibility in a special way. Here we remain aware, however, that a universal consensus on many disputed individual ethical questions (from bio- and sexual ethics through mass media and scientific ethics to economic and political ethics) will be difficult to attain. Nevertheless, even for many questions still disputed, differentiated solutions should be attainable in the spirit of the fundamental principles jointly developed here.

In many areas of life a new consciousness of ethical responsibility has already arisen. Therefore, we would be especially pleased if as many as possible national or international professional organizations, such as those for physicians, scientists, business people, journalists, and politicians, would compose up to date codes of ethics.

Above all, we would welcome it if individual religions also would formulate their very specific ethic: What they on the basis of their faith tradition have to say, for example, about the meaning of life and death, the enduring of suffering and the forgiveness of guilt, about selfless sacrifice and the necessity of renunciation, compassion and joy. All these will be compatible with a Global Ethic, indeed can deepen it, make it more specific and concrete.

We are convinced that the new global order will be a better one only in a socially-beneficial and pluralist, partner-sharing and peace-fostering, nature-friendly and ecumenical globe. Therefore on the basis of our religious convictions we commit ourselves to a common Global Ethic and call upon all women and men of good will to make this Declaration their own.

A UNIVERSAL DECLARATION OF HUMAN RESPONSIBILITIES

(PROPOSED BY THE INTERACTION COUNCIL)

1 September 1997

Introductory Comment

IT IS TIME TO TALK ABOUT HUMAN RESPONSIBILITIES

Globalization of the world economy is matched by global problems, and global problems demand global solutions on the basis of ideas, values and norms respected by all cultures and societies. Recognition of the equal and inalienable rights of all the people requires a foundation of freedom, justice and peace—but this also demands that rights and responsibilities be given equal importance to establish an ethical base so that all men and women can live peacefully together and fulfil their potential. A better social order both nationally and internationally cannot be achieved by laws, prescriptions and conventions alone, but needs a global ethic. Human aspirations for progress can only be realised by agreed values and standards applying to all people and institutions at all times.

Next year will be the 50th anniversary of the Universal Declaration of Human Rights adopted by the United Nations. The anniversary would be an opportune time to adopt a Universal Declaration of Human Responsibilities, which would complement the Human Rights Declaration and strengthen it and help lead to a better world.

The following draft of human responsibilities seeks to bring freedom and responsibility into balance and to promote a move from the freedom of indifference to the freedom of involvement. If one person or government seeks to maximise freedom but does it at the expense of others, a larger number of people will suffer. If human beings maximise their freedom by plundering the natural resources of the earth, then future generations will suffer.

The initiative to draft a Universal Declaration of Human Responsibilities is not only a way of balancing freedom with responsibility, but also a means of reconciling ideologies, beliefs and political views that were deemed antagonistic in the past. The proposed declaration points out that the exclusive insistence on rights can lead to endless dispute and conflict, that religious groups in pressing for their own freedom have a duty to respect the freedom of others. The basic premise should be to aim at the greatest amount of freedom possible, but also to develop the fullest sense of responsibility that will allow that freedom itself to grow.

The InterAction Council has been working to draft a set of human ethical standards since 1987. But its work builds on the wisdom of religious leaders and sages down the ages who have warned that freedom without acceptance of responsibility can destroy the freedom itself, whereas when rights and responsibilities are balanced, then freedom is enhanced and a better world can be created.

The InterAction Council commends the following draft Declaration for your examination and support.

Universal Declaration of Human Responsibilities
(Proposed by the InterAction Council)

Preamble

Whereas recognition of the inherent dignity and of the equal and inalienable rights of all members of the human family is the foundation of freedom, justice and peace in the world and implies obligations or responsibilities,

whereas the exclusive insistence on rights can result in conflict, division, and endless dispute, and the neglect of human responsibilities can lead to lawlessness and chaos,

whereas the rule of law and the promotion of human rights depend on the readiness of men and women to act justly,

whereas global problems demand global solutions which can only be achieved through ideas, values, and norms respected by all cultures and societies,

whereas all people, to the best of their knowledge and ability, have a responsibility to foster a better social order, both at home and globally, a goal which cannot be achieved by laws, prescriptions, and conventions alone,

whereas human aspirations for progress and improvement can only be realized by agreed values and standards applying to all people and institutions at all times,

Now, therefore,

The General Assembly

proclaims this Universal Declaration of Human Responsibilities as a common standard for all peoples and all nations, to the end that every individual and every organ of society, keeping this Declaration constantly in mind, shall contribute to the advancement of communities and to the enlightenment of all their members. We, the peoples of the world thus renew and reinforce commitments already proclaimed in the Universal Declaration of Human Rights: namely, the full acceptance of the dignity of all people; their inalienable freedom and equality, and their solidarity with one another. Awareness and acceptance of these responsibilities should be taught and promoted throughout the world.

Fundamental Principles for Humanity

Article 1
Every person, regardless of gender, ethnic origin, social status, political opinion, language, age, nationality, or religion, **has a responsibility to treat all people in a humane way.**

Article 2
No person should lend support to any form of inhumane behavior, but all people have a responsibility to strive for the dignity and self-esteem of all others.

Article 3
No person, no group or organization, no state, no army or police stands above good and evil; all are subject to ethical standards. Everyone has a responsibility to promote good and to avoid evil in all things.

Article 4
All people, endowed with reason and conscience, must accept a responsibility to each and all, to families and communities, to races, nations, and religions in a spirit of solidarity: **What you do not wish to be done to yourself, do not do to others.**

Non-Violence and Respect for Life

Article 5
Every person has a responsibility to **respect life**. No one has the right to injure, to torture or to kill another human person. This does not exclude the right of justified self-defense of individuals or communities.

Article 6
Disputes between states, groups or individuals should be resolved without violence. No government should tolerate or participate in acts of genocide or terrorism, nor should it abuse women, children, or any

other civilians as instruments of war. Every citizen and public official has a responsibility to act in a peaceful, non-violent way.

Article 7
Every person is infinitely precious and must be protected unconditionally. The animals and the natural environment also demand protection. All people have a responsibility to protect the air, water and soil of the earth for the sake of present inhabitants and future generations.

Justice and Solidarity

Article 8
Every person has a responsibility to behave with **integrity, honesty and fairness**. No person or group should rob or arbitrarily deprive any other person or group of their property.

Article 9
All people, given the necessary tools, have a responsibility to make serious efforts to overcome poverty, malnutrition, ignorance, and inequality. They should promote sustainable development all over the world in order to assure dignity, freedom, security and justice for all people.

Article 10
All people have a responsibility to develop their talents through diligent endeavor; they should have equal access to education and to meaningful work. Everyone should lend support to the needy, the disadvantaged, the disabled and to the victims of discrimination.

Article 11
All property and wealth must be used responsibly in accordance with justice and for the advancement of the human race. Economic and political power must not be handled as an instrument of domination, but in the service of economic justice and of the social order.

Truthfulness and Tolerance

Article 12
Every person has a responsibility to **speak and act truthfully.** No one, however high or mighty, should speak lies. The right to privacy and to personal and professional confidentiality is to be respected. No one is obliged to tell all the truth to everyone all the time.

Article 13
No politicians, public servants, business leaders, scientists, writers or artists are exempt from general ethical standards, nor are physicians, lawyers and other professionals who have special duties to clients. Professional and other codes of ethics should reflect the priority of general standards such as those of truthfulness and fairness.

Article 14
The freedom of the media to inform the public and to criticize institutions of society and governmental actions, which is essential for a just society, must be used with responsibility and discretion. Freedom of the media carries a special responsibility for accurate and truthful reporting. Sensational reporting that degrades the human person or dignity must at all times be avoided.

Article 15
While religious freedom must be guaranteed, the representatives of religions have a special responsibility to avoid expressions of prejudice and acts of discrimination toward those of different beliefs. They should not incite or legitimize hatred, fanaticism and religious wars, but should foster tolerance and mutual respect between all people.

Mutual Respect and Partnership

Article 16
All men and all women have **a responsibility to show respect** to one another **and understanding** in their partnership. No one should subject another person to sexual exploitation or dependence. Rather, sexual partners should accept the responsibility of caring for each other's well-being.

Article 17
In all its cultural and religious varieties, marriage requires love, loyalty and forgiveness and should aim at guaranteeing security and mutual support.

Article 18
Sensible family planning is the responsibility of every couple. The relationship between parents and children should reflect mutual love, respect, appreciation and concern. No parents or other adults should exploit, abuse or maltreat children.

Conclusion

Article 19
Nothing in this Declaration may be interpreted as implying for any state, group or person any right to engage in any activity or to perform any act aimed at the destruction of any of the responsibilities, rights and freedom set forth in this Declaration and in the Universal Declaration of Human Rights of 1948.

Endorsement

The proposed Universal Declaration of Human Responsibilities have the endorsement of the following individuals:

I. The InterAction Council Members
Helmut Schmidt (Honorary Chairman)
> Former Chancellor of the Federal Republic of Germany

Malcolm Fraser (Chairman)
> Former Prime Minister of Australia

Andries A. M. van Agt
> Former Prime Minister of the Netherlands

Anand Panyarachun
> Former Prime Minister of Thailand

Oscar Arias Sanchez
> Former President of Costa Rica

Lord Callaghan of Cardiff
> Former Prime Minister of the United Kingdom

Jimmy Carter
> Former President of the United States

Miguel de la Madrid Hurtado
> Former President of Mexico

Kurt Furgler
 Former President of Switzerland
Valery Giscard d'Estaing
 Former President of France
Felipe Gonzalez Marquez
 Former Prime Minister of Spain
Kenneth Kaunda
 Former President of Zambia
Lee Kuan Yew
 Former Prime Minister of Singapore
Kiichi Miyazawa
 Former Prime Minister of Japan
Misael Pastrana Borrero
 Former President of Colombia (deceased in August)
Shimon Peres
 Former Prime Minister of Israel
Maria de Lourdes Pintasilgo
 Former Prime Minister of Portugal
Jose Sarney
 Former President of Brazil
Shin Hyon Hwak
 Former Prime Minister of the Republic of Korea
Kalevi Sorsa
 Former Prime Minister of Finland
Pierre Elliott Trudeau
 Former Prime Minister of Canada
Ola Ullsten
 Former Prime Minister of Sweden
George Vassiliou
 Former President of Cyprus
Franz Vranitzky
 Former President of Austria

II. Supporters
Lester Brown, President, Worldwatch Institute
Andre Chouraqui, Professor in Israel
Takako Doi, President, Japan Socialist Democratic Party
William Laughlin, American entrepreneur
Rabbi Dr. J. Magonet, Principal of the Leo Baek College
Robert S. McNamara, Former President, World Bank
Konrad Raiser, World Council of Churches
Paul Volcker, Chairman, James D. Wolfensohn Inc.

III. Participants (in preparatory meetings in Vienna, Austria, in March 1996 and April 1997) and special guests at the 15th Plenary Session in Noordwijk, The Netherlands, in June 1997)

Hans Küng (academic advisor to the project), Tübingen University
Thomas Axworthy (academic advisor to the project), CRB Foundation
Kim, Kyong-dong (academic advisor to the project),
      Seoul National University
Cardinal Franz Koenig, Vienna, Austria
Anna-Marie Aagaard, World Council of Churches
M. Shanti Aram (died in June), World Conference on Religion & Peace
A. T. Ariyaratne, Sarvodaya Movement of Sri Lanka
Julia Ching, University of Toronto
Hassan Hanafi, University of Cairo
Nagaharu Hayabusa, The Asahi Shimbun
Yersu Kim, Division of Philosophy and Ethics, UNESCO
Peter Landesmann, European Academy of Sciences
Lee, Seung-Yun, Former Deputy Prime Minister and Minister of Economic Planning Board of the Republic   of Korea
Flora Lewis, International Herald Tribune
Liu, Xiao-feng, Institute of Sino-Christian Studies
Teri McLuhan, Canadian author
Isamu Miyazaki, Former Minister, Economic Planning Agency of Japan
James Ottley, Anglican observer at the United Nations
Richard Rorty, Stanford Humanities Center
L. M. Singvi, High Commissioner for India
Seiken Sugiura, House of Representatives of Japan
Koji Watanabe, Former Japanese Ambassador to Russia
Woo, Seong-yong, Munhwa Ilbo
Alexander Yakovlev, Former Member, Presidential Council of the
      Soviet Union

IV. Sponsors
Shinyasu Hoshino, President, National Institute for Research Advancement
Ayako Sono, Chairperson, Nippon Foundation
Kim, Woo-Joong, Chairman, Dae-Woo Corporation

A Universal Declaration of Human Responsibilities
Report on the Conclusions and Recommendations by a High-level Expert Group Meeting, Vienna, Austria (20-22 April 1997)
Chaired by Helmut Schmidt

It is time to talk about human responsibilities

The call by the InterAction Council for a Universal Declaration of Human Responsibilities is timely. Although traditionally we have spoken of human rights, and indeed the world has gone a long way in their international recognition and protection since the Universal Declaration of Human Rights was adopted by the United Nations in 1948, it is time now to initiate an equally important quest for the acceptance of human duties or obligations.

This emphasis of human obligations is necessary for several reasons. Of course, this idea is new only to some regions of the world; many societies have traditionally conceived of human relations in terms of obligations rather than rights. This is true, in general terms, for instance, for much of Eastern thought. While traditionally in the West, at least since the 17th Century age of enlightenment, the concepts of freedom and individuality have been emphasized; in the East, the notions of responsibility and commu- nity have prevailed. The fact that a Universal Declaration of Human Rights was drafted instead of a Universal Declaration of Human Duties undoubtedly reflects the philosophical and cultural background of the document's drafters who, as is known, represented the Western powers who emerged victorious from the Second World War.

The concept of human obligations also serves to balance the notions of freedom and responsibility: while rights relate more to freedom, obligations are associated with responsibility. Despite this distinction, freedom and responsibility are interdependent. Responsibility, as a moral quality, serves as a natural, voluntary check for freedom. In any society, freedom can never be exercised without limits. Thus, the more freedom we enjoy, the greater the responsibility we bear, toward others as well as ourselves. The more talents we possess, the bigger the responsibility we have to develop them to their fullest capacity. We must move away from the freedom of indifference towards the freedom of involvement.

The opposite is also true: as we develop our sense of responsibility, we increase our internal freedom by fortifying our moral character. When freedom presents us with different possibilities for action, including the choice to do right or wrong, a responsible moral character will ensure that the former will prevail.

Sadly, this relationship between freedom and responsibility is not always understood clearly. Some ideologies have placed greater importance on the concept of individual freedom, while others concentrate on an unquestioning commitment to the social group.

Without a proper balance, unrestricted freedom is as dangerous as imposed social responsibility. Great social injustices have resulted from extreme economic freedom and capitalist greed, while at the same time cruel oppression of people's basic liberties has been justified in the name of society's interests or communist ideals.

Either extreme is undesirable. At present, with the disappearance of the East-West conflict and the end of the Cold War, humankind seems closer to the desired balance between freedom and responsibility. We have struggled for freedom and rights. It is now time to foster responsibility and human obligations.

The InterAction Council believes that globalization of the world economy is matched by globalization of the world's problems. Because global interdependence demands that we must live with each other in harmony, human beings need rules and constraints. Ethics are the minimum standards that make a collective life possible. Without ethics and self-restraint that are their result, humankind would revert to the survival of the fittest. The world is in need of an ethical base on which to stand.

Recognizing this need, the InterAction Council began its search for universal ethical standards with a meeting of spiritual leaders and political leaders in March 1987 at La Civiltà Cattolica in Rome, Italy. The initiative was taken by the late Takeo Fukuda, former Prime Minister of Japan who founded the InterAction Council in 1983. Again in 1996, the Council requested a report by a high-level expert group on the subject of global ethical standards. The Council at its Vancouver Plenary Meeting in May 1996, welcomed the report of this Group, which consisted of religious leaders from several faiths and experts drawn from across the globe. The findings of this report "In Search of Global Ethical Standards" demonstrated that the world faiths have much in common and the Council endorsed the recommendation that "in 1998, the 50th anniversary of the Universal Declaration of Human Rights, the United Nations should convene a conference to consider a Declaration of Human Obligations to complement the earlier crucial work on rights."

The initiative to draft a Universal Declaration of Human Responsibilities is not only a way of balancing freedom with responsibility, but also a means of reconciling ideologies and political views that were deemed antagonistic in the past. The basic premise, then, should be that humans deserve the greatest possible amount of freedom, but also should develop their sense of responsibility to its fullest in order to correctly administer their freedom.

This is hardly a new idea. Throughout the millennia prophets, saints and sages have implored mankind to take its responsibilities seriously. In our century, for example, Mahatma Gandhi preached on the seven social sins:

1. Politics without principles
2. Commerce without morality
3. Wealth without work
4. Education without character
5. Science without humanity
6. Pleasure without conscience
7. Worship without sacrifice

Globalization, however, has given new urgency to the teaching of Gandhi and other ethical leaders. Violence on our television screens is now transmitted by satellites across the planet. Speculation in far away financial markets can devastate local communities. The influence of private tycoons now approaches the power of governments and, unlike elected politicians, there is no accountability for this private power except for their own personal sense of responsibility. Never has the world needed a declaration of human responsibilities more.

From Rights to Obligations

Because rights and duties are inextricably linked, the idea of a human right only makes sense if we acknowledge the duty of all people to respect it. Regardless of a particular society's values, human relations are universally based on the existence of both rights and duties.

There is no need for a complex system of ethics to guide human action. There is one ancient rule that, if truly followed, would ensure just human relations: the Golden Rule. In its negative form, the Golden Rule mandates that we not do to others what we do not wish be done to us. The positive form implies a more active and solidary role: Do unto others as you would have them do unto you.

Bearing in mind the Golden Rule, the Universal Declaration of Human Rights provides an ideal starting point from which to consider some of the main obligations which are a necessary complement to those rights.

- If we have a right to life, then we have the obligation to respect life.

- If we have a right to liberty, then we have the obligation to respect other people's liberty.

- If we have a right to security, then we have the obligation to create the conditions for every human being to enjoy human security.

- If we have a right to partake in our country's political process and elect our leaders, then we have the obligation to participate and ensure that the best leaders are chosen.

- If we have a right to work under just and favorable conditions to provide a decent standard of living for ourselves and our families, we also have the obligation to perform to the best of our capacities.

- If we have a right to freedom of thought, conscience and religion, we also have the obligation to respect other's thoughts or religious principles.

- If we have a right to be educated, then we have the obligation to learn as much as our capabilities allow us and, where possible, share our knowledge and experience with others.

- If we have a right to benefit from the earth's bounty, then we have the obligation to respect, care for and restore the earth and its natural resources.

As human beings, we have unlimited potential for self-fulfilment. Thus we have the obligation to develop our physical, emotional, intellectual and spiritual capacities to their fullest. The importance of the concept of responsibility towards attaining self-realization cannot be overlooked.

The expert-group, which was convened in Vienna in April 1997, worked on a declaration of human responsibilities. The results of this work were summarized and condensed by the three academic advisors: Prof. Thomas Axworthy, Prof. Kim Kyong-dong and Prof. Hans Küng. Prof. Küng provided a very helpful first draft as the starting point for the discussion. They made recommendations to Helmut Schmidt, who chaired the meeting, Andries van Agt and Miguel de la Madrid. Oscar Arias, a member of the Council, who could not be present, contributed a welcome substantive paper.

The results of this work are contained in the draft proposal for the United Nations entitled "A Universal Declaration of Human Responsibilities." The group submits with pleasure the attached draft to the InterAction Council and the world community at large.

List of Participants

InterAction Council Members

H. E. Mr. Helmut Schmidt
H. E. Mr. Andries van Agt
H. E. Mr. Miguel de la Madrid Hurtado

Academic Advisors
Prof. Hans Küng, Tübingen University
Prof. Thomas Axworthy, Adjunct Faculty in Public Policy at Harvard University
Prof. Kim Kyong-dong, Seoul National University

High-level Experts
Cardinal Franz Koenig, Vienna, Austria
Prof. Hassan Hanafi, University of Cairo
Dr. Ariyaratne, President of the Sarvodaya Movement of Sri Lanka
The Rt. Rev. James H. Ottley, Anglican observer at the United Nations
Dr. M. Aram, President, World Conference on Religion & Peace (MP, India)
Dr. Julia Ching (Representing Confucianism)
Dr. Anna-Marie Aagaard, World Council of Churches
Dr. Teri McLuhan, Author
Prof. Yersu Kim, Director of the Division of Philosophy and Ethics, UNESCO
Prof. Richard Rorty, Stanford Humanities Center
Prof. Peter Landesmann, European Academy of Sciences, Salzburg
Ambassador Koji Watanabe, Former Japanese Ambassador to Russia

Journalists
Ms. Flora Lewis, International Herald Tribune
Mr. Woo Seung-yong, Munhwa Ilbo

Project coordinator (IAC Tokyo Secretariat)
Keiko Atsumi

InterAction Council, Tokyo Secretariat
3-16-13-706, Roppongi, Minato-ku, Tokyo 106, Japan
Tel: 813-3505-4527 Fax: 813-3589-3922
E-mail: infoplus@mail.asianet.net

THE AFRICAN CHARTER ON HUMAN RIGHTS: AN AFRICAN CONTRIBUTION TO THE GLOBAL ETHIC PROJECT

MUTOMBO NKULU

I. *Status Quaestionis*[1]

IN 1992, PROFESSOR SWIDLER called for a "Global Ethos Research Center"[2] that would be charged with the task of drawing together the research and reflection on a global ethic into a Universal Declaration of a Global Ethic. It is in response to this project that I came to think about the situation of Africa in the light of the tragic events happening in this continent. What do African people have to do with a Global Ethic elaborated outside of their continent and perhaps without taking into account their situation and difficulties? Does Africa even need a Global Ethic? What contribution could Africa bring to the project? To answer these questions, it is important to know first of all the real situation of African societies today in terms of human rights and ethics. Some recent events can help us to situate the debate of a "global ethic" in Africa.

In fact, the last decade from 1981 to 1991 will probably remain in African history an important period which can be qualified as a period of "Human Rights Revolution" or "The Rise of Democracy." Two important events marked this period: on the one hand, the publication of The African Charter on Human and Peoples' Rights in June 1981 by the Organisation of African Unity(OAU) and, on the other hand, the end of the "single party era" under the storm of democratization which started to blow in East Europe, Africa and Asia between 1989 and 1991 with the rise of Gorbatchevian perestroika. In fact, since 1989, in several countries of Africa, the word "democracy" is becoming everybody's favorite song. Independent newspapers are growing everywhere. People talk openly against dictatorship and organize demonstrations. In many countries, men and women, priests, believers and non-believers march into the streets and die for freedom and justice. In January 1991, Jacques Pelletier, French Minister of the Cooperation, said that among 29 countries of Black Africa traditionally "friends of France," only five had not yet started seriously the process of democratization.[3] In this process of democratization, one phenomenon has struck our attention: the role played by the churches to support democracy. In more than four countries, Christian bishops have been elected president of the "National Conference," a kind of "special Parliament," organized to lead countries from totalitarianism toward democratic governments in a non-violent way. Many African bishops, as in Zaïre,[4] have clearly taken a position in favor of democracy and pluralism against dictatorship and the single party regime which prevailed in many countries since the independence era of '60s. In several pastoral letters the Zairian National Conference of Catholic Bishops called clearly for the end of the dictatorship of President Mobutu and for the rise of "democracy." In February 1992 the National Catholic Conference of Bishops in the United States sent a "statement on massacre of marchers in Zaïre" sustaining the efforts of Archbishop Monsengwo to lead the country to a democratic regime:

> Dear Archbishop Monsengwo Pasinya,
>   I write to express condolences on behalf of the United States Catholic Conference on the deaths of the Christian protest marchers who where killed on Sunday, February 16, in Kinshasa in their prayerful and non-violent attempt to vindicate their rights as a people. I would like as well to offer you, Archbishop, in your capacity as president of the National Conference, the support of the USCC in your

work on behalf of national reconciliation and peaceful change. The church in the United States stands in solidarity with the church in Zaïre in its struggle for freedom, peace and justice.

We will be communicating our concern over the Kinshasa massacre with the embassy of Zaïre and with the US Department of State. If there is any way in which we can show our solidarity with your efforts on behalf the transition to democratic government, we would welcome hearing from you.[5]

This letter shows us the importance of "international solidarity" to solve African problems today. And the project of a Global ethic may be helpful in the same way. The African struggle for democracy and for the respect of human Rights may be understood as a result of, at least, five factors:

1. The United Nations' Universal Declaration of Human Rights

2. The vigilant action of Amnesty International

3. The pressure of the US government urging the respect of human rights as a *sine qua non* condition for any economic help to african countries. This pressure became very powerful under the Carter administration.

4. The end of the Cold War which has slowed down the support given to African dictators by the former Soviet Union, the United States and many former colonial powers (mainly Great Britain, France and Belgium). Therefore the weakness of dictators has liberated the energy of people who can now organize marches and call for change toward new political regimes committed to the respect of human rights and the guarantee of freedom, justice and welfare for at least the majority of the people.

5. The "African Humanism" expressed in different political and philosophical movements like Panafricanism, Negritude, Authenticity and *Ujamaa* or African Socialism. This African Humanism is the traditional African passion for life expressed in the Bantu philosophy under the term *Force Vitale*, a passion which has always made African people able to survive under oppressions, to claim freedom and justice and to fight slavery, colonialism, racism and now dictatorship.

The conjunction of all these factors defines the New Era of Africa, a new era which will surely be marked by the promotion of human rights. We use the expression of "New Era" also because the Africa of ethnocentrism and nationalism is developing a new way of life dominated by a "global vision" and "global interaction." In fact, even for an African who has never traveled abroad, it is clear today that the World has become a "global village." I still remember how the people of my small village were excited at the event of the first man marching on the moon in 1969. In African languages we created songs to sing "Apollo XI" while some boys of my village preferred to be called "Apollo." From their villages, Africans remain connected to the entire world through radio and through the contact with thousands of "outsiders" visiting Africa or working there. Many Africans are now accustomed to seeing all kinds of American Peace Corps workers, Westerns tourists, scientists, businessmen, teachers, engineers, soldiers, missionaries, and foreign governments' agents. Many of these non-Africans have been living there for a long time, some of them even marry Africans, become members of African religions like Kimbanguism, receive traditional initiations, and so on.

Also, Near and Far Eastern people—mainly Indians, Chinese, Koreans, Japanese, Arabs and Jews—have been present on the African continent for generations and generations. In brief, the so-called "Black Continent" is inhabited by peoples from all over the world. That situation raises the question of "the conditions of the possibility" of "living together" peacefully and in friendship for people from different ethnic groups, races, customs, religions and ethical backgrounds. Such as a question makes the project of a global ethic relevant, in the African context.

But before talking about a global ethic, we should first ask whether Africa has a systematic ethic. When we read books published on "African Philosophy" and "African Theology," it is clear that we still do not have an "African Kant." Nevertheless, some efforts have been made to systematize the ethics of different ethnic groups, and some authors, like John Mbiti,[6] have attempted to bring this system to the level of the whole continent. Furthermore, a global direction is found everywhere, from academic researches to public symposiums. In Zaïre, for instance, since 1972, the Catholic Faculty of Theology every year holds two kinds of symposia called "Philosophical Week of Kinshasa" and "Theological Week" which have produced an abundant literature on the issue of African ethics and human rights. Published works from these proceedings include: *Liberation and African Philosophy* (1977), *Ethic and African Society* (1980), *Human Rights and African Philosophy* (1982), *Development and African Philosophy* (1985), *Christian Ethic and African Societies* (1987), *Social Order and African Philosophy* (1988).[7]

In December 1992, a "Pan-African Workshop on Justice and Peace and Human Rights" was organized in Kumasi (Ghana). In the keynote address delivered during that symposium by Rt. Rev. Peter K. Sarpong, Catholic Bishop of Kumasi, we can clearly perceive the move towards a global ethic:

> At the beginning of this last decade of our millennium, the global community, suddenly awakened to the gross injustices in our world, came up with such slogans as "Education for all by the year 2000," "Water for all by the year 2000," "Food for all by the year 2000," "Health for all by the year 2000," to captivate the imagination of humankind. They were designed to address inequalities in the world and hopefully to stem the wave of violence and hostilities everywhere. At a time when once unimaginable strides are being made in science, technology and social communications, our globe is sinking gradually but surely into the abyss of destruction. The world is revelling in wrong-doing, resulting in the degradation of the human person, sometimes to a level below that of the brute animal. One may ask why we intelligent and free human beings can not discern what is wrong from what is right, reject the former and adopt the latter?[8]

Today, in many countries we have several national organizations dealing with ethical themes, such as the Association of Physicians, Association of Philosophers, Association for the Defense of Human Rights and Association of Moralists. Beside these non-religious organizations we have also the Ecumenical Association of African Theologians and the Ecumenical Association of the Third World Theologians[9] which carry on a significant dialogue on African values and on the issues of justice and freedom. Members of the Catholic theology and the Protestant Churches developed a dialogue open also to African Religions and to other religions like Islam. Unfortunately all these organizations have not yet produced a general text in the spirit of a global ethic including believers and non-believers.

Until now, the African Charter on Human and Peoples' Rights remains the unique text bringing Africans of all beliefs to some common principles on human rights. This text is foundational for the comprehension of ethics in Africa. That is why in this paper we want to see how this text can be used in the project of a global ethic. In fact, in our world it is not enough to have "peacelovers," we need "peacemakers"; it is not enough to think in a "global way" or to have a kind of "universal mind." What is required is "to act in a global way and with a global perspective" by treating in each human being the entire humanity, to paraphrase both Kant's and the ancient rabbinical principle. The survival of our world urges us to keep in mind the unity of the "human family" in each of our actions. It is in this way that we can understand the project of global ethic and its importance for African people.

We will limit our analysis to a special text which is more meaningful: the African Charter on Human and Peoples' Rights.[10] This text will be analyzed in connection with three other texts, the Universal Declaration of Human Rights and the Swidler and Kung Global Ethic draft declarations presented in this volume.[11]

After a brief presentation of the "African Charter on Human and Peoples' Rights," we will focus our attention on the contribution of this African Charter to the project of a Global Ethic. This Charter has been commented on and analyzed in several books and reviews dealing with international law such as the *American Journal of International Law*, the *Encyclopedia of Public International Law*, *Revue Universelle des Droits de l'Homme*, *Rivista Internazionale dei Diritti dell'Uomo*, *Cooperazione Giuridica Internazionale*, *Afrique 2000*. *Revue Africaine de Politique Internationale*, *Présence Africaine*, *Zaïre-Afrique*.[12] Our paper intends to bring another kind of commentary, from the perspective of a Global Ethic.

II. What is the *African Charter of Human and Peoples' Rights*?

A. Definition

The African Charter of Human and Peoples' Rights is a declaration of human rights published by the Organisation of African Unity in June 1981. This Charter intends to define human rights in the context of the African continent as a whole and from the African world view. In a sense, this Charter seems to be a correction, an interpretation, and an amplification of the UN Declaration of Human Rights. In other terms it is an application of the UN Declaration of Human Rights to the African situation, also taking into account the evolution of the concept of human rights since 1948. It is written by Africans and for Africans.

B. Genesis of the text

The African Charter on Human and Peoples' Rights is not an invention *ex nihilo*. It has a long history behind it. Beside the contribution of the UN Declaration of Human Rights, the immediate history of the African Charter is rooted in the Carter administration and the action of the Association of African Jurists.

The conflict between African governments and the United Nations' Universal Declaration of Human Rights constitutes the starting point of the process of creating the African Charter of Human Rights. Created in 1963, in a context of war against colonialism, the OAU focused its attention on the eradication of colonialism and *apartheid*. To avoid conflict between member states, the OAU emphasized the principle of noninterference in "internal affairs." Soon, the abuse of power by the presidents of newly independent African states becomes an internal affair so that President Sekou Touré could claim that the OAU was not a tribunal which could sit in judgement on any member state's internal affairs.[13] For a long time the OAU kept silence on the violation of human rights by Africans. The massacres of thousands of Hutu in Burundi in 1972 and 1973 were neither discussed nor condemned by the OAU, which regarded them as matters of internal affairs.[14]

Even though the OAU Charter reaffirms in its preamble and purposes the principles of the UN Charter and the Universal Declaration of Human Rights, many African presidents came to think that the UN Declaration, written without their participation, does not reflect the African vision of human rights and is in a certain way another form of colonization. Then in the name of "African identity" and "African tradition" they refused to recognize any European denunciation of violations of human rights, claiming that they were acting according to "the African vision of human dignity" and the African interpretation of the UN Declaration of Human Rights. The OAU charter itself was responsible for that confusion because, as many African jurists pointed out,[15] it missed a significant emphasis on human rights, making only passing reference to the UN Charter in its preamble and in Article II.

But during the course of the years, the abuse of power by African politicians became more and more problematic because the "oppression of Africans by their fellow Africans" became so evident and intolerable. If the independent states were few in the 1960s, their number increased in the 1970s and the responsibility of Africans for the violation of human rights became much more evident and even increased. In fact, as Umozurike[16] pointed out, during the 1970s the violation of human rights reached its acme in Africa with the terrible behavior of presidents like Idi Amin Dada in Uganda (1971-1979), Marcias Nguema in Equatorial Guinea (1969-1979) and Jean-Bedel Bokassa in Central African Republic (1966-1979). The terror set up by Idi Amin and Bokassa and its resonance in Western media created a great deal of indignation. In 1975, the Helsinki Final Act signed by the United States, Canada, and 33 European countries emphasized respect for human rights.

When President Jimmy Carter took office in 1977, he found Africa in serious trouble. The same decade was also marked by the phenomenon of "boat people" in Southeast Asia. Coming to the White House after the Helsinki Act was signed in 1975 by the United States, President Carter made respect of human rights a *sine qua non* condition for any economic help to third world countries. But indignation did not come only from the outside. On their side, African jurists decided to revise the role of the OAU in such matters. Before the development of Western pressure and concern about abuse of human rights in African independent states, African jurists, already aware of the gross abuse of human rights during the colonial period, gathered in Lagos in 1961, under the auspices of the International Commission of Jurists and suggested an African Human Rights Charter under which would be created a court to which individuals or groups could have recourse.[17]

A similar call was made in Dakar by jurists from French-speaking African states in 1967. The African Bar Association later proposed a commission of human rights to operate along the same line as Amnesty International in London and the International Commission of Jurists in Geneva. In 1967 Nigeria proposed at the 23rd session of the Commission on Human Rights that the UN establish regional commissions where none existed. The idea was accepted and the Commission then invited the UN Secretary-General to organize seminars in those regions where no human rights commission existed. At the commemoration of the 20th anniversary of the UN Declaration of Human Rights held in Tehran in 1968, Nigeria renewed its campaign for the establishment of regional commissions. In 1969, during a UN seminar held in Cairo and attended by 19 African states, the creation of an African Commission of Human Rights with the collaboration of the OAU was decided upon.[18]

Finally under international pressure and the pressure of the Carter administration, the OAU decided in 1979 to address the issue of human rights. That happened also because the General Secretary of the OAU at that period happened to be Edem Kodjo, a jurist more sensitive to the issue of human rights and a citizen of Togo where human rights were terribly violated. In February 1979, Edem Kodjo organized a colloquium on the topic "Les perspectives du développement de l'Afrique à l'horizon 2000". The conclusion of that symposium stated clearly that "no development was possible in Africa without the guarantee of human rights."[19] Then the OAU set in motion studies of an African Charter of Human Rights. From 28 November to 8 December 1979, a committee of experts met in Dakar to draw up a draft charter. The Secretary-General of the OAU enjoined them to take cognisance of the "African concept of Human Rights"[20] in order to make the proposed charter distinct from other conventions already adopted in other regions. For that reason the Secretary-General proposed to the experts:

1. To give importance to the principle of non-discrimination;
2. To lay emphasis on the principles and objectives of the OAU;
3. To include peoples' rights besides individual rights;
4. To determine the duties of each person towards the community in which he lives and more particularly towards the family and the state;
5. To show that African values as well as morals still have an important place in our societies;
6. To give economic, social and cultural rights the place they deserve.[21]

After many amendments the draft gave birth to the African Charter on Human and Peoples' Rights that was finally adopted by the eighteenth summit of the OAU in Nairobi, Kenya in July 1981, the year that President Carter left the White House!

C) The Text

The text of the African Charter of Human and Peoples' Rights is divided into three parts introduced by a general preamble. The second and the third parts deal with the "Organization of the African Commission of Human Rights." The first part and the preamble are more important for the issue of a global ethic. The first part is divided into two chapters. The first chapter defines in 26 articles the rights of human beings (arts. 1-18) and the rights of peoples (arts. 19-26). The second chapter completes the list of rights by defining the duties of each individual (arts. 27-29). The preamble defines the spirit and the source of the Charter as based on the "African tradition," the "Universal Declaration of Human Rights," and other international conventions.

Among the important articles for the issue of human rights we have articles 17, 18 and 27, which present ethics as indispensable and as the key to the interpretation of any human right. We have also article 8 which guarantees the liberty of conscience and religion. Articles 10, 11, 12 and 13 are also very interesting because they open the door for "democracy." The word "democracy" is not used in the Charter, but article 13 guarantees the right to participate in government either directly or through freely chosen representatives and protects access to public property and services on the basis of non-discrimination. Also interesting for a global ethic is the constant reference of the Charter to ethics which appears several times in the text.

III. Contribution of the African Charter to a Global Ethic

A. Contribution as Ethics

The first question to be addressed is to know whether this text can qualify as an "ethical text." When we look at the story and the context of the text, we find that it has been promulgated neither by an association of African moralists nor by churches but by politicians—by heads of states gathered in the OAU, which is a political organization. But an attentive analysis of the content of the text reveals that the text is not totally lacking in an ethical atmosphere. What do we mean by ethics in that context?

Swidler reminds us that "Ethic" refers to "the fundamental attitude toward good and evil, and the principles to put it into action."[22] Understood in that sense, an ethic is present in the ACHPR. First of all we perceive that there are many similarities between the ethical principles of a Global Ethic formulated by Swidler and Küng. In these two texts of a Global Ethic, the foundation of a global ethic rests on the concept of "good and evil" and on "the dignity of the human being," which implies the respect of human rights. Küng's text states clearly:

> We recall to mind the 1948 Universal Declaration of Human Rights of the United Nations. What is formally proclaimed on the level of rights we wish to confirm and deepen here from the perspective of an ethic: the full realization of the intrinsic dignity of the human person, of inalienable freedom, of the equality in principle of all humans, and the necessary solidarity of all humans with each other.

For its part, Swidler's text says:

> This document presupposes and affirms the rights and corresponding responsibilities enumerated in the 1948 Universal Declaration of Human Rights of the United Nations as a Universal Declaration of a Global Ethic which we believe must undergird any affirmation of human rights and respect for the Earth. In accord with that first UN Declaration we believe there are five general presuppositions which are indispensable for a global ethic: every human possesses inalienable and inviolable dignity, everyone is obliged to do good and avoid evil. . .

In the African Charter of Human and Peoples' Rights, we find, *mutatis mutandis*, the same presuppositions. The preamble states clearly that the African Charter takes into account the UN Declaration of Human Rights and specifies that in this African Charter the fundamental rights "stem from the attributes of human beings" (*les attribus de la personne humaine*). That is to say, in concurrence with the general notion of human rights, that in the African world view human rights are not defined on the basis of the family or the collectivity, but one has rights by the fact of being a human being. Completing this foundation, article 4 affirms the "inviolability" of the human person and article 5 emphasizes that each individual has a dignity inherent in her person.

It appears then that the Global Ethic declaration (as defined in Swidler's and Küng's texts) and the African Charter of Human and Peoples' Rights have a common vision in the fact that:

1. They perceive human rights as based on the notion of "human nature."

2. They consider that "human nature" has an intrinsic value and inviolable dignity.

3. They consider that this "common human nature" is the foundation of the principles of equality, justice, freedom and fraternity or solidarity which constitute the foundation of all human rights.

In the two Global Ethic documents and ACHPR, we find the primacy of ethics and its expression in a fundamental rule, a kind of golden rule as an indispensable key to any definition and understanding of human rights and to any possibility of "living together" in the world.

In the ACHPR we do not have the golden rule in the same words used by Swidler and Küng like, "What you do not wish done to yourself, do not do to others or what you wish done to yourself, do to others." But we clearly have the same rule in article 27 which states powerfully that all rights and liberties defined in the Charter must be put into action by each person only in the respect of the right and the security of others and in the respect of the morality: "The rights and freedoms of each person shall be exercised with due regard to the rights of others, collective security, morality and common interest" (art. 27, #2).

The concept of respect of others means that people must avoid to do to others what is not good. It corresponds to the golden rule in the expression of "What you do not wish done to yourself, do not do to others." The article also specifies that each individual has duties toward his or her family, toward the society and toward the international community: "Every individual shall have duties toward his family and society, the State and other legally recognised communities and the international community" (art. 27; #1).

By duties we should understand "the good to do to other people." An attentive reading shows clearly that this article 27 is the key to the interpretation of all human rights defined in the African Charter. It is then normal and logical to think that we have here a "fundamental rule," a "golden rule." We have then a major similarity of logic between the ACHPR and the Global Ethic. This similarity continues also in other articles of the Charter. It is easy to draw a parallelism between the Global Ethic defined by Swidler and the African Charter, where we find the same key words and key notions or principles: dignity, equality, justice, respect, freedom, solidarity. The great majority of "ethical principles" defined by Swidler and Küng are present in the human rights defined by the ACHPR: freedom of religion and conscience (art. 8), freedom of thought and speech (art. 9), law (arts. 3, 13), decision making (art. 13), property (art. 14), work (art. 15), education (art. 17), information (art. 9), peace (art. 23).

All that demonstrates that the ACHPR is in a certain way an "ethical text" for the following reasons:

1. Like any ethic, the African Charter deals with "action." It is not a metaphysical text. It shows what must be done and what must not be done in the behavior of people, churches, any kind of group or association, and governments.

2. The word "moral" and cognates, which deal clearly with ethical issues, appears several times in the text.

3. The text gives a great importance to ethic (arts. 17 and 27); it has a clear ethical vision, it contains in a sense some ethical principles ("dignity of human being. . . "), and it considers ethics the foundation of the genuine way of exercising human rights and freedom.

Even though the words "good" and "evil" are not present in the text, it is clear that this text prescribes the good to do and the evil (violation of freedom and human rights) to avoid. All we have seen in our analysis allows us to say that in the ACHPR we have in a certain way a kind of a "Declaration of African Ethics" which can then be analyzed in relationship to the project of a Global Ethic.

B. Contribution as a "Global" Project

We now focus our analysis on the concept of "globality." Our thinking will follow three steps: African continent, relationship between Africa and other continents, relationship between African ethics and the text of the Universal Declaration of a Global Ethic.

1. First step: Within Africa

If the nature of the "Global Ethic" is to be a consensus from different "ethical traditions" of humankind, it is clear that it would be easier to deal with a text that already is a consensus of African peoples than to deal with the ethics of each single African ethnic group. The "ethical situation" of Africa is a very complex one. Africa is a huge continent of 53 countries and more or less 660 millions people speaking about two thousands languages, having different customs and worshipping God in several religions. As John Mbiti pointed out,[23] we find in the African continent mainly Christianity, Islam, Judaism, Hinduism and several "African religions" along with sects from all over the world, mainly from USA and Asia like the Baha'i Faith and Jehovah Witnesses.

The so-called "African religions" is a group of different churches practicing the traditional religions or mixing Christianity and traditional spirituality. According to Gerhard J. Bellinger, in his article in *Knaurs Grosser Religionsführer,*[24] the African population in 1986, was 60 million members of tribal religions (12% of African population and 70% of all members of the traditional religions of the World), 40% Muslims and 45% Christians. According to Rik De Gendt,[25] who used the data furnished by the AIMIS (Agence d'Information Missionnaires) of Rome, in 1990 the continent had 81,883,000 Roman Catholics (13.4% of the whole African population), and in 1992 Africa had more than seven thousand "Afro-Christian" churches with 15 million believers.

Such a situation does not make the building of a global ethic easy. Even though Christians and Muslims have been developing a dialogue, there are many violent religious conflicts, mainly in Nigeria and in Sudan. And in South Africa, the "Black theology" opposing and the "White theology" justifying *Apartheid*[26] demonstrated how some Blacks and some Whites disagree on the conception of human rights and ethics. Among Black people there is no agreement on all ethical issues. In some ethnic groups of Zaïre, for instance, to have a child before marriage is considered a good thing, a proof of fertility for a girl, while in other ethnic groups, like the Baluba, it is a sign of "prostitution," and a great obstacle to marriage.

Within this ethical situation of commonalities and differences among African ethics, the African Charter of Human and Peoples' Rights brings a consensus on "how should we treat with our fellow human beings." By bringing African peoples from different ethical backgrounds to a consensus on human rights, the text constitutes a first step towards a global ethic. If this first step consists in bringing one African people together with other African peoples, the second step consists in bringing all African peoples to a dialogue with peoples of other continents.

2. Second step: Africa and the International Community

African people are already collaborating with many international institutions, and some belong to the predominant religions of our world such as Christianity and Islam. But the ACHPR plays an important role in bringing this international relationship to the level of a global ethic, as we can show in the following analysis.

The preamble of the ACHPR says clearly that the African Charter takes into account human rights defined by the Universal Declaration and also the rights of human beings and peoples defined by various institutions of the United Nations and by the Nonaligned Movement, which brought together the "Third World" of Africa, Asia and South and Central America. In dealing with Asia and Western countries, African peoples have been challenged to revise their traditions and customs, to revise their conception of "marriage," of "the dignity of women and children," of "family" and the humanistic values of "non-believers." Taking into account the legacy of modernity, the African Charter on Human and Peoples Rights appears to be a genuine bridge of dialogue between African peoples and the international community on the issues of human rights. In fact, the text already contains some common elements between African Ethic and the Global Ethic to be built. The African Charter goes beyond many practices of the traditional African way of life. That is the case for instance concerning religion, women, democracy, and human beings as individuals.

a) About religion

Many scholars, Africans and Westerns, have pointed out that Africans are notoriously religious.[27] In fact, historians tell us that in ancient African empires such as Ghana, Mali, Luba, Lunda, Kuba, and Zulu the political principle of the separation between State and the Religious institutions did not exist. In almost all the cases, we find the belief in the "divinity" of the King who considered also himself the High Priest or the supreme authority of "religious affairs."

But when we come to the African Charter we find that there is no mention of God and no reference to God as the foundation of political power. Even "human dignity" is not based on the notion of creation of humankind by God. The Charter says that the basic rights of human beings have their foundation in the "attributes of the human person." We have in that expression not the religious language of African religion, but clearly the language of the Western metaphysics or rationalism. Despite the speculation of some commentators, like the Italian Giovanni Michele Palmieri[28] pretending that the African Charter is characterized by "animism," the text appears clearly secular on that specific point. While African ethics are predominantly marked by the religious belief, the Charter does not have the language and characteristics of a religious text. In that way this charter opens the African conception of human rights to a global dialogue including non-believers.

b) About Women

Some Scholars interested in the history of Africa before Christianity and before Islam have recently developed a new understanding of African philosophy, showing that the dignity of women was never radically denied in African traditions. That is true to some extent. No African thinker developed a systematic sexism or racism, going so far as to question, for instance, whether some human beings are really human or whether they have a soul. Nevertheless the practices in social life do not correspond to the ideal. For centuries, women have been forced to occupy a low place in society and have been forbidden to participate in government. The African Charter clearly guarantees the "rights of women" (art. 18) and condemns any kind of discrimination based on sex (art. 2;18). The Charter does not provide space for speculation on a possible "African way of understanding the dignity of women." The Charter guarantees to African women the same dignity and rights universally recognized for other women of our planet. Such an equality of rights between men and women is clearly a modern notion and not a characteristic of African traditions. The Charter abolishes many African traditions in that regard and brings the Africans into a genuine dialogue with other peoples in the context of modern civilization.

c) Democracy

Since the independence of Africa, many African leaders have manipulated the African traditions to banish pluralism and free elections and to justify their monoparty regime, even to make themselves "president for life." In Zaïre, for instance, Mobutu, who proclaimed the ideology of "authenticity," said that he should keep power until the end of his life because "according to our ancestors' practice," there is no place for "political antagonism" in African order of power, but only a place for one, unique Chief who must be obeyed unconditionally. But the African Charter, which defends the "traditional values recognized by the community" (art. 18), strongly guarantees the right of all citizens to participate in the government through freely chosen representatives and guarantees freedom of speech and freedom of association. Here again, the Charter brings African peoples to join the international community in the "democratic system" of government.

d) Human Beings

In traditional societies we had the primacy of the family, the clan or the collectivity over the individual. But even though the African Charter recognizes the social dimension of being human and defines the rights of "peoples," it also brings about a fundamental revolution in the African conception of being human by recognizing specific rights to each human being as an individual. This vision of "human rights" based not on the family or the clan but upon the "attributes of human person" (Preamble) goes far beyond the traditional vision of "Ujamaa" and brings African peoples to a common understanding of human rights with the international community.

That is to say, that the African Charter, which brings together African peoples with other African peoples, also brings Africa to join the international community on the issue of human rights. In that way it opens the door to a "global ethic."

3. Third step: Contribution of the ACHPR to a Global Ethic

First, it is not easy to realize what the African Charter can bring to the Global Ethic in terms of novelty or innovation. When we read the text, we realize that many elements of the African Charter are already present in one way or another in the UN Declaration of Human Rights and in the two texts of Global Ethic written by Leonard Swidler and Hans Küng. The African Charter itself does not claim any radical originality in its formulation of human rights. The preamble of the ACHPR clearly acknowledges the influence of the Universal Declaration of Human Rights on the African Charter.

But when we read the African Charter more closely and carefully, we realize that it is not simply mimicking the Western formulation of human rights or Global Ethic. The Universal Declaration of Human Rights and the two texts of a global ethic are in many ways different from the African Charter.

First of all the name of the title is different in a very significant way. The text of the French Revolution was called "Declaration of Human and Citizens' Rights," the Universal Declaration carries in its title the expression of "human rights" while the African Charter adds to human rights something new in the title: "Peoples' Rights."

Secondly the African Charter has some specific articles defining "Duties" in the connection with "Rights."

The third important difference consists in the source of the Charter. While the Global Ethic considers itself like a kind of ethical extension of the Universal Declaration of Human Rights, the African Charter claims that its source is "African tradition," which includes "virtues of African historical traditions" and "values of the African civilization." Finally, the Charter talks about some "new rights," like the right to development and the right of peoples to own their natural resources. It is mainly in these differences and "novelties" that we can find a contribution of ACHPR to a Global Ethic.

Many specialists of international law have tried to define the specificity and originality of the ACHPR. According to Emmanuel Wonyu,[29] the originality of the ACHPR lies in the fact that it links in an indissoluble way human rights and rights of peoples, defines human rights by understanding the human being both as individuals and as members of a society, and in the fact that the African Charter adds to the traditional or classical human rights some new human rights developed in the second half of the twentieth century, such as the right to the existence of any people, the right for each people to liberation by using all means accepted by the international community, and the right for each nation to utilize its natural resources. Like Wonyu, Umozurike also thinks that the African Charter has created something new in the field of the classical definition of human rights as it "has combined an impressive array of individual rights and duties, group rights, and state rights and duties. Some of these, like the right to development and the right to national and international peace and security, appear to be new additions to the list of internationally recognised rights."[30]

But when we read commentaries made by non-African authors, the tone is a bit different. Giovanni Michele Palmieri, an Italian, contends that the contribution of African Charter lies in its "animism."

Our perception differs from the above commentators. We do not think that the contribution of African Charter to a Global Ethic depends only on its originality, even though an original creativity may well be there. There are many ways of contributing to something. We may contribute to a project by expressing our agreement or our disagreement on some specific points, or by bringing some new elements to the project.

In my opinion, the first contribution lies in the acceptance or recognition of the Universal Declaration of Human Rights. Through this common ground with the Universal Declaration the African Charter makes a global ethic meaningful for African peoples, bringing to the project the agreement of more or less 700 million African people!

The second contribution consists in the "amplification" and the "explicitation" of some rights. The African Charter brings a new perception of traditional rights by making explicit what was implicit, by stating in a precise manner or by emphasizing what the Global Ethic or the Universal Declaration of Human Rights consider in a general way. Because of the difference in the experiences of life between African peoples and Westerners, what Africa considers priority rights are not always priorities for Western countries such as the right to development or to utilize one's natural resources or the right of other people to existence or the rights of parents. Then the African Charter formulates in "clear articles" what the Universal Declaration declaration or the Global Ethic does not thus express. For instance, the Global Ethic (according to Küng's and Swidler's texts) states that it is not good to kill or to steal. The African Charter extends these rights and formulates them as clear articles. The "not to steal" is extended to "the right of peoples to freely dispose of their wealth and natural resources" and "the right for the dispossessed people to the lawful recovery of its property as well as to an adequate compensation, in case of spoliation." The "not to kill" is extended to "the survival of peoples" and to the protection of their traditional culture, while the right to freedom is extended to the right for colonized and oppressed people to defend themselves by using all means recognized by the international community.

The creativity of the African Charter can be perceived more clearly in three important fields: the rights of peoples, the rights to property and the right to development.

a) The Rights of Peoples

It seems clear that the major contribution of the African Charter consists in the definition of the "Rights of peoples." The French Declaration of Human Rights and the Universal Declaration carried out a definition of human rights based on the individualistic vision of human beings. The Global Ethic defined by Swidler is mainly based on the Universal Declaration's vision of human rights. For that reason, there is a kind of primacy of the individual over the society, even though some references to the society seem to correct that vision.

With the African Charter we have a definition of human rights intrinsically connected to the rights of peoples. That is the result of the specific history of African peoples marked by slavery, colonialism and neocolonialism and which peoples feel and fear the danger of disappearing as peoples. The African Charter brings to the project of a global ethic a sensibility to the social dimension of human beings. It calls the attention to the "dignity of peoples" who cannot exist without a specific "culture" and situates the issue of ethics at a much more global level, including the behavior of peoples towards other peoples. In that way the discourse of a global ethic can be significant to many peoples of the Third World who suffer "cultural alienation," "political domination," and "economical exploitation."

But this vision of human rights brings a correction not only to the Western vision of being human but also to the African tradition. Even though hospitality to foreigners is considered a great value in the African tradition, the idea of family as centered on "blood affiliation," the clan and the tribe, has created, in some cases, a spirit of self-esteem that led people to despise the members of other ethnic groups simply because they were different, spoke a different language and behaved in different ways. In an important study, *Die auserwählten Völker. Eine christliche Deutung der Welt*, Father Walbert Bühlmann has shown that "the theology of chosen people" is a universal phenomenon, often used as a weapon against other people.[31] In Africa, most persons who identify with an ethnic group believe that they are "the best people in the world." This is one of the reasons for so many ethnic conflicts.

The African Charter preaches respect for all tribes. As Maurice Massengo-Tiassé pointed out, the right of equality of peoples means that neither tribes or ethnic groups have the right to dominate others.[32] As we can see, this right of equality of peoples is a major contribution to world peace and to the project of a Global ethic.

b) The Right to Property

The African Charter has developed a new vision of property that is not in the Universal Declaration nor in the Global Ethic. The African Charter protects the right to property, but provides that it may be encroached upon in the interest of public need or the general interest of the community and in accordance with the provisions of appropriate laws. The right to property also implies the moral commandment: do not still the goods of another. Here the African Charter has developed the "right to compensation" and the right of peoples to freely dispose of their national wealth and resources."

There is no clear mention of compensation in the UN Declaration nor in the Global Ethic texts in African philosophy the goal of the ethical code is not only to prevent evil action but also the reparation of the "broken order" by compensation. Finally the African Charter brings out the notion of what I call "global property" by defining the right of peoples to "equally enjoy the common patrimony of humankind."

In this way the African Charter genuinely covers all the aspects of "property" we need to take into account in a fair discussion of a global ethic.

c) The Right to Development

According to Umozurike,[33] the right to development is a specific African contribution to the international community. It was first enunciated by the President of the Senegal Supreme Court, Keba M'baye, in an address to the Institute of International Law of Human Rights in Strasbourg in 1972. Keba M'baye suggested then that all rights are intertwined with the right of existence, with a progressively higher standard of living, and therefore with development. In 1978, as President of the International Commission of Jurists, he further commented on the right at the Dakar Conference on the Development of the Law of Human Rights. Finally, at the request of the Commission of Human Rights, the UN Secretary-General made a study in which he concluded that a large number of principles based on the UN Charter and human rights texts and declarations confirm the existence of the right to development in law. This conclusion was later confirmed by the UN General Assembly. Keba M'baye referred to Articles 55-56 of the UN Charter and 22-27 of the Universal Declaration of Human Rights, and to the statutes of the specialized agencies in which international cooperation and solidarity are important. From the African world view he came to conclude that "the right to development" is a "human right." This right implies the negative duty not to impede the development of states and the positive duty to aid such development. In our century, the right of peoples to development seems the genuine way to address the issue of "international injustice," and thus the issue of a global ethic, because it is in the context of the development of peoples that we can best understand how the issue of good and bad behavior has reached a global level. This new global situaion makes urgent the development of a global ethic without which the world has no way to avoid a "global catastrophe." It is in this way that we can understand Hans Küng when he opened his project of a Global Ethic with this expression: "No survival without a world ethic."[34] Or in Swidler's terms: "the future offers two alternatives: death or dialogue."[35]

d) The Right to Traditional Values

The articles 17 and 18 of the African Charter powerfully call for the protection and the promotion of "morality and traditional values." We have here something that does not exist in the Universal Declaration of Human Rights nor in the texts of a Global ethic written by Swidler and Küng. Obviously when one thinks that the defense of human rights is a product of the twentieth century and is something new in the history of humankind, it would appear contradictory that the African Charter consider the promotion of "traditional African values" as a defence of "human rights." And yet it appears for Africans that their traditions are not completely empty of any notion of human rights. The Charter does not say what those "traditional values" are. But we can illustrate them by analyzing the traditional code of African ethics. Doing so allows us to see how it is easy for Africans to accept the project of a Global Ethic because it already has some elements in common with the traditional African ethic. I will try to follow John Mbiti and confirm his view by the Luba ethic of my own tradition.

1. The Notion of Human Rights

Among the Baluba I do not find the notion of "human rights" in its modern sense as defined in the Universal Declaration. The expression "human rights" itself is absent from the Kiluba language as well as from many other Bantu languages. But the notion of human dignity is there. The Bantu anthropology reveals ten basic concepts used in the Kiluba language that can help us to understand the issue of human rights:[36]

The nature of BEING	About the notion of DIGNITY
BUMI: life (any kind of life)	*BULEME*: respect, dignity
LUFU: death	*BUYA*: goodness, beauty
MUNTU: human being	*BUBI*: bad, evil, ugly
KINTU: thing	*BUHIKA*: alienation, slavery
BUMUNTU: essence of human being	*BUBINE*: truth

In the Bantu philosophy,[37] "being" is divided into two categories:

- *MUNTU* (*BANTU* in plural; existing being-of-intelligence; human-being)
- *KINTU* (existing being-without-intelligence; animal, plant, thing).

Animals, vegetation and minerals belong to the category of *KINTU* while God and human beings belong to the category of *MU-NTU*. But when a human being behaves badly he falls into the category of *KINTU* and people refer to him differently, as the following figure shows:

The *MU-NTU* category: good morality and intelligence	The *KI-NTU* category: bad morality and stupidity
MUNTU (good, respectable person)	*KI-NTU* or *KI-MUNTU* (one not deserving respect)
TATA (a good father)	*KI-TATA* (a bad father)
MAMA (a good mother)	*KI-MAMA* (bad mother)
MWANA (a good child)	*KI-MWANA* or *KYANA* (bad child)
MULOPWE (good king)	*KI-LOPWE* (tyrant, stupid king)

The term *KI* means that a human can empty her or his essence, his or her humanness by doing evil, by saying or thinking in a wrong way. The criterion used to measure the "humanness" is "intelligence" or "wisdom" and mainly "moral conduct."

2. The Traditional Ethic

According to the traditional ethic, moral conduct is evaluated according to the attitude toward *BUMI* (life). That is good which protects and promotes human life, and that is evil which destroys or alters human life. That is why in Luba society the devil *par excellence* is the *Mfwintshi* (Sorcerer). *BUMI* is the supreme value in the Luba ethic, which is completely concentrated on the "respect of human life." For the Baluba, as for many other African peoples, religion and ethics are so anthropocentric that Mbiti could say: "In Africa, it is as if God exists for the sake of man."[38] The Africans are so deeply concerned about the preservation and the promotion of human life that religion itself becomes a tool to reinforce the "respect for human life." It is this concern for *BUMI* that gives African ethics and religion this dimension called by some scholars "utilitarianism" and expressed by Mbiti in this radical way:

> African faith is utilitarian, not purely spiritual; it is practical and not mystical. The people respond to God in and because of particular circumstances, especially in times of need. Then they seek to obtain what He gives, be that material or spiritual; they do not search for Him as the final reward or satisfaction of the human soul or spirit. Augustine's description of man's soul being restless until it finds its

rest in God, is something unknown in African traditional religious life.[39]

This concern for "human life" is possible only because the Baluba believe strongly in the "dignity" of every human being. This notion of "dignity" is expressed by two words: *BUMUNTU* and *BULEME*. The concept of *BULEME* is the key to understand the Luba notion of human rights. It means "weight," "solid," "consistence," as in the Hebrew notion of the "Kabod of Yahwe." In the Luba ethic, a person (*MUNTU*) fulfill her/his humanness (*BUMUNTU*) when s/he is capable of respect (*BULEME*) for her/himself (*KWILEMEKA*) and for others. Whenever a person does not "respect" the life and dignity of other persons, s/he automatically empties his/her *BUMUNTU* (essence of a genuine human being) because the *BULEME* is the essence of the *BUMUNTU*. It is the notion of *BULEME* that constitutes the foundation of all Luba ethics. Any conduct that does not respect the dignity of human life is bad. What contributes to the protection and the intensification of human life is good.

The same can be said for other African cultures, as we can see in the "African ethic" described by Mbiti. In fact, according to Mbiti,[40] among the basic principles of "African ethics" we find: truth and rectitude as essential virtues, justice, generosity (the opposite of selfishness), hospitality, protecting the poor and weak, giving honor and respect to older people, chastity before marriage and faithfulness during marriage, avoiding hypocrisy, stealing, and falsehood, and keeping a covenant. This is verified for instance in the Luba society where ethics is based on two poles: *BUBI* (evil, bad, sin, ugliness) and *BUYA* (goodness, righteousness, purity, beauty). The Baluba distinguish the *MUNTU MUBI* (bad person) from the *MUNTU MUYAMPE* (a good person) or *MUNTU WAMPIKWA KATONYE* (a person without stain).

The *MUNTU MUYAMPE* has the plenitude of *BUMUNTU* (the being-human; the essence of being human) while the characteristics of the *MUNTU MUBI* are those which destroy human dignity, as the following figure shows:

Characteristics of the *MUNTU MUYAMPE* (good person)	Characteristics of the *MUNTU MUBI* (bad person)
1. *LUSA* (compassion)	*MUSHIKWA* (hate)
2. *BUSWE* (love)	*BUTSHI* (Witchcraft, sorcery)
3. *BULEME* (dignity, respect, integrity)	*BWIVI* (robbery)
4. *BOLOKE* (righteousness)	*BUNZAZANGI* (hypocrisy)
5. *BUBINE* (truth, integrity, honesty)	*BUBELA* (falsity)
6. *BUNTU* (generosity)	*MWINO* (selfishness)
7. *KANYE* (compassion)	*BUSEKESE* (fornication)
8. *BUYUKI/NGENYI* (wisdom, intelligence)	*BULEMBAKANE/BUVILA* (stupidity)
9. *BUTALALE* (peace)	*BULOBO/BUKALABALE* (violence)
10. *BUKWASHI* (help)	*NTONDO* (discrimination)
11. *BUTUNDAILE* (hospitality)	*LWISO/MALAKA* (absence of control of one's desire and emotions)
12. *BWANAHABO/BULOHWE* freedom, autodetermination, being one's own king, nobility)	*BUHIKA* (slavery)

This ethic is not only anthropocentric but much more sociocentric. Because in the African worldview bad behavior is not a "private matter." Any bad conduct destroys "social relations," and for that reason, African ethics takes seriously into account the principle of "reparation": anyone who has done evil must confess publicly his fault and repair what he has destroyed in order to restore the broken order or harmony of social life. This social dimension of human life—"to be with," "to be in communion with"—what Nyerere calls *UJAMAA* (togetherness, fraternity or family spirit) is so important in Africa that some languages like Kiluba do not even have a specific word to express the verb "to have." In Kiluba, as in many other Bantu languages,[41] the verb "to have" is expressed by the verb "to be" followed by "with" (*NE*). The verb *KWIKALA* means to be; *KWIKALA NE* means "to have" (literally "to be with"). To have a child = to be with a child (*KWIKALA-NE-MWANA*). To have a house = to be with a house (*KWIKALA-NE-NJIBO*).

This spirit of "togetherness" generates a spirit of hospitality and solidarity which distinguishes African ethics from the Marxist notion of "class struggle." As Nyerere tells us:

> The true African socialist does not look on one class of men as his brethren and another as his natural enemies. He does not form an alliance with the 'brethren' for the extermination of the 'non-brethren.' He regards all men as his brethren—as members of his ever-extending family. *UJAMAA*, then, or 'familihood,' describes our socialism."[42]

Our survey may give the impression that the African traditions are perfect. That is not the case at all. We know that the daily life of people does not always correspond to the ideal. The purpose of this response was to deal with "the system of values" and not the behavior of individuals. To study "African ethics" we must distinguish between the conduct of people and the "abuses" of the traditions from the genuine "spirit of the African tradition" that the African Charter calls the positive African traditional values. From our brief analysis we can understand clearly why the African Charter appeals for the promotion of these "positive traditional values" that predispose Africans to be interested in a debate on a global ethic to which Africans cannot come as a "*tabula rasa.*" It is for that reason that the African Charter states in its preamble that Africa has "traditionally" reserved for "human rights and freedom" a primordial importance.

IV. Conclusion

As Arlene Swidler pointed out, human rights represent what is probably the primary ethical concern in the world today.[43] When we say "the world," we also include the "African world." My opinion, at the end of this survey, is that Africans are today very much concerned with the issue of human rights and cannot reject a project such as a Universal Declaration of Global Ethic, a project that helps to end the violation of human rights in the world.

The project of a Global Ethic finds its justification and meaning in the course of events which characterize our world today. With the collapse of the communist regimes in Eastern Europe, with the storm of democracy in the Third World, with the economic crisis and the wave of xenophobia in Western countries, our world is today in a very dangerous situation, a kind of "social earthquake." The African continent, more and more neglected by the masters of world economy while its governments fall apart and Africans suffer starvation and ethnic cleansing, is not in a good situation. This "lost continent" as some pessimistic scholars call it again, need such a thing as a Global Ethic that can rescue it from its own diseases and save it through a "global solidarity." At the same time its experience of suffering and struggle for survival may be fruitful for other peoples. For suffering is a privileged instance for the understanding of human rights.

If the United Nations, through the Universal Declaration of Human Rights, and the Vatican Council II were built without Africa, perhaps at the edge of the third millennium the Universal Declaration of Global Ethic may receive an African contribution. But what kind of contribution, some could ask? When we consider the great influence of Western civilization on African culture during the last four centuries it is easy to challenge Africans: "What do you have that you have not received?" (1 Cor 4:7). Given the constant violation of human rights on the African continent, one could even remain skeptical about the notion of an "African ethic" and could say like Nathaniel, "Can anything good come from Nazareth?" (Jn 1:46)

But it is also true that the continent has already produced three Nobel Peace Prizes: Albert Luthuli (1960), the Anglican bishop Mgr. Desmond Tutu (1984) and Mandela-De Klerck (1993). It is also significant that the Winner of the Nobel Prize for literature in 1986 was the Nigerian writer Wole Soyinka, well known for his struggle against dictatorship in Africa. It is a fact that African people are becoming more and more aware of human rights. And this process of awareness has increased since 1989 in the direction of democracy. In many countries, bishops, priests and people in general strongly urge politicians to build democratic institutions. Africa is clearly joining the international community in this matter. In that process of "democratization," the African Charter on Human and Peoples' Rights plays a key role. This African Charter does not claim any radical originality in its formulation of human rights. In fact, many African languages do not have a clear expression for "human rights." Nevertheless the concept of "human being" (*MUNTU*) and "human dignity" (*BULEME, BUMUNTU*) is clearly asserted in the African tradition, as we have pointed it out above in our analysis of the Bantu philosophy.

What is important in the African Charter is first of all the strong recognition of the Universal Declaration of Human Rights as something valid and good for African people in the way of dealing with their fellow Africans and in their contact with other human beings that populate the earth. The second merit is that this text makes easy the project of a global ethic by bringing African people from different ethical traditions to a general consensus on human rights. The third is the African sensibility to the issues of colonialism, racism, economic exploitation and sensibility to the issue of the survival of human beings as members of a specific group (a nation, a race) whose culture must be protected as an important part of human identity. That is why the "Rights of Peoples" can be considered a major contribution of the African Charter to the project of a Global Ethic. The African Charter pays close attention to the "social dimension" of being human and is for that reason better able to deal with ethical issues without losing time in casuistic speculations about the definition of concepts. Even though it is important to define concepts in order to know clearly what we want to do, it is true that a Global Ethic can find its just place in the interaction between people and not in a conception of human rights based on the primacy of the individualistic dimension of human beings. I believe that ethics deals basically with "what we do to others and what others do to us."

The African Charter is not perfect. We wanted to focus our paper on "the possible contribution of the African Charter" rather than making a critical analysis of its weakness and incoherences. For that reason we came to stress much more the positive aspects rather than the negative aspects of the African Charter. If some rights have not received as much attention in the African Charter, it may also be because it already emphasizes its solidarity with the Universal Declaration of Human Rights. In that way some repetitions had to be avoided. The African Charter has already been criticized by many African philosophers or jurists for its lack of clarity on certain points. For instance, the emphasis on duties seems, to some people, a problematic point because it may be used by governments to curtail human rights and also because it puts conditions and restrictions on "liberties."[44] But despite all its weaknesses, the African Charter remains a very important step towards the respect of human rights and towards a consensus on a "Universal Declaration on Global Ethic." It is the first text in African history that draws on principles of good and evil and principles of how to treat human beings, and that reflects a general consensus beyond all kind of differences that divide African peoples. This can be considered an "African Charter of Ethics" which can be usefully used, *mutatis mutandis*, in the project of a Global Ethic.

Footnotes

1 Abbreviations: AOTA: Association oecuménique des Théologiens Africains (Ecumenical Association of African Theologians); EATWOT: Ecumenical Association of Third World Theologians; ACHPR: African Charter on Human and Peoples' Rights (we will also use the expression "African Charter").

2 Leonard Swidler, *The Meaning of Life at the Edge of the Third Millennium*, (New York: Paulist, 1992), p. 69. In fact, in 1995, Professor Swidler did establish a "Center for Global Ethics," with an attached Internet network: G-ETHIC.

3 R. Gendt, "Le christianisme africain dans l'opinion publique européenne," in *Concilium. Cahier spécial: Vers le Synode Africain*, No. 239, février, 1992, p. 140.

4 The Zairian Conference of Catholic bishops has taken position against the dictator Mobutu and called for the building of democracy in different documents. We found some of those documents in three periodicals: *La Documentation Catholique* published in France (No. 2006, 20 mai 1990; No. 2020, 20 Janvier 1990; No. 2070, 18 avril 1993); *Zaïre-Afrique* and *Renaître* (two reviews published by Jesuit fathers of Zaïre to promote justice and democracy). We have analyzed the following documents:

1. "Déclaration de l'Episcopat sur la situation présente." (1975)
2. "Notre foi en Jésus-Christ." (1977)
3. "Tous solidaires et responsables." (1977)
4. "Appel au redressement de la Nation." (1978)
5. "Notre foi en l'homme, image de Dieu." (1981)
6. "Message et déclaration des Evêques du Zaire à l'occasion du 25e anniversaire de l'Indépendance." (1985)
7. "Education nationale." (1986)
8. "Le Chrétien et le développement de la Nation." (1987)
9. "Mémorandum des Evêques du Zaïre au Chef de l'Etat." (1990)
10. "Nécessité d'une campagne d'information sur la démocratie." (1990)
11. "Libérés de toute peur, au service de la Nation. Message des évêques du Zaire aux Chrétiens Catholiques et aux hommes de bonne volonté."
12. "Libérer la démocratie: Message et Déclaration des Evêques du Zaire aux chrétiens catholiques et aux hommes de bonne volonté." (carême 1991)
13. "Déclaration de l'Episcopat du Zaïre à propos de la Conférence Nationale." (1991)
14. "Message des Eglises Catholique, Orthodoxe, Protestante et Kibanguiste." (1991)
15. "Message de la Conférence Episcopale du Zaïre au Peuple Zaïrois et aux hommes de bonne volonté" (1991)
16. "Pour la poursuite de la démocratisation au Zaïre." (Kinshasa, 12 décembre 1992
17. "Sauvons la Nation." (1993).

5 Nkulu-N'Sengha Mutombo, "Les Eglises face à Mobutu: réflexion sur le rôle démocratique de la religion" in *FORUM ZAIROIS. Bulletin Culturel de la Communauté Zaïroise des Etats-Unis*, Philadelphia, Vol. I, No. 4, Février 1993, p.12.

6 John Mbiti, *African Religions and Philosophy* (New Hampshire: Heinemann, 1990).

7 *Théologie Africaine. Bilan et Perspectives (Actes de la Dix-Septiéme Semaine Théologique de Kinshasa)* (Kinshasa: Facultés Catholiques de Kinshasa, 1989), p.6.

8 We refer here to a document published by the AFJN (Africa Faith and Justice Network) based in Washington D.C.

9 Mushete Ngindu, *Les thèmes majeurs de la théologie africaine* (Paris: L'harmattan, 1989), p.19. EATWOT (Ecumenical Association of Third World Theologians) was created in 1976 in Dar-es-Salaam (Tanzania). During its second meeting held in Accra (Ghana) in 1977, the AOTA (Association

Oecuménique des Théologiens Africains) which is a part of EATWOT, was created.

10 We use in this paper the complete text of the African Charter published in Amadu Sesay, Olusola Ojo, and Orobola Fasehun, *The OUA After Twenty Years* (Boulder, CO and London: Westview Press, 1984), pp.109-124, and the French version of the same charter published in the Jesuit review *Zaïre-Afrique*, No. 236, Juin-Août 1989, pp. 295-299.

11 For the texts of a "Global Ethic," we use in our paper the copy of Professor Swidler's published in this volume and the one by Professor Küng translated by Professor Swidler and made available in his seminar "Global Ethos-Human Rights-World Religions" at Temple University, Spring, 1993. It was subsequently published in Hans Küng and Karl-Josef Kuschel, eds., *A Global Ethic. The Declaration of the Parliament of the World's Religions* (New York: Continuum, 1993) and is included in this volume as well.

12 Giovanni Michele Palmieri, "Il sistema regionale africano di promozione e di protezione dei diritti dell'uomo e dei popoli: profili istituzionali." *Rivista Internazionale dei Diritti dell'Uomo*, Anno IV, gennaio-aprile, 1991, pp. 53-87. Emmanuel Wonyu, "Un support juridique pour la démocratie en Afrique: la Charte Africaine des Droits de l'Homme et des Peuples" in *Afrique 2000: Revue Africaine de Politique Internationale* (Institut Panafricain de Relations Internationales), No. 8, Janvier-Février-Mars, 1992, pp. 29-50. U. O. Umozurike, "The African Charter On Human and Peoples' Rights," in *American Journal of International Law*, vol.77, 1983, pp. 902-912. "Charte africaine des droits de l'homme et des peuples (27 juin 1981)" in *Zaïre-Afrique*. Juin-Août, 1989, pp. 295-299.

13 Umozurike, "The African Charter," p. 903.

14 Idem.

15 Idem, p.90.

16 Idem, pp. 902f.

17 Idem, p. 903.

18 Idem, p.904.

19 Wonyu, "Un support juridique," p.30.

20 Sesay, et al., *The OAU After Twenty Years*, p. 84.

21 Idem.

22 Swidler, *The Meaning of Life*, p. 67.

23 John Mbiti, *African Religions and Philosophy*, pp. 223-256.

24 We used the Italian translation of the book: G. Bellinger, *Enciclopedia delle religioni* (Milano: Garzanti, 1989), p. 17.

25 Gendt, "Le Christianisme africain," pp. 142-44.

26 Bruno Chenu, *Théologies Chrétiennes des tiers mondes. Latino-américaine, noire américaine, noire sud-africaine, africaine, asiatique* (Paris: Le Centurion, 1987), pp. 107-110.

27 Mbiti, *African Religions and Philosophy*, p. 1.

28 Palmieri, "Il sistema regionale africano," p. 56.

29 Wonyu, "Un support juridique," p. 31.

30 Umozurike, "The African Charter," p. 911.

31 I have used the Italian translation: Walbert Bühlmann, *I Popoli eletti. Un'interpretazione cristiana del mondo*. (Milano: Edizioni Paoline, 1987).

32 M. Massengo-Tiassé, *Comment peut-on vivre libre et digne en Afrique. Africains: vos droits et vos devoirs* (Paris: Michel de Maule, 1988), pp. 37-39.

33 Umozurike, "The African Charter, pp. 906f.

34 Hans Küng, *Global Responsibility. In Search of a New World Ethic* (New York: Crossroad, 1991), p. xv.

35 Leonard Swidler, *Death or Dialogue? From the Age of Monologue to the Age of Dialogue* (Philadelphia: Trinity Press International, 1990), p. vii.

36 For the Luba culture and the Kiluba language, which is my mother tongue, I am trying to create my own systematization of the "Bantu-Luba anthropology." The Luba culture is important within the study of African philosophy because that is the culture which refers to the "Philosophie Bantu," considered the starting point of the modern debate on African philosophy. This book, written by a missionary from Belgium, Father Placide Tempels, was published in 1947 by the famous "Présence Africaine," the historical organ of expression of the "Négritude Movement" based in Paris.

37 E. A. Ruch, *African Philosophy. An Introduction to the main philosophical trends in Contemporary Africa* (Rome: Catholic Book Agency-Officium Libri Catholici, 1984), p. 156.

38 Mbiti, *African Religions*, p. 90.

39 Idem, p. 67.

40 Idem, p. 207.

41 Théophile Obenga, *Les Bantu: langues, peuples, civilisations*, (Paris: Présence Africaine, 1985), pp. 184f.

42 Valentin Yves Mudimbe, *The Invention of Africa. Gnosis, Philosophy and the Order of Knowledge* (Indianapolis: Indiana University Press, 1988), p. 95.

43 Arlene Swidler, ed., *Human Rights in Religious Traditions* (New York: Pilgrim Press, 1982), p. vii.

44 Sesay, *The OAU After Twenty Years*, p. 88.

Toward a Universal Declaration of a Global Ethic: A Protestant Comment

John Hick

Leonard Swidler is undoubtedly right—as also is his colleague Hans Küng—in thinking that the time is ripe to begin the worldwide process of formulating a basic global ethic; and we must be grateful to them for having taken the initiative embodied in this draft. For we are all conscious today that our world has become a virtual communicational unity, that its nations and regions are increasingly economically interdependent, and that war is insanely destructive. The survival and flourishing of the human family requires at this moment in history the articulation of at least a basic ethical outlook, and if possible a set of ethical principles, on which all the major streams of human culture concur, and which can be used to influence their behavior. We need to uncover and cultivate the ground of human unity beneath the multiplicity of nations, cultures, social systems, religions and ideologies among which and between which conflicts are so common.

The difficulty in offering a distinctively Christian comment on Leonard Swidler's draft is that it is already in an important sense a Christian document. For since the European "Enlightenment" of the eighteenth century Western Christianity has been increasingly suffused with the individualistic, democratic, liberal, historically-minded, science-oriented outlook of the Enlightenment, an outlook that constitutes what can comprehensively be called the ethos of "modernity." Indeed Christianity, as a cultural influence, is identified in the minds of many Christians, particularly when they make comparisons with other religions, with these liberal ideals of modernity.

From an historical point of view, this is paradoxical. For what has happened is that secular modernity has transformed the outlook of most of the Christian world, rather than that Christianity has out of its own distinctive religious resources introduced these modern liberal values into Western culture. Indeed during much the greater part of its history Christianity has been neither democratic, nor liberal, nor science-oriented, nor historically-minded or individualistic in the modern sense. In saying, then, that Leonard Swidler's is a Christian draft I merely mean that it comes out of contemporary Western Christianity and embodies the spirit of post-Enlightenment culture. Anyone reading it can readily identify its provenance, reflecting as it does the concerns and presuppositions of modernity. (Let me add at this point that the currently fashionable notion of "post-modernity" has been given such different meanings by different writers and schools of thought that its use would merely be confusing in the present context, and I recommend that we avoid it).

Christianity, as an historical-cultural movement, has through the centuries absorbed and been changed by a series of external cultural forces—neo-Platonism in the early centuries, then the revival of Greek learning and of the enquiring rational spirit in the Renaissance, later the Enlightenment and the impact of modern science, then Darwinism and also the historical study of ancient scriptures in the second half of the nineteenth century, and liberal secularization in the twentieth century. All these influences have as their present end-product the modern Western outlook that is roughly coterminous with the vaguely Christian culture of North America and Europe and some of their colonial extensions.

The fact that modernity developed first in the West, and has largely remade the social ethos of Christianity in its own image, is basic to our situation today; whilst the correlative fact that this modern ethos is linked to Christianity through the contingencies of history, rather than being intrinsically Christian in any exclusive sense, may be crucially relevant to the project of a global ethic.

For it may be that some at least of the same influences are at work throughout our increasingly unified world, transforming the other religious, and also officially anti-religious, cultures of the earth, so that the kind of ethic proposed in Leonard Swidler's draft may prove to be acceptable more or less universally.

But on the other hand this may prove to be only very partially the case. Some, but not all, of the influences that have gone into the formation of the Christian version of modernity are affecting the other traditions. And there may well be yet other influences upon them that have not affected Christianity. There may thus be significant variations of outlook within an increasingly "modern" global mind-set. And these variations may quite possibly affect the basic framework and structure of a global ethic and the presuppositions that are reflected in it.

For this reason this first draft, produced by Leonard Swidler (and likewise the basically similar draft produced by Hans Küng), must not stand as the one official draft which is to be amended, added to, and developed by contributions from the rest of the world. It is essential that as early in the process as possible other independent initial drafts be forthcoming from within the cultures of China, Africa, Russia, India, the Islamic world, the Buddhist world, the "primal" life-streams. Only then, with the comparison and interaction of these perhaps significantly different drafts, will the movement towards a genuinely global Declaration be able to proceed beyond its present initial state. At least as important, then, as the organizing of intensive discussion of our Western draft must be the eliciting of Asian, African, Pacific and other drafts.

To set this wider and more pluralistic process in motion obviously requires resources. Might UNESCO be the agent? or might an initiative be taken by religious leaders (the Pope, the Dalai Lama. . .), or by academics? Or might some major sponsor concerned with the larger welfare of the world be approached—the Aga Khan, or one of the major U.S. Foundations, or the Spanish Fundacion BBV. . . ? Or several of these in collaboration? I can, alas, only ask but cannot answer these questions.

The West today is largely secular, with only a marginal religious influence in addition to that which has floated down through the culture. Much of the rest of the world is much more strongly religiously influenced. But in the West as well as elsewhere the main voice of moral consciousness, formulating and propagating whatever ethical principles we recognize, remains that of the religions. Their teachings thus constitute the natural starting point for the search for a global ethic. The recognition (which Leonard Swidler emphasizes in his Introduction) that all the major traditions teach a form of the "Golden Rule" of treating others as one would oneself wish to be treated, is thus enormously important. This will almost certainly become recognized globally as the basic principle of morality. For it seems to be a virtually universal human insight that to be a moral person is to regard others as having essentially the same value as oneself. The differences in ethical outlook then consist in different assumptions about who the "others" are—family, tribe, caste, nation, religious community, human species?

In his section IV Leonard Swidler formulates ethical principles which follow from the Golden Rule. His eight Basic Principles sound right to me, as one sharing his modern Western liberal outlook. But I should (as I am sure Leonard Swidler would also) like to see independent attempts from within the Chinese, Indian, African and other cultures to spell out the implications of the Golden Rule. It could be that these will all be broadly consonant with his draft. Or it could be that significant differences will emerge, which would then give rise to important dialogues. And, as Leonard Swidler says in his Introduction, a Universal Declaration of a Global Ethic "must be arrived at by consensus through dialogue."

Swidler's ten Middle Principles also sound right to me. For, once again, they reflect our modern Western cultural ideals. Do they also reflect a universal point of view, common to the peoples of all cultures? I do not know. This is something that only a wider inter-cultural dialogue can establish. For the aim of a Universal Declaration must be to express an existing, or now forming, common outlook, not to impose that of one culture upon others. It may turn out that the existing common outlook does not at present go so far as some of Swidler's Middle Principles. Or it may be that it does; or again, that in the process of dialogue it might develop in that direction. Or it may be that some quite different principles will emerge.

I return in conclusion to my main point. In this first stage of the search for a global ethic, rather than getting the peoples of other cultures to debate our Western draft, agreeing or disagreeing with it as the only document on the table, we should say: "Here is the kind of draft that comes naturally to us in the industrialized West. What kind of draft comes naturally to you, and to you, and to you?" And then the next stage beyond this should be to bring a plurality of drafts together and see what comes out of the interaction between them.

I do not think that in any of this I am differing from what Leonard Swidler has in mind. I want particularly to stress, however, the need to move as soon as possible from a one-draft to a multi-draft situation. So long as we only have a modern Western draft there will be the danger of the whole project looking like an act of Western cultural imperialism. This has never been the intention. And the danger can be avoided by directing every effort to get people from within the other great cultural streams of human life to participate in the search from their own independent points of view.

It cannot count as a legitimate criticism that the search for a global ethic has originated in the West; for it had to originate somewhere! And the West probably contains more abundantly than elsewhere the practical resources required to launch and promote the process. But it would be a ground for legitimate criticism if the search remained concentrated around our Western contribution to it. The challenge is now to find ways of opening the discussion up on an equal basis within all the great traditions of the earth.

The Universal Declaration
of a Global Ethic:
A Jewish Response

Michael S. Kogan

I. The Image of the Imageless God

From the first chapter of Genesis, the authors of the Hebrew Scriptures are engaged in a profound and complex investigation into the natures of two distinct but inseparable realities. The theological goal of this quest is the nature of God; anthropologically considered, the search is for the nature of the human. But theology and anthropology are two aspects of the same investigation. This is true because of the Bible's fundamental conception of the relationship of the divine and the human.

> Then God said, "Let us make humankind in our image, after our likeness. . . " (Genesis, 1:26)

Has there ever been—could there ever be—a more exalted conception of the human? As the earthly image of God, the human person reveals the divine face. This is a stunning and unique definition, but on closer analysis it may turn out to be not a definition at all. It is true that the text goes on to explain, in some sense, what the image of God means. ". . . let them have dominion . . . over all the earth. . . " (Genesis, 1:26). To be human is to exercise dominion, to rule on earth as God rules the universe. We are to engage in responsible stewardship over what has been given us, to tend the earth as if it were God's own garden. But while this commission reveals humanity's position in relation to the created order, it says little about human nature itself. Perhaps the view of humanity as the earthly image of God functions as a warning against any further definition, against any conception of human nature at all.

What must be remembered is that if the human is the image of the divine, then the reverse is also the case: the divine is—must be—the image of the human. What we can say about the human person, inso-far as s/he reflects the divine reality, must also be said of God. But what does Scripture say about the essence of God—the face of God—which we are said to image forth in the world? The issue is re-visited in Exodus, 33-34.

> Moses said, "I pray thee, show me thy glory." And God said, "I will make all my goodness pass before you, and I will be gracious to whom I will be gracious, and will show mercy on whom I will show mercy. But," he said, "you cannot see my face; for man shall not see me and live." (Exodus, 33:18-20)

Moses, Israel's greatest teacher and God's foremost prophet, having led the people in the exodus and through the theophany at Sinai, asks to look upon the divine glory itself, the very face of God. The Holy One's response is clear enough; no human shall—can—look upon "my face."

The prophet Isaiah delivers a similar message.

> In the year that King Uzziah died I saw the Lord sitting upon a throne, high and lifted up; and his train filled the temple. Above him flew the seraphim; each had six wings: with two he covered his face, and with two he covered his feet and with two he flew. And one called to an-other and said:
> "Holy, holy, holy is the Lord of hosts;
> The whole earth is full of his glory." (Isaiah, 6:1-3)

Isaiah "sees" God, but it is the King's train he describes, never the divine face. Even the seraphim cover their eyes, unable to look on the glory of God. Their angelic chorus proclaims the holiness of the One whose face is not to be seen by them or by us.

Again in Ezekiel we find a vision of God on the throne-chariot:

> . . . and seated above the likeness of a throne was a likeness as it were
> of a human form. And upwards from what had the appearance of his
> loins I saw as it were gleaming bronze, like the appearance of fire
> enclosed roundabout; and downward from what had the appearance
> of his loins I saw as it were the appearance of fire . . . such was the
> appearance of the likeness of the glory of the Lord. (Ezekiel,1:26-28)

This is a description which is not a description. The likeness of a
human form? Perhaps, but how to picture such a "likeness," composed,
as the prophet tells us, of "the appearance of fire." Of course no face is
even hinted at. Ezekiel is urgent in his desire for us to understand that
his imagery does not offer us a picture of God at all. He insists that he
saw "as it were" only the (1) appearance of the (2) likeness of the (3)
glory of the Lord. What he looked upon was at three removes from the
glory itself . . . from the face of God.

Through these texts and others we are presented with the paradox
of an imageless image of God. This is a God who, in God's holiness, can
never be imaged forth. Yet humanity *is* the divine image. If this is so,
then the human is to be conceived as created in the image of an imageless
God. Thus the human is itself imageless and the Bible's initial definition of divinity and humanity is, both theologically and anthropologically a negative definition. Or, better, it is a non-definition, an absence
of definition.

To say that we reflect the image of a God who is imageless is to say
that, like God, the human is indefinable, irreducible, un-namable, in-
exhaustible. As there is no knowable, absolute divine nature, so there
is no universal human nature. Both the divine and the human are
open-ended and cannot be enclosed in a static nature or limiting conception. God and the human transcend all definition, escape all images.[1]

That being said, the Bible goes on to say much about the charac-
ters of the divine and the human. But does this not contradict all we
have said above? A return to Moses' exchange with God in Exodus,
33-34 may be helpful. As quoted above (vs. 19), God tells Moses that "I
will be gracious to whom I will be gracious, and will show mercy on
whom I will show mercy." Does this mean God is gracious and merci-

ful? Not in any way we can count on or expect in some particular situation.[2] God retains absolute sovereignty to dispense divine grace and mercy how and to whom God pleases. Thus there is no absolute sense in which these qualities can be predicated of God in any way human beings can comprehend. Again, a non-definition for an imageless God.

But the conversation does not end there. God has more to say to Moses and to us. The next day, at God's command, Moses goes up again onto Sinai. As God has promised, Moses is placed in the cleft of a rock (vs. 22-23). ". . . And I will cover you with my hand, and you shall see my back; but my face shall not be seen." In this moving, evocative passage the glory of God, the face of God, remains hidden; but something is revealed which is referred to as God's "back." The meaning of this obscure reference is revealed in 34:6-7.

> The Lord passed before him and proclaimed, "The Lord, the Lord, a God merciful and gracious, slow to anger, and abounding in steadfast love and faithfulness, keeping steadfast love for thousands, forgiving iniquity and transgression, and sin, but who will by no means clear the guilty. . . . "

Having denied Moses the right to look upon the glory of God (some absolute, universal nature of the divine), now God reveals to Moses and to us exactly what the Holy One desires us to know—not the "face" of God, but the "back." The latter consists of God's activities as revealed to Israel in its sacred history. What any people can know of God— *all that they can know*—is how God interacts with *them* in the particularity of their historical, religious and cultural situation. Within these parameters much can be said about God and human beings. And the Bible says it.

Having held that the face of God cannot be seen, and that there is therefore no "absolute image of humanity," the Scriptures go on to discuss at great length the natures of God and the human as revealed within the context of the experience of the people Israel. At no point does the Bible reveal any "nature of God" as God may be, unrelated to the people of God. Moses, Isaiah and Ezekiel see only the God who is revealed to Israel in uniquely Israelite visions. Each people, each culture must fill in the image of the imageless God in a manner dictated by the lived experience of that people. No such image is exhaustive or can be imposed on any other people or transferred to any other cultural context.

II. The Declaration and Its Assumptions

Our reading of the Bible's discussion of divine and human images leads us to a positive evaluation of the proposed "Universal Declaration of a Global Ethic." This despite the fact that such a title could be quite misleading. One might be led to suspect an attempt by one tradition to impose its values on another, to engage in the kind of ethical imperialism that has so marred and distorted the "missionary" projects of the past. But, beyond the title, one quickly learns from the introductory text that what we have here is no exercise in Western triumphalism. Although the scope is global, the project rests on the assumption that each culture is unique and that each must develop its own particular ethical system even as each must generate its own religious self-understanding. All this is recognized within a new and larger context which is given a three-fold analysis.

A. The Contemporary Paradigm Shift

All truth is "relational," de-absolutized by the particular situation of the knower who is limited by language and point of view. This is a truth for him and for those sharing his temporal, spatial and cultural context. Every truth is contextual and is therefore not a bare description but an interpretation.[3] All these insights are elements of the post-modern mindset now dominant in so many fields of thought.

What does Judaism say about all this? It says: "Let every nation walk in the name of its god; we will walk in the name of the Lord our God forever" (Micah, 4:5). This means that Jews do not attempt to "win the world" for their faith. Judaism encourages other cultures to develop ethical structures of their own which will bring out the best qualities of their peoples. Jews respect the paths others have taken. Judaism seeks both to affirm and to transcend itself. It encourages its own people to live in the larger human community in the way people should live when God is their Ruler. Thus Israel becomes a "witness people," teaching by example, never by coercion.

The ultimate Jewish project, the upbuilding of God's Reign on earth, is not envisioned as the imposition of one set of social structures or religious rules on everyone. Rather, Jews seek to join hands with others, working to create a humane environment which will take various forms in different societies. The Declaration's stress on each religio-cultural community's individual development of its own version of the

"Golden Rule" provides a starting point in each distinct society from which to encourage development of standards which will grow organically out of many soils. The insistence that all aspects of the Declaration will be open to discussion and input from all participants insures a balance of universal and particular elements. Such thinking allows us to respect the contextual and relational character of truth without ending up in ethical or cultural solipsism.

B. A New Axial Age of Global Consciousness

This reading of the current state of world consciousness is highly questionable. It seems to me that, paradoxically, global consciousness is not itself global but is a particular phenomenon of the Western mind. Examples of the opposite tendency outside the Western world abound. Eastern Europe and the former Soviet Union come most readily to mind. These new or newly liberated states are caught up in a process of fragmentation which is the negative legacy of the attempt by Communist authorities to impose unity from the top down. The introduction to the Declaration recognizes the futility of such artificial movements of forced consensus. The current drive toward re-tribalization in this region is the inevitable reaction to the tyranny of sameness which Marxism's economic and social theories attempted to force on organically distinct ethnic and cultural groups.

But there is more than simple reaction going on here. The peoples of Eastern Europe had been unique and separate in their self-conceptions long before the Tsarist and then the Soviet yoke was imposed upon them. It is difficult to discern among these Eastern European peoples any movement whatever toward global consciousness. Racial, religious and cultural fragmentation seem to be the order of the day. They have combined to turn the former Yugoslavia into one of the world's most ghastly killing-fields.

And where can we discern any movement even toward regionalism, much less global consciousness, in Africa or South America? What was once a disparate agglomeration of states and peoples loosely grouped under the heading "Third World" has now ceased to claim even that dubious common ground. Here too ethnic fragmentation, often fanatical nationalism and primitive tribalism seem to dominate these regions.

The Arab world presents a different picture. United by a common faith these countries seem to be achieving a strong regional consciousness. But it is a consciousness intent on stopping far short of any universal self-conception. Arab unity is still aborning and seems unsure of its own defining terms. In this century pan-Arabists have tried first Westernization, then Arab Socialism and now recrudescent Islam as vehicles of Arab unity. The terms keep shifting and each tendency has had its holdouts, but the impulse remains strong. The latest trend, Islamic orthodoxy, or rather, Islamism, seems, of all of them, to be the most heavily weighted with anti-outsider attitudes and self-isolating tendencies. It is to be hoped that the developing peace process between Israel and its Arab neighbors will modify these trends and open the Arab world to a greater participation in the global community. But there is little sign of that today.

On the other side of the picture Western Europe, long plagued by wars brought on by virulent nationalism, is on the way to a new regional unity. But unlike that of the Arab world this trend is fully open to larger participation in the global community. The same could be said of the United States and Canada as they move toward greater integration of markets. Their cultures are already all but indistinguishable. The full participation of Mexico in a larger relationship with the two nations to its north remains a hope rather than a reality.

It must be said at this point that the present attitudes of major elements of the African-American community run counter to the trend toward regional and global consciousness in North America as a whole. The tribal consciousness of this group seems to be intensifying. This is one example of a number around the world in which a minority culture-within-a-culture engages in a psychological withdrawal from identification with the larger society within which it lives. That there are such tribal holdouts even within the most cosmopolitan nations cannot be denied, but in the West the growth of regional consciousness within a global context seems inevitable.

It is important that Westerners not delude themselves that this movement involves the great masses of the world's peoples. Their identities remain at the most national, at the least tribal; their passions are for causes and ideals often limited to the length and breadth of their home village. What may mislead us into believing that global consciousness is itself a global phenomenon is that the Western-educated and oriented elites in most countries share it with us. Their tribal, ethnic and national identities have been de-absolutized by Western philosophies of individualism and universalism. These elites are much more in tune with the middle and upper classes of the Western democracies than they are with their own peoples.

C. The Age of Monologue Gives Way to the Age of Dialogue

No community is more acutely aware of the truth of this analysis than is the people Israel living in the Western world. For us it is a recent truth, but nevertheless an all encompassing and transformative one. We have seen a religious revolution in the last three decades in the relations between Jews and Christians. This troubled relationship of rival siblings has been in the past heavily weighted with historical tragedy and theological enmity. Today it is on the mend as it has been for thirty years of fruitful Jewish-Christian dialogue. Led by the Roman Catholic Church of Pope John XXIII, the mainstream churches of Christendom have radically shifted their attitudes toward Jews and Judaism. In a mere three decades these churches have come to view Jews not as candidates for conversion but as partners in dialogue. Once the lessons of the Holocaust had sunk in and with the Israelite state reborn on its ancient soil, the churches were led to re-examine attitudes which had marginalized, even demonized Jews and consigned them to eternal wandering, theologically and geographically.[4]

Religions have always encountered their most difficult challenge in attempting to deal with "the other." This is especially true in the case of Western religious systems which make universal claims. For the Church the very existence of Jewry and Judaism represented a challenge to a universal Christianity which had grown out of Jewish soil but had failed to win over the very people from whom Christ had sprung. As the need for a dialogic stance emerged out of the Jewish tragedy/ triumph of the 1940's, the Church began to wrestle with the problem of how to reaffirm the truth of Christ while not delegitimizing the people and faith of Israel with all the ghastly consequences produced by that attitude in the past.

Today Christians are still struggling with this question, but the mainstream churches have come far. Virtually all of them have endorsed the central proposition of the Jewish faith that God has entered into an eternal covenant with the people Israel and has commissioned them to be God's witnesses in the world. They have further recognized that Judaism, the life of Torah, continues, after the Christ event, to be a fully valid and divinely ordained relationship between the people Israel and their God—the same God revealed to Christians in Jesus of Nazareth.

For their part, Jewish theologians have responded to this revolution in Christian thought by searching into ways for Judaism to uphold its own truth without denying that of Christianity.[5] This is a complex and delicate theological task still in its beginnings, but the way leads upward toward a fuller and more fruitful mutual appreciation in which each faith makes room for the other, realizing for the first time that neither can understand itself and its calling without taking into account the complementary work of the other. This is true dialogue indeed.

It must be noted that this extraordinary dialogue is a strictly Western phenomenon involving two Western religions. It is true that both these faiths have in the past claimed to be the sole repository of divine revelation. These competing claims have put them on paths of collision with each other. But it is also true that those who differ over the same issues or make competing claims have at least something in common to talk about. In the Hebrew Scriptures (Christianity's Old Testament) Jews and Christians have a common text over which to differ. This makes dialogue difficult but it also makes it possible. The task is eased by the fact that, increasingly, Jews and Christians share a common Western culture. Or perhaps one should say that those in the Jewish and Christian communities who do share that culture are the ones who are engaging in dialogue.

More recently some Jews have found themselves involved in hitherto unexpected political negotiations. After a half-century of mutual hostility Arabs and Israelis in the Middle East may at long last be on the road to peace. Here we have an example of enlightened self-interest at its best. Israeli Jews do not want to raise yet another generation of children expert in the use of the *Uzi*. Jews did not return to their ancient soil to live in a garrison state. Nor do they desire to rule over another people and thus compromise the moral authority of their faith and culture. For their part Palestinians do not want to raise their children as perennial exiles. They want to be masters in their own house.

These political and military negotiations bear no resemblance to the true dialogue being carried on by Jews and Christians in the West. The goal here is not mutual enrichment and understanding. Neither side is interested in learning anything from the other. Unable to live together they have agreed to separate, to live in contiguous states in peace. Since neither side can completely subdue the other, they have no choice other than non-belligerency. Both peoples will benefit from the peace if and when it comes. But this will be a triumph of classic political negotiation rather than of any new dialogic consciousness in the region. Both groups are struggling to find a way to realize their respective aspirations. Each must give up dreams of regional hegemony. They must learn to share the earth, to live if not as brothers, at least as good neighbors for the benefit of all. That they appear to be doing this is perhaps the single most hopeful development on the contemporary world political scene. It is to be hoped that the present process will continue apace and that the lessons of reconciliation between peoples will set an example for others.

III. A Jewish Comment on the Declaration

It must be clear from what has been said above that I cannot agree with the view that a "Second Axial Age" of global consciousness "is happening simultaneously around the earth." I believe that the evidence indicates that the move from a paradigm of monologue to one of dialogue is real enough, but that it is confined to the middle and upper classes of the Western world and to the westernized elites which are in positions of power in non-Western regions. Westerners meet them at international conferences and may come to believe that they represent the masses of their people. There is, however, no evidence of this whatever. Ghandi, Sadat and Reza Pahlavi each gained popularity in the West but met similar ends, demonstrating how out of touch they were with their own populations.

As an American I believe in the ideal of human moral progress; as a Jew I hold that history ultimately aims at a messianic fulfillment. This culmination will involve a universal recognition of the sanctity of all life and the respect of all for all in the human community. My rather pessimistic reading of the present state of mind of most of the world, of the fragmentation and re-tribalization obtaining in so many places, does not lessen my enthusiasm for the present attempt to reverse current trends. The messianic work must often be carried on despite the dominant conditions in human society. One strand of Jewish thought conceives of a world moving inexorably upward toward the messianic consummation; another views history as a steady decline from Eden.[6] But the worse things become, the greater the need (thus the greater the likelihood) of the Messiah's advent.

Is it possible that today conditions are becoming both better and worse? Better because we have seen the collapse of global tyrannies, Fascism and Communism and their like; worse because social disintegration seems to be the order of the day. Positive ideas regarding global unity seem as impotent to influence peoples as negative ones—at least outside the world of the Western elites. "Nevertheless," said the Rabbis, "nevertheless, make straight the path of the Messiah".[7]

Earlier I spoke of the human as the earthly image of the imageless God. This iconoclastic non-definition of the divine and the human leaves each culture free to discover images for both appropriate to its particular lived experience. These images are usually found in the narratives which both shape and are shaped by the collective individuals we call societies. Such narratives have been produced by smaller societies (cultures) or by larger ones (civilizations), but never by a world civilization, since no such thing has ever existed. And, if I am correct, no such thing is in the offing today.

This leaves us with the problem of what to do with the universal claims about humanity in general that so many religions make. Certainly the great monotheistic systems have done so in the past, Judaism included. The Jewish faith as a whole may be for the Jewish people alone, both those born into the community and those who join it, but crucial elements of it reach beyond that community to embrace all human beings. If we ignore this self-transcending dimension then Judaism becomes a strictly local phenomenon with nothing to say to the rest of the world.

But monotheism itself makes such Jewish isolationism impossible. There is one God over all peoples. And if that monotheism is ethical monotheism, the same foundational ethical principles must be applicable to all. Judaism has managed to affirm these truths without engaging in religious imperialism. Each people must develop its own ethical system, but there are certain minimum standards to which all will come. According to the Rabbis both Adam and Noah, the first and second fathers of humanity, were required to observe seven commands, five of which fall under the category "ethics." Broadly stated they are as follows. All societies must establish functioning justice systems, and all peoples must abstain from homicide, robbery, sexual misconduct and cruelty to animals.[8] This is not a program to be imposed by one society on another, but is rather a set of minimal guidelines which must surely inform any ethical system worthy of the name. These texts clearly indicate that the idea of a universal declaration of minimal ethical standards is very much in the Jewish tradition.

This universal stress continues as the primeval history of Genesis 1-11 gives way to Israel's story beginning in the next chapter. Here the Holy One calls Abraham out of his native land with an eternal promise:

> And I will make of you a great nation . . . and in you shall all the families of the earth be blessed. (Genesis, 12:3)

Every part of this promise depends on every other part. Israel's greatness is its calling to bring blessing to all humanity. Both directly (through Judaism) and indirectly (through Christianity and Islam), Israel will speak to the world of its vision of the divine and the human. There can be no national life for Israel without this international witness.[9] That witness inevitably involves ethical ideals. It is as witnesses to these principles that the Holy One has scattered Israel abroad in many lands. And so, once again, the idea of a global ethic is fully compatible with Judaism's world mission.

All this having been said, it should be pointed out that the agreement of Jewish tradition with the Universal Declaration before us could hardly be otherwise. If global consciousness is a peculiarly Western development then it should come as no surprise that Judaism, the oldest ethical religion of the West, should share that consciousness. Indeed the Jewish conception of ethical monotheism gave it birth. The Judeo-Christian civilization which has grown from Israelite (and Ionian) roots has cultivated this vision. But, as noted earlier, there are other civilizations and other visions.

In a significant essay, "The Clash of Civilizations?"[10] Samuel P. Huntington predicts that the next world struggle will be between seven world civilizations now coming to the fore as Cold War divisions fade. He points to the weakening of national consciousness and the revival of religion as the dominant characteristic of these emerging civiliza-

tions.[11] It is along the "fault lines" between these seven civilizations
that world conflict will continue to take place. His argument is a powerful one and presents a new post-Cold War paradigm which accounts
for many of the events of contemporary history. There are certain weaknesses: he passes over the absence of strong regional consciousness in
Africa and South America and, in his original essay, he does not discuss
the forces of racial and ethnic disintegration threatening the integrity
of the United States. However, in the follow-up essay in which he answers his critics, he discusses the internal dangers to our country with
considerable insight.[12] Since America is not alone in facing this threat,
Huntington would do well to speak to this more fully in his upcoming
book.

Whether we face a period of tribalism, nationalism or regionalism
or a poisonous brew of all three, global consciousness remains a distant ideal. But that is the nature of ideals—to be distant. They summon
us toward them like the horizon which tantalizes but retreats before
us. But if the horizon were not there we would be without a goal. Horizons may not be reachable by human effort alone, but much ground
can be covered en route. Our task is to cultivate the seeds of a universal
religious humanism wherever we find them, to inform ourselves regarding the various ways different civilizations engage in their own
versions of self-affirmation and self-transcendence and to encourage
those in all cultures who share our ultimate vision of a global community. The Universal Declaration of a Global Ethic represents a step toward the horizon which is our goal and our hope. Success in the short
range is unlikely, but we are sustained by the messianic promise and
encouraged by the words of Rabbi Tarphon:

> He used to say, "it is not thy duty to complete the work, but neither
> are you free to desist from it."[13]

Footnotes

1 Moses asks God at the burning bush to reveal the divine name. God
responds: "I am what I shall be." (Exodus, 3:14)

2 Maimonides' doctrine of the negative attributes of God is helpful here.
His concern is to establish the absolute sovereignty and unity of the Holy
One. This involves God's indefinability.

3 "The Torah speaks in the language of men." (*Sifré* to Numbers, 1:12)

4 A number of official church statements on Jews and Judaism are listed in Michael S. Kogan, "Jews and Christians: Taking the Next Step," *Journal of Ecumenical Studies*, Fall, 1989.

5 Michael S. Kogan, "Toward a Jewish Theology of Christianity," *Journal of Ecumenical Studies*, Winter, 1995.

6 This latter theme was first articulated by Philo (first century CE), *On the Creation*, 49:140, and echoed in *Genesis Rabbah*'s discussion (fifth century CE) of Adam's perfection and the steady degradation of all the following generations.

7 This Rabbinic passage was quoted by Rabbi Judah Nadich in a sermon delivered at the Park Avenue Synagogue perhaps fifteen years ago. At this point neither he nor I remembers the source of the quote.

8 *Tosefta* (2nd century CE), *Genesis Rabbah* 16:6 (5th century CE).

9 Many Rabbinic passages speak of God's and Israel's concern for the peoples of the world and of the salvation awaiting the righteous of all nations. E.g., *Suk.* 55b, *Ber.* 40b, and *Tosefta Sanh.* 13:2.

10 Samuel P. Huntington, "The Clash of Civilizations?" *Foreign Affairs*, Summer, 1993, pp. 22-49.

11 Nietzsche's madman was aware that he came "too soon." Apparently it was *much* too soon. Westerners should not be surprised at the news of God's resurrection. I am reminded at a popular graffito on college campuses in the 1960's: "God is dead, signed—Nietzsche; Nietzsche is dead, signed—God."

12 Samuel P. Huntington, "If Not Civilization, What?," *Foreign Affairs*, Nov., Dec., 1993.

13 Talmud:*Avot*, 2:21.

LEONARD SWIDLER'S
DRAFT OF A GLOBAL ETHIC:
A MUSLIM PERSPECTIVE

KHALID DURAN

FOR A COMMENTATOR IT may be the wrong
thing to do, but I should like to say right at the start that I fully support
Leonard Swidler's project of drafting a global ethic and winning acceptance for it, global acceptance, if possible.

Islam, as we know, is not only a faith with a theology, philosophy
and mysticism, but also a culture and a social phenomenon of global
character—with a history of more than fourteen hundred years. If today one speaks of "the Islamic perspective," further information is
needed in order to know what is meant. Hence, when I as a Muslim say
that I have no difficulties with Leonard Swidler's presentation of a universal global ethic, then of course I must add that I represent only one
of many possible perspectives within the Islamic spectrum. Indeed,
there is the famous saying of our Prophet, according to which: One day
his community will be splintered into 72 sects; only the 73rd will be
saved. Now, fortunately I belong to that 73rd!—but of course my rep-
resentativeness is thereby limited. On the other hand, as a historian of
religion I believe I am in a position to say some things at least partially
authoritative about Islam and a universal global ethic.

I believe that there are a number of reasons for Muslims to endorse a universal global ethic, first and foremost being the fact that Islam itself was originally intended as something like a global ethic. The Prophet Muhammad did not wish to found a new religion. He was driven by the desire to bring people back to the original faith of Abraham. He understood that the various types of Christianity and sects of Judaism all sprang from the same source. Since they had come to differ amongst themselves considerably, he saw his task in re-establishing the original Abrahamic religion, called Islam. This may sound odd to someone who associates the word *islám* with the religion of Islam as we know it today, or even with the world community of Islam as a social phenomenon. We might forget about Islam in this sense for a moment and bear in mind that the word *islám* has a meaning in Arabic. It signifies submission to the will of God, and peace. In that sense *islám* is the same as *salám*, which is the same as the Hebrew *shalom*, meaning peace, with the special connotation of soundness, wholesomeness.

Muhammad made it his mission to bring people back to *islám* in that original sense. He did not intend to convert people to his own religion; he wanted to convert them to the religion of Abraham. To this end the prototype of Abrahamic religion had to be reconstructed, and that became the religion of Islam as we know it today, at least in its ideal sense, as enshrined in the revelation of *Al-Qur'án* (Koran). Hence, I must once again emphasize that the Prophet Muhammad originally did not think of the creation of a new faith community. He was first of all concerned to unite the various groups of believers in God on a platform that was common to all. He proceeded on the assumption that the various sects of Jews and Christians as well as the other monotheists all formed a single family which through unfortunate accidents fell into dispute with one another. Consequently, he took as his task the reestablishment of that prototype of Abrahamic religion, monotheism.

It is in my opinion no accident that a new religion like that of Baha'i grew specifically out of Islam. It is similar with the Sikh religion, despite its "local color," for behind the Indian facade is hidden an original drive for unity, for a synthesis of Islam and Hinduism. As already earlier with Muhammad, so also with Guru Nanak in India and Baha'u'llah in Persia, nothing came from this drive—nothing of this bringing together of the different faith communities. In each case a new religion arose, that is, precisely the opposite of what was at first aimed at. Nevertheless, this original motive, the unity of all believers, never was completely lost, at least not in the mystical tradition.

Sufism, with many regional differences, was for a long time dominant in the Islamic world. Today as well Sufism is still stronger that militant Fundamentalism. Wherever Sufism plays a roll, the unity of all religions is on the agenda. In this sense Sufism and Fundamentalism are diametrically opposed to each other. The Fundamentalists put up fences, dividing walls, they separate, preferably with an Iron Curtain. On the contrary, the Sufis seek to tear down everything that divides.

In interreligious dialogue, therefore, there is a problem of a particular sort with many Muslims, and especially those who are Sufi-oriented. Interreligious dialogue definitely does not wish to work syncretically. Indeed, it has a special need to differentiate itself from syncretic streams, to defend itself against the accusation of syncretism. The fear of syncretism is a restrictive limit for many who otherwise are fully in favor of dialogue. Hence, the *Dialogue Decalogue* of Leonard Swidler to a large extent excludes syncretism.

Many Muslims, on the other hand, especially those who are Sufi-oriented, ask themselves, what is really so terrible with syncretism? For many the ideal is *wahdat al-wujúd* (the "unity of all being"). Others have difficulties with the pantheism that is implied therein, but would like to stress the essential unity of all religions. Hence, there is the revision that is dominant among our mystics: *wahdat ash-shuhúd* (the "unity of witnesses").

Why do I relate all this? I am concerned to illustrate the fundamental readiness to accept the drafted universal ethic. The current exclusivist positions fought for by a strengthened Fundamentalism, the cultural Apartheid striven for by the Islamists (Muslim Fundamentalists), the anti-Western xenophobia of our fanatics are all factors which easily can give the impression that Muslims *qua* Muslims are less open to such universalist goals.

I do not hesitate to maintain that precisely the opposite is the case. Islamism, that is, Fundamentalism, has indeed increased in strength, but it still remains a minority phenomenon. The majority of Muslims are especially receptive to universalistic undertakings—with, naturally, differences conditioned by specific historical experiences and varying interpretations of Islam. As a rule, however, a draft like this universal global ethic will not only encounter open ears but will also stimulate religious echos.

"Come here for a word which is in common between you and us," it says in the Qur'an. There we have a literal translation of "dialogue," i.e., a "word between" (*dia-logos*) conversation partners. And there also we have the presentation of a common platform of all believers; for the special word between the believers of all religions, that word which is common to all of them is the confessing of God.

From this expectation Muslims can only welcome the hoped-for establishment of a universal global ethic. It doesn't need any theological tricks. For this one needs no new theology.

Islam was to do justice to both major purposes with which the term religion is usually associated, viz. an explanation of the world and an ethics. In Islam, as in Judaism, the emphasis is a little more on ethics. Given the fact that Islam, in its capacity as the reborn faith of Abraham, was meant to be a platform for Jews, Christians and other monotheists, it had to be universal. It was not a message to any particular people, not a religion for Arabs exclusively. Quite the contrary, the basic assumption underlying Muhammad's message, one that is clearly and frequently stated in *Al-Qur'án*, is that God sent messengers to all peoples. Every people has had its messenger. Jesus was understood as a messenger to the Jews primarily. Finally there was to be a messenger for all humanity, Muhammad.

Accordingly, the ethics of this prototype of Abrahamic religion *had* to be universal. The express purpose was to do away with particularisms. Not without reason have anthropologists accused Muslims of cultural levelling and creating a *homo islamicus*, enforcing a high degree of uniformity on otherwise very diverse parts of our world.

From the viewpoint of a cultural anthropologist it is certainly regrettable that the national costumes of many peoples have come to be replaced by a set of Middle Eastern gowns, creating monotony in place of creativity. I personally share this regret and seek solace in the fact that many local traditions have been able to hold their own despite that monotonous Middle Easternization following in the wake of Islam's advance.

I relate all this to illustrate what is meant by the creation of a *homo islamicus*, a kind of uniform human being, more conditioned by Islam than by any other tradition or particularism. Many scholars hold the view that it is law which has brought about that uniformity more than anything else. Islamic law, the *sharí'a*, is in fact much more than law as Westerners today understand law. The *sharí'a* is rather a comprehensive code of behavior. A modern slogan calls the *sharí'a* "complete code of life." That is not wrong, although our Fundamentalists misuse this slogan in such a way that many Muslims have become allergic to it.

A complete code of life comprises ethics, and many common believers in various parts of the Muslim world do in fact understand the term *sharí'a* to be roughly equivalent with *akhláq*, the Arabic word for ethics. I guess this problem of distinguishing, or not distinguishing, between law and ethics exists in other cultures too. In the case of Islam, ethics came first. The law was formulated later in order make ethics prevail. That is a rather complex affair because in the course of time these two tend to drift apart. Among Muslims that has been a debate for centuries. We have our scholars of the law, *sharí'a*, and we have scholars of ethics, *akhláq*. There is an age-old conflict between the scholars of the law and the teachers of ethics who feel that stagnation of the law has led to what are, from an ethical point of view, absurdities.

We might speak of a history of revolt against the law in Islam, a revolt in the name of ethics, a series of uprisings of the proponents of *akhláq* against the professors of *sharí'a*. This is what comes to mind immediately upon hearing Leonard Swidler talk of global ethics. Muslims who put ethics above and the law beneath will be thrilled to hear of this project. Those who take the *sharí'a* as their shield without understanding the difference between *sharí'a* and *akhláq* will be apprehensive.

It will not be easy for any Muslims, including the Islamists, to say an outright "no" to such a project of a global ethic. However, the *sharí'a* advocates will want the *sharí'a* to be the global ethic. Confusing the law with ethics, they cannot but seek to impose their exclusivist vision on others. To sum up, there will be Muslims truly committed to the project and others who will seek to exploit it as a means of proselytizing.

What good is there in a global ethic, the defenders of the *sharí'a* will argue, if it is not enacted—in other words, if the ethical principles or teachings are not converted into a law? At the same time they cannot accept any law other than the *sharí'a*. Perhaps I am stating an extreme. We do, of course, have many scholars of the law who hold very rational views about the *shari'a*, who approach it from a historical angle and analyze it as a product in the making of which many outstanding personalities participated over a span of at least two centuries. In actual fact, the *shari'a* is the product of what was then an Islamic melting pot of races and cultures. Our Islamists, however, claim divine origin for the *shari'a*. What is divine is superior to what is human-made. Leonard Swidler's project of a global ethics can only result in a human-made product—hopefully a product made by as many women and men as possible.

Further difficulties lie, in my opinion, in the details of any universal global ethic, that is, in the difficult balance between universality and its specific binding force. Nothing is easier than to line up universal principles and have them approved. Then everyone goes about their implementation in his or her own manner. For example, we have just experienced with the collapse of the Soviet block how every concept has received a new meaning: The "peoples friendship" between East Germany and Poland was not the same as the "peoples friendship" between West Germany and France. The "freedom of the press" of the Communist *Neues Deutschland* was like the "freedom of the press" of the Nazi *Völkischer Beobachter*, but had nothing to do with the "freedom of the press" of the West Berlin *Spandauer Volksblatt*, etc.

We cannot avoid conceptually specifying the general principles and thereby going somewhat into detail. If tomorrow in Tajikstan the "Peoples' Democracy" were replaced by an "Islamic Democracy" à la Iran, we would have an experience of still more democratic rigamorole, but we would have even less of the substance of democracy. Today, however, we are passing through a phase not very different from that of Soviet rule when a particular brand of Communism was enforced. Under that ideology many terms of our vocabulary became perverted. Rather than admit that they could not care less for democracy, the Soviets insisted on being the best of democrats, and more than that, "people's democrats." This was imitated by not a few Muslim countries. A dictatorial regime in Algeria proclaimed a "Democratic and Popular Republic." Linguistically speaking that means the same thing three times. The Libyan People's *Jamáhiriya* means one and the same thing—a dozen times.

As for our Islamists, we are better off with the radical ones who openly say that there is "no democracy in Islam" and "Western" concepts of human rights cannot be reconciled with Islam. Much worse are those who speak of an "Islamic democracy" and "Islamic republic," but mean essentially the same that the Communists meant while talking about "popular democracy" and "people's republic." A group of so-called moderate Islamists even drafted an "Islamic Declaration of Human Rights." As a Muslim I would be less hesitant about signing a "Hindu Declaration of Human Rights" or a "Jewish Declaration of Human Rights." I know that there are Islamists around who just wait for someone like Leonard Swidler, eager to hijack his global ethics.

No one has proclaimed in words so loudly in favor of the emancipation of women as the *Mullahcracy* in Iran. The most radical devotee of radical feminism could learn something from them. Even the German radical feminist publication *Emma* could not keep up with Khomeini. But what does that mean in practice? Almost the exact opposite. As gun-toters and as prison guards the women of Iran and the Sudan are good. That then is lifted up as progress beyond the traditionalist society, which never had such. Under the aegis of the *New Ideology of Islamism*, which is everything other than the *Old Religion of Islam*, a complete emptying of concepts of their content takes place. There, in the name of the Islamic Republic and its emancipation of women, women are sprayed with acid because a single lock of hair slipped out a little from under the required head covering.

Saudi Arabia has no state constitution because it allegedly needs none. "We have the Qur'an," it is said. That is a fatuous fiddling with the Holy Book. This forces us, then, to really define, in pedantic manner, what we are claiming and what we want to achieve. Otherwise the same will happen to us as to those concerned with human rights. For example, it is insisted that no religious minority has it so good as do the Christians of Pakistan. This ideal solution is expressed in separate election lists: Muslims may vote only for Muslim candidates, Christians only for Christian. A Hindu may not receive any more votes than there are Hindu voters, even if the majority of the Muslims might prefer to vote for him because he is the most capable candidate, because he is more honest than the Muslim candidate.

Perhaps some Germans still remember Adolf Hitler's *Mein Kampf*, where it is so beautifully stated: "The male stork goes to the female stork, the male wolf to the female wolf, house mouse to house mouse and field mouse to field mouse" (*Der Storch geht zur Störchin, der Wolf zu Wölfin, Hausmaus zu Hausmaus und Feldmaus zu Feldmaus).*

In the "ideological state" of the Islamists the rights of women are better maintained than in any other system, and specifically through the fact that a few women were named as representatives of womanhood in the parliament. Men elect only men and women only women, if at all. Women Prime Ministers such as Khalida Zia in Bangladesh, Benazir Bhutto in Pakistan, Tansu Çiller in Turkey are symptoms of a devilish Westernization, *gharbzadegi*, as the Islamists say. *Gharbzadegi* means something like "being dazzled by the glitter of the West and giving oneself over as a slave to it," with the resulting immorality.

The proponents of Islamism, the ideology of the nineties, would gladly be the first to sign the draft of a universal global ethic, as long as a long series of individual issues were not specified therein. They are also eagerly the first to engage in interreligious dialogue, to monopolize it so other Muslims—for instance, "heretics" like us—cannot participate. Afterwards in their publications in Arabic and Urdu, concerning interreligious dialogue they proclaim: That is the latest trick of the Christian missionaries after all other means to convert Muslims have failed. Concerning the draft of a universal global ethic, their comments behind closed doors would hardly be other.

What to do? A draft of global ethics cannot go into too much detail as this would jeopardize universal acceptance. But if it remains too unspecified, too vague, it will lead nowhere, because the first ones to sign will be the perpetrators of genocide, such as Milosevic and Karadzic, Rafsanjani and Turabi. How, then, can one work out in detail such a global ethic and be just to all sides—I do not mean here the Islamists or similar Fundamentalists among Jews, Christians, Buddhists, Hindus and others. Let us leave that marginal group on the side, for it is already extraordinarily difficult to reach a consensus among the majority streams. An yet, it should be attempted. We should not limit ourselves to safe ground, but rather venture further—otherwise nothing will be gained. There is no longer a lack in our global village of well-intentioned declarations by the most various of committees of different concerns on the fundamental issues of the world community.

I mean that Leonard Swidler's initiative deserves to be taken seriously, that is, consistently worked out—which of course demands an immense amount of work, which would presume world-wide intensive discussions in Buddhist monasteries, in the Vatican, in the Qarawiyí

(Morocco's theological university with an influence throughout West Africa), in the 'Ulamá Academy of Lahor in Pakistan, among Hindu Pundits and Chinese Party Ideologues.

For this purpose we must wrestle with the question whether the different cultures really think in thought categories which are different from one another, as the Fundamentalists on all sides eagerly maintain. In my opinion it makes an immense difference whether one speaks of the differing concepts of the different cultures, or of different thought categories. One can translate concepts or at least find approximate correspondents in other cultures. With thought categories it is more difficult.

I do not wish categorically to deny that there are such fundamentally different thought categories. On the contrary, everything which enriches human thought should be welcomed. But I have experienced how the slogan of different thought categories can be misused, how every discussion can be made impossible, how every understanding of one another can be sabotaged, for our Fundamentalists obstinately insist that "true Islam" cannot be understood or analyzed with the help of Western structures of thought. Nevertheless, they propose an unanalyzable unity which can be grasped only with their own categories—not, of course, through the comparative method.

Now and again all this will be presented in a significantly more learned manner than I am doing here. But the end effect is always the same, namely, the tireless pursuit of the distortion of the meaning of concepts and the dislocation of all such universalistic attempts as that by Leonard Swidler.

I gladly grant that as a Sufi-influenced Muslim I am not especially concerned about my uniqueness. However, I believe I can bring a certain understanding for those who in their religion are first of all concerned to maintain their uniqueness and their distinctness from others. The overcoming of this hurdle is certainly the most difficult barricade on the path to a global ethic, for with many there arises the fear that through such a global undertaking they could lose something of substance, could lose holding on to "their own." That is not absolutely the same as the above-mentioned rejection of syncretism. Rather, it is a very simple question: If we all contribute something, how much from me, then, will be taken up, how will it maintain itself alongside the other elements, will it play any role at all, or will it be hardly visible any more among the multiplicity of contributions?

I once wrote a dissertation on a modern Egyptian historian and language reformer who was also a religious scholar and reform thinker. During the forty years of his activity as editor of the cultural periodical *Ath-Thaqáfa*, Ahmad Amín (d. 1954) concerned himself tirelessly with the thought of a "global marriage" of East and West ("Islamic Orient and Christian Occident"). In this he constantly asked about what would be brought along. What in our cultural heritage is appropriate to be taken up into the family community? What do we possess which we do not wish to give up, or indeed cannot give up? How do we adapt and how do we maintain our identity?

Those are all questions which will unhesitantly be posed. Even when we give our signature to the draft because we have nothing further to add, we nevertheless would like to be visible in the final version.

I should like to explain a little more why I, as a Muslim, feel so affirmative about this project. After all, I am not a contemporary of the Prophet Muhammad, when *islám* was still to be written with a small "i," as the prototype of Abrahamic religion, not *Islam* with a capital "I," the world community of today, fourteen centuries later.

Our philosophical tradition knows of a famous parable which inspired three great minds who all wrote a book on Hayy Ibn Yaqzán, an Arabic name which in English means *The Living One, Son of the Awake.* Being of Andalusian ancestry, I feel closest to the version presented by our twelfth-century philosopher Ibn Tufail. His Hayy Ibn Yaqzán is a human being growing up on an uninhabited island, reared by animals ever since he was placed there as a baby. In the course of a long life he discovers many laws of nature by sheer observation and by dint of his natural intelligence. Observation of animal life teaches him the rules of society and the reasons of social conduct. He becomes a deeply ethical being.

Late in his life *The Living One, Son of the Awake* finally manages to get to another island with a large population and a social hierarchy. Society over there abides by a code of ethics taught to them by a prophet who had received it in the form of revelations from God. Hayy Ibn Yaqzán is wonderstruck to discover that those revelations say exactly the same as the conclusions he arrived at during his contemplations in complete solitude.

Ibn Tufail and the other philosophers wanted to tell us that ethics, to be true, must be universal. Whether we see their origin in the laws of nature or in divine revelations, the test of their truth is their universality. It is also a way of telling us to respect the ethics of other peoples, no matter whether they originate in a revelation from on high or whether they are the product of the human genius which, after all, we believe to be of divine grace too.

Without wanting to stretch the argument too far, I have sometimes asked myself whether there was not, at the back of our philosophers' minds, a realization of the oneness of humanity. As Muslims they had to believe in that anyhow, but it was a matter of taking practical steps in that direction. Islam had become yet another religion. Though it had brought a large chunk of humanity together, it was no longer exactly the platform for all to stand on, as the Prophet had envisioned it. It is now one more faith, in addition to those that always existed, plus some even younger ones. What, then, about the primordial aspiration to provide a common base for all?

I cannot vouchsafe that philosophers such as Ibn Tufail, Ibn Sínā and Suhrawardī, who all wrote about *The Living One, Son of the Awake*, felt that the recognition of other peoples' ethical thought as equal with ours could be such a platform. Much less can I aver that they, and other Muslim philosophers, aimed at something like a global ethic. But at least I see no rejection of such a project. On the contrary, they were apparently heading in that direction.

I do expect objections to this project from a different corner, and that may be both Muslim and Non-Muslim. Leonard Swidler is a Catholic and an American. He is the Editor-in-Chief of the *Journal of Ecumenical Studies* and the author of the *Dialogue Decalogue*. As I have noted, Islamists eagerly participate in interreligious dialogue while warning against it in their Arabic and Urdu press as the latest trick of Christian missionaries wishing to convert Muslims. They tell their followers to participate in interreligious dialogue in order to use it against the Christian missions, in order proselytize for Islam. It is important to be aware of this attitude because this is precisely the spirit with which they will approach the global ethic project. It may be possible to convince one or the other amongst them that the intention underlying the project is a very different one, but it would fallacious to entertain any illusions and to be taken in by Islamist professions of interest in the project. Their wrongly conceived misgivings about it need to be addressed again and again.

Others will allege that such a project is typical of the rich North that can engage in such pastimes. Whether they call the United States "the West" or "the North," there will be objections to the project's provenance: The much maligned West/North never ceases to impose itself culturally on the underdogs in the East/South. This widespread notion will cause much resistance to the project, resistance that would not exist if Leonard Swidler were a native of Chad or a Hindu divine from the Tamil part of Sri Lanka. It seems advisable to preempt such antagonisms by addressing them beforehand.

Leonard Swidler and his collaborators from the Christian West simply should above all not allow themselves to be driven onto the horns of a dilemma. The protests against Western patronizing which are raised by some against his draft really appears to me to be rather threadbare. I *know* that many in the world of Islam, indeed, probably the majority, fundamentally have no problem with the project. Naturally there are also those who react to it allergically simply because it comes from America or from an American. However, we should not overreact, we should not thereby allow ourselves to be deterred. From the USA there comes not only Patriot and Stinger Missiles but also healing experiments in thought. The sooner people outside of America learn that, the better.

Toward a Global Ethic: A Baha'i Response

Moojan Momen

I. Introduction

Baha'u'llah, the founder of the Baha'i Faith, lived in the nineteenth century, just at the dawn of the modern age. In his writings, he addresses many of the problems that the present world faces. Baha'u'llah describes himself as the "Divine Physician" and states that the purpose of his mission is to diagnose the disease and prescribe the remedy for the ills of the world:

> The All-Knowing Physician hath His finger on the pulse of mankind. He perceiveth the disease, and prescribeth, in His unerring wisdom, the remedy. Every age hath its own problem, and every soul its particular aspiration. The remedy the world needeth in its present-day afflictions can never be the same as that which a subsequent age may require. Be anxiously concerned with the needs of the age ye live in, and center your deliberations on its exigencies and requirements. (Baha'u'llah: *Gleanings*, no. 106, pages 212-213)

In the introductory essay to this book, Leonard Swidler lists three ways of describing the radical change occurring in our world that necessitates the development of a global ethic. Concerned as he is with bringing about the unity and harmony of the peoples of the world, Baha'u'llah's writings presage these three descriptions of modernity and also many of the points that appear in Swidler's proposed draft Universal Declaration of a Global Ethic. Where Baha'is may disagree is with some of the underlying presuppositions of the draft.

II. A Macro-Paradigm Shift

Swidler describes the major paradigm shift that Küng considers has occurred in the world. In his writings, Baha'u'llah has signalled to the world the need for a major paradigm shift in the affairs of humanity. Whereas in the past human beings had thought of themselves as part of a tribe or nation or religious community, Baha'u'llah declared that it was time put aside all sources of alienation, of intra-communal and inter-communal prejudice, disunity and hatred:

> The Great Being saith: O well-beloved ones! The tabernacle of unity hath been raised; regard ye not one another as strangers. Ye are the fruits of one tree, and the leaves of one branch. (Baha'u'llah: *Gleanings*, no. 112, pages 218-219)

More specifically, in relation to the paradigm shift in our view of the truth that Küng/Swidler describes, "the fundamental principle which constitutes the bedrock of Baha'i belief" is "the principle that religious truth is not absolute but relative, that Divine Revelation is orderly, continuous and progressive and not spasmodic or final" (Shoghi Effendi: *World Order of Baha'u'llah*, pages 115-116).

III. Second Axial Period

Swidler describes Ewart Cousins assertion of the need for humanity to return to a global consciousness. This concept of the globalization of the affairs of humanity is one that finds strong support in the writings of Baha'u'llah:

> Of old it hath been revealed: "Love of one's country is an element of the Faith of God." The Tongue of Grandeur hath, however, in the day of His manifestation proclaimed: "It is not his to boast who loveth

his country, but it is his who loveth the world." Through the power released by these exalted words He hath lent a fresh impulse, and set a new direction, to the birds of men's hearts, and hath obliterated every trace of restriction and limitation from God's holy Book. (Baha'u'llah: *Gleanings*, no 43, pages 95-96; cf. Swidler, Basic Principle no. 4)

IV. The Age of Dialogue

Swidler has described the need for humanity to move to an age of dialogue. The need for a dialogue among the peoples of the world is also clearly asserted in the writings of Baha'u'llah. He writes of the need to put aside all of those traditions and prejudices that lead human beings to revile and shun one another and of the need for the peoples of all religions to consort with each other:

> Through each and every one of the verses which the Pen of the Most High hath revealed, the doors of love and unity have been unlocked and flung open to the face of men. We have erewhile declared—and Our Word is the truth—: "Consort with the followers of all religions in a spirit of friendliness and fellowship." Whatsoever hath led the children of men to shun one another, and hath caused dissensions and divisions amongst them, hath, through the revelation of these words, been nullified and abolished. (Baha'u'llah: *Gleanings*, no. 43, p. 95)

On one occasion, an eminent Indian Zoroastrian wrote to Baha'u'llah asking questions regarding the relationship of the religions to one another. As part of his response, Baha'u'llah writes that human beings, even those from different religious communities, should regard one another as brothers and sisters. He then goes on to say that the requirements of love among siblings are many. The first is that whatever one desires for oneself, one should desire for one's siblings (i.e., the Golden Rule). The second, and this relates more specifically to the manner in which inter-faith dialogue should be carried out, relates to the question of how one should set about offering to others the truths that one holds dear. In a parallel passage in another text, Baha'u'llah states:

If ye be aware of a certain truth, if ye possess a jewel, of which others are deprived, share it with them in a language of utmost kindliness and good-will. If it be accepted, if it fulfill its purpose, your object is attained. If anyone should refuse it, leave him unto himself, and be-seech God to guide him. Beware lest ye deal unkindly with him. A kindly tongue is the lodestone of the hearts of men. It is the bread of the spirit, it clotheth the words with meaning, it is the fountain of the light of wisdom and understanding. (Baha'u'llah: *Epistle to the Son of the Wolf*, pp. 15-16)

V. The Principles Outlined in the Universal Declaration of a Global Ethic

Turning now to the text of the Declaration that Leonard Swidler has submitted for discussion, one must first commend him for his efforts in this respect. In 1985, the Universal House of Justice, the highest authority in the Baha'i Faith, challenged the religious leaders of the world to undertake such enterprises:

> The challenge facing the religious leaders of mankind is to contem-plate, with hearts filled with the spirit of compassion and a desire for truth, the plight of humanity, and to ask themselves whether they cannot, in humility before their Almighty Creator, submerge their theological differences in a great spirit of mutual forbearance that will enable them to work together for the advancement of human understanding and peace. (*Promise of World Peace*, a statement is-sued in October 1985)

Swidler uses the Golden Rule as the initial principle of the Decla-ration. Baha'u'llah's writings fully support the Golden Rule as Swidler has noted in the quotation that he cites.

Furthermore, Baha'is have been advocating for most of the twenti-eth century many of the Middle Principles that the Declaration espouses. Thus, for example 'Abdu'l-Baha has confirmed the principle of equal-ity before the law (Middle Principles, no 1).

> The Laws of God are not imposition of will, or of power, or pleasure, but the resolutions of truth, reason and justice.
> All men are equal before the law, which must reign absolutely. . .
> Kings must rule with wisdom and justice; prince, peer and peasant

alike have equal rights to just treatment, there must be no favour shown to individuals. A judge must be no "respecter of persons," but administer the law with strict impartiality in every case brought before him. (`Abdu'l-Baha: *Paris Talks*, pp. 154)

The Declaration speaks in the Middle Principles (no. 5) of the need for equality between men and women. This principle was advocated before audiences in the West by 'Abdu'l-Baha, the son of Baha'u'llah, in the second decade of the twentieth century.

And among the teachings of Baha'u'llah is the equality of women and men. The world of humanity has two wings; one is women and the other men. Not until both wings are equally developed can the bird fly. Should one wing remain weak, flight is impossible. Not until the world of women becomes equal to the world of men in the acquisition of virtues and perfections, can success and prosperity be attained as they ought to be. (*Selections from the Writings of 'Abdu'l-Baha*, sec. 227, p. 302)

'Abdu'l-Baha emphasized in particular the link between this principle and peace (Middle Principle, no. 9).

Another fact of equal importance in bringing about international peace is woman's suffrage. That is to say, when perfect equality shall be established between men and women, peace may be realized for the simple reason that womankind in general will never favor warfare. Women will not be willing to allow those whom they have so tenderly cared for to go to the battlefield. When they shall have a vote, they will oppose any cause of warfare. ('Abdu'l-Baha: *Promulgation of Universal Peace*, p. 167)

The draft Declaration also speaks of the need for the education of children (Middle Principles, no. 8). This principle has been strongly advocated in the Baha'i teachings, especially in relation to moral education.

The education and training of children is among the most meritorious acts of humankind . . . for education is the indispensable foundation of all human excellence and alloweth man to work his way to the heights of abiding glory . . .

If, in this momentous task, a mighty effort be exerted, the world of humanity will shine out with other adornings, and shed the fairest light. Then will this darksome place grow luminous, and this abode of earth turn into Heaven . . .

For the inner reality of man is a demarcation line between the shadow and the light . . . With education it can achieve all excellence; devoid of education it will stay on, at the lowest point of imperfection.

Every child is potentially the light of the world— and at the same time its darkness; wherefore must the question of education be accounted as of primary importance. (*Selections from the Writings of 'Abdu'l-Baha*, no. 103, pp. 129-130)

VI. The Presuppositions Upon Which the Declaration is Based

While Baha'is would certainly support the general aim of this Declaration and the specific goals outlined in the "Middle Principles", there remains some questions about the underlying assumptions upon which this Declaration is based. It seems to me that this Declaration has its foundation in the areligious humanism of the Western Liberal Tradition. It assumes that all human beings are inherently good, but just different, something with which most religious traditions would disagree. It omits any reference to a transcendental dimension to human life and the influence of this upon the attitude of religious people to such questions. Lacking a religious basis, it has no universal standard by which to judge what is good and what is evil. For these reasons, most religious persons (except those at the extreme liberal end of the spectrum) would be somewhat uneasy about signing up wholeheartedly to such a document, however much they may approve of its intentions. We will examine each of these points in turn.

1. The assumption that all human beings are good.
Following the Western Liberal Tradition, this Declaration is based on the assumption that people are inherently good. This assumption is manifested in phrases such as: "such an ethic presumes a readiness and intention on the part of people to act justly." In fact most religious traditions do not agree with this humanist viewpoint. The whole point of the mission of the founders of the world's religions is to guide people

away from their natural tendency towards selfishness and towards detachment, away from materialism and towards spirituality. This natural tendency or condition of humanity is described in various ways in the religions of the world: Christians have the concept of original sin; Muslims maintain that human beings will tend to stray if not guided by God; and the first Noble Truth of the Buddha's teaching is that human beings have a tendency to crave and grasp for the pleasures and rewards of this world and from this comes attachment and that is the source of suffering.

In the Baha'i teachings, human beings are regarded as potentially good, but this potentiality can only be manifested through the guidance and teachings of the founders of the world's religions. Without such guidance, humanity remains at the level of "savagery":

> The Prophets and Chosen Ones have all been commissioned by the One True God, magnified be His glory, to nurture the trees of human existence with the living waters of uprightness and understanding, that there may appear from them that which God hath deposited within their inmost selves . . . The purpose of these Educators, in all they said and taught, was to preserve man's exalted station. (Baha'u'llah: *Aqdas: Questions and Answers*, no. 106, p. 139)

> The Prophets of God are the first Educators. They bestow universal education upon man and cause him to rise from the lowest levels of savagery to the highest pinnacles of spiritual development. ('Abdu'l-Baha: *Promulgation of Universal Peace*, ibid., pp. 84-85)

2. Need for a universal standard

Another way in which the Declaration proposed by Swidler is at odds with the way that many religious people think is in the assumption that what is good and what is evil is self-evident to all (similarly for what is just, Middle Principles, no. 1). What religion claims to bring is a standard to which all in that culture can assent. Without such a universal standard, we are left with only the whims of our individual consciences to guide us. While we may be quite happy to be at the receiving end of actions generated by Swidler's conscience, one can scarcely be so confident about the actions of many others.

Swidler also appears in this Declaration to assent to any ideology or culture that a group of people have espoused (Basic Principles, no. 7). Are we then to assume that the espousal of Nazi or racist ideologies is acceptable provided that enough people accept them? Are we to accept the ill-treatment and virtual enslavement of women in some societies just because that is the norm and accepted practice of a culture? If the answer to these question is "no", then we are back to the problem of how to set universal ethical standards.

In the past, it has been religion that has set the ethical standards within each cultural world. But it has set these standards within the framework of a total conceptual world that explains and justifies the ethical standards of a society. It has made its ethical standards part of overall framework of reality for that culture. What Swidler is trying to do is to extract the ethical principles from this framework and make them stand up by themselves. Is it possible to have the ethics without the metaphysics? Without the metaphysics to explain and justify the ethics, will ordinary people feel themselves bound by the ethics?

3. The lack of a transcendent dimension.

In each religion, there is a transcendent dimension which is the motivating force for ethical behavior. In the Baha'i Faith, for example, there are several factors promoting ethical behavior. First, human beings are described as being essentially spiritual. Ethical behavior is enjoined because it is conducive to the spiritual development of the individual. Second, ethical behavior is described as the natural result of the love of the believer for the object of his or her devotion.

> O Son of Man! Neglect not My commandments if thou lovest My beauty, and forget not My counsels if thou wouldst attain My good pleasure. (Baha'u'llah: *Arabic Hidden Words*, no. 39)

In the Declaration, under "Basic Principles" and "Middle Principles", many of the statements start with a reason "Because . . . " and then go on to a declaration of principle. While the Declaration of principle may be acceptable to many religious people, the initial reasoning is frequently based on areligious humanist thinking. Thus for example the first of the Basic Principles begins: "Because freedom is of the essence of being human, every person is free to exercise and develop every capacity . . ." For a religious person, the two halves of this statement are not necessarily connected. Human beings do have free will, but according to religious teaching, this is not something that should be given free reign. It should be disciplined through the teachings of religion. It is this transcendent or spiritual dimension that is, for the religious person, missing from the Declaration.

Human society is not possible without some shared conceptual world which explains and justifies the way things are and on the basis of which decisions are made. In the past (and still today in many parts of the world), it is religion that provides the framework of this shared conceptual world. During the present century, however, religion has lost its position as the generator and maintainer of the conceptual world in the West, and increasingly in the rest of the world also. Various ideologies have tried, during the course of this century to take the place of religion in this respect: nationalism, racism, and communism. These have, however, proved disastrous failures, leading to two World Wars and the bankrupt economies of the former communist states. And yet human society cannot exist without some framework of reality. As we draw towards the close of the twentieth century, the search is on for an alternative ideology. Some have espoused religious fundamentalism as a way of re-establishing the situation that existed before the present century; for others individualism and hedonism are ways of trying to ignore this question; still others try to resurrect a neo-tribalism in the form of gangs and fan clubs. Without a central ideology to hold it together, however, human society literally falls apart.

I would maintain that it is impossible to know what a declaration of ethical principles means without making some assumptions about the total conceptual world within which it has been framed. Thus, for example, I can envisage what Swidler means when he speaks of "good" and "evil" but can we assume that everyone will mean the same? After all, in the not-so-distant past many upright citizens of cultures that thought themselves at the forefront of civilization have considered slavery, racism and child labor to be acceptable practices. Only a few decades ago, citizens of Nazi Germany were able to observe the persecution of Jews and gypsies and not find this to be "evil" in their conceptual world.

What I am trying to argue is that the draft Declaration cannot be made to stand up independent of some conceptual framework—either religious or secular. It is only within such a framework that words such as "good" have a meaning and that there is an impulse to make the Declaration effective.

In commenting on the need for a transcendental dimension to the Declaration, I am, of course, aware that part of the reason that Swidler has not taken such a line is that to base the Declaration on any metaphysical assumptions would be very difficult in view of the great differences in the metaphysical systems of the various religions. As Hans Küng has put it: "If we, for example, were to speak `in the name of God,' we would *a priori* exclude the Buddhists." The fact that it is difficult to find a consensus on this aspect does not however mean that we should not try (see below).

VII. The Text of the Universal Declaration of a Global Ethic

There are yet other ways in which the draft Declaration may be unacceptable to many of those from other cultures and religions. Apart from the principles that Swidler enunciates, there are a number of terms that Swidler uses that need comment. We need to be sure about what exactly is meant when they are used.

Among the values that Swidler puts forward as being universal is "democracy" (in Rationale, third paragraph). One wonders what exactly Swidler has in mind by this. If he means an elective process for choosing the leaders of society and for decisions to be reached by consultative processes, then Baha'is would agree with this. But words have a history and a lot of baggage that they carry around with them. And if, Swidler means, as one suspects that he does, the full-blown American phenomenon with divisive party politics, the large financial resources needed by candidates, and the manipulation of the process by business interests and the media, then certainly Baha'is and one suspects many others would refrain from whole-hearted endorsement of this.

Similarly, Swidler puts forward "liberty" as a "positive value" (Middle Principle, no. 9). Again, this is a word that appears innocuous at first reading. If by this word, Swidler means certain basic freedoms for the individual, then this would be supported by Baha'is and many others. Liberty has become, particularly in the United States of America, however, the rallying cry of many who wish to assert their right to carry out acts of racism (e.g., the Klu Klux Klan), sexual excesses (e.g., pornography, paedophilia, etc.) and to pollute the environment. The noble principle of liberty for the individual has been degraded to a charter for libertines. Many peoples in other parts of the world may feel that the American obsession with liberty has gone too far. Baha'u'llah states:

> Know ye that the embodiment of liberty and its symbol is the animal. That which beseemeth man is submission unto such restraints as will protect him from his own ignorance, and guard him against the harm of the mischief-maker. Liberty causeth man to overstep the bounds of propriety, and to infringe on the dignity of his station. It debaseth him to the level of extreme depravity and wickedness.

> Regard men as a flock of sheep that need a shepherd for their protection. This, verily, is the truth, the certain truth. We approve of liberty in certain circumstances, and refuse to sanction it in others. (Baha'u'llah: *The Kitab-i-Aqdas*, v. 124-5 p. 63)

Swidler lists "conservation of the earth" as one of the concerns to be found universally among the religions of the earth. Among Baha'is, the preferred term is "stewardship" since conservation implies a maintenance of the status quo, an attempt to freeze the situation as it is. This is an unrealistic expectation in this area. What is needed is a concerned and responsible stewardship over the resources of the earth.

In the Middle Principles, no. 3, regarding honesty and the avoidance of inappropriate intrusions into personal privacy, this is applied to the "media, artists, scientists, politicians and religious leaders." It would perhaps be highly relevant in today's world to make this apply also to business leaders (especially executives of big businesses), the police and security forces, and all those in positions of responsibility and authority over others (e.g., civil servants as well as politicians).

In the Middle Principles, no. 5, on the status of women, it would be relevant to add after "to full development of their talents" the phrase "and equal access to opportunities to use them."

Presupposition no. d also raises questions. Is the implied converse of this statement (i.e., that communities and social organisations that do not "contribute to the good of humans" do not have a right to exist) also to be upheld?

VIII. Some Proposals for the Way Forward

Despite the above criticisms of the draft Declaration, I believe that it does form the basis of a useful advance in the process of bringing together the people of the world. I will now try to put forward, from a Baha'i perspective, some suggestions for how this process can be carried forward.

It seems to me that the starting principle that Swidler has used, the Golden Rule, is very much along the right lines since, as he has shown, it is one on which all religions can agree. It would seem therefore that the best course would be to pursue this line and see what other areas there are upon which there would be general agreement. If a Declaration of Ethics can be built up from elements that all religions have in common, then each religion will provide the conceptual framework and the metaphysical support for the principles. In this way you can have both the ethics and the metaphysics.

One teaching that is universal among the religions is the need for the individual to detach himself or herself from the things of this world. It is greed for the things of this world or for power that is the source of much that is evil in the world. The religions of the world are agreed that human beings should strive to free themselves from their attachment to worldly things. In the Baha'i scriptures, there are many references to this:

> O Son of Man! Thou dost wish for gold and I desire thy freedom from it. Thou thinkest thyself rich in its possession, and I recognize thy wealth in thy sanctity therefrom. By My life! This is My knowledge, and that is thy fancy; how can My way accord with thine? (Baha'u'llah: *Arabic Hidden Words*, no. 56)

The religions of the world encourage their followers towards a life marked by virtuous conduct. Among the virtues that can be found encouraged in most of the scriptures of the world, and which are of particular relevance to a Universal Declaration of Ethics are purity, sincerity, trustworthiness, benevolence, humility, and justice.

All religions state that failure on the part of human beings to follow a virtuous life results in spiritual penalties. One would not expect a Declaration of a Global Ethic to include sanctions or punishments for those who fail to live up to it, but there is no reason why it could not contain a statement along the following lines: "Failure to make progress along the path towards acquiring virtues involves a spiritual penalty; it makes us less human."

Lastly, all religions demand that these virtues should be manifested in concrete action. It is not enough merely to speak of spiritual matters and noble aspirations. One's spirituality must be seen in one's generosity to the poor, one's comforting of the distressed, one's patience with the tiresome, and one's humility towards all.

> Be generous in prosperity, and thankful in adversity. Be worthy of the trust of thy neighbor, and look upon him with a bright and friendly face. Be a treasure to the poor, an admonisher to the rich, an answerer of the cry of the needy, a preserver of the sanctity of thy pledge. Be fair in thy judgment, and guarded in thy speech. Be unjust to no man, and show all meekness to all men. Be as a lamp unto them that walk in darkness, a joy to the sorrowful, a sea for the thirsty, a haven for the distressed, an upholder and defender of the victim of oppression. Let integrity and uprightness distinguish all thine acts. Be a home for the stranger, a balm to the suffering, a tower of strength for the fugitive. Be eyes to the blind, and a guiding light unto the feet of the erring. Be an ornament to the countenance of truth, a crown to the brow of fidelity, a pillar of the temple of righteousness, a breath of life to the body of mankind, an ensign of the hosts of justice, a luminary above the horizon of virtue, a dew to the soil of the human heart, an ark on the ocean of knowledge, a sun in the heaven of bounty, a gem on the diadem of wisdom, a shining light in the firmament of thy generation, a fruit upon the tree of humility. (Baha'u'llah: *Gleanings*, no. 130, p. 285)

IX. A Practical Example

Finally, one contribution that the Baha'i community can make to progress towards a Global Ethic is its example. In the Baha'i community, we can observe several million people, many of them poor and uneducated, in every country of the world who have voluntarily espoused principles of the oneness of humankind, the necessity of world unity, and the need to abandon prejudices and resolve causes of conflict. Many Baha'i communities have gone beyond the mere espousal of such principles and are actively working towards the betterment of the moral, social, and economic state of the world around them. The Baha'i community is living proof that such a global ethic can be taken up and acted upon by every type of person from every kind of background. As the Universal House of Justice said in its message on World Peace in 1985:

> The experience of the Baha'i community may be seen as an example of this enlarging unity. It is a community of some three to four million people drawn from many nations, cultures, classes and creeds, engaged in a wide range of activities serving the spiritual, social and economic needs of the peoples of many lands. It is a single social organism, representative of the diversity of the human family, conducting its affairs through a system of commonly accepted consultative principles, and cherishing equally all the great outpourings of divine guidance in human history. Its existence is yet another convincing proof of the practicality of its Founder's vision of a united world, another evidence that humanity can live as one global society, equal to whatever challenges its coming of age may entail. If the Baha'i experience can contribute in whatever measure to reinforcing hope in the unity of the human race, we are happy to offer it as a model for study (*Promise of World Peace*, a statement issued in October 1985).

FOR DIALOUGE ON A GLOBAL ETHIC: A CONFUCIAN/TAOIST VIEW

ZHAO FU SAN

I. A Global Retrospect

SOMETIMES ONE MAY WONDER: How would future historians review our present century? Those emphasizing material progress may point to the rapid progress of science and technology in the twentieth century that has greatly enhanced the growth of world economy and the living conditions of a large part of the humankind. Those focusing on political changes may point to the countless wars and revolutions that marked this century involving almost every people in the world. As its result, the five-century long world colonial system came to its end, and in its place are now a large number of newly emergent nation states. Among historians some could be optimists, while some others, pessimists. After all, academics seldom agree with one another. However, they may agree on one point that is, the historic changes in the twentieth century and its rapidity far surpassed the previous centuries, and the price humankind paid for them are also unprecedented.

In the eyes of a cultural historian, the beginning of the twentieth century was permeated by a spiritual, cultural despair over the status quo. The *Boxers Uprising,* the *Republican Revolution* and the *May Fourth Politico-cultural Movement* of China, Nietzschean philosophy and Oswald Spengler's lamentation of *The Decline of the West* mirrored the mood of that age. The two World Wars in the first half of the century, the rise of Hitlerism and the revolutions in more than a dozen of the East European and East Asian countries were its consequences. Now these wars and revolutions have all passed, leaving people querying: Has the spiritual and cultural despair of the early twentieth century also evaporated? The two World Wars having taken a toll of tens of millions of lives in our "civilized" world, are we now determined to shun the use of military power in political controversies? In countries that had gone through revolutions and independence movements, are their people now full of faith and hope in their societies and their future? In the developed countries, are people there living in security and happiness and looking confidently into their future? Facts seem to show that, after experiencing the material progress and social-political upheavals people become disenchanted and lose the hopes they entertained at the beginning of these changes. In the early days of the century, those in despair were still able to attach their hopes to the changes. And now, hopes vanished, despair remains if not intensified.

People in the West, by and large, have been tuned to historical optimism since the Industrial Revolution and the Enlightenment of the eighteenth century. When James Watt improved the steam engine, thus making it possible to replace family workshops with factories, large-scale production coupled with a new world market laid the foundation of modern industrial society. Correspondingly, in his book *The Wealth of Nations,* published in 1776, Adam Smith tried to show that while everyone works for his self-interest, its overall effect is to push forward economic growth, thus benefiting the entire society. In other words, economism, materialism and egocentrism are intrinsically good. They are the driving force of social progress. It was on the basis of the Industrial Revolution and the corresponding notions that the concepts of "modernization," "modern civilization" and "historical progress" took their meanings. Historical progression became a synonym of historical progress in the nineteenth century. However, this has been increasingly questioned in the course of this century. So, the disillusionment in perennial historical progress implies also a shattering of the fundamental cultural convictions for many in the West.

For the developing countries that never experienced a period of the development of their own national capital due to colonial rule in the past two to four centuries, their historical vision was one of anti-imperialism, anti-colonialism and anti-feudalism. To many in the developing countries, Marxism was more a program for modern development through revolution than an ideology taken as their identity. Since 1960s the rapid economic growth of East Asian countries has pushed aside both the classic Marxist theory of Socialism and the classic capitalistic modernization theory summarized by Talcott Parsons. However, though these East Asian countries do not subscribe to either free-market economy, or Western style liberal democracy, they are still under the sway of economism, materialism and egocentrism prevalent in the West. Following the globalization of commodity economy, the supremacy of self-interest, a growing indifference of public well-being, the erosion of law and order also prevailed. Anyone visiting North America, Europe, East and South Asia as well as Sub-Sahara African countries will note that the "developed" countries and the "developing" countries differ only in their levels of economic development, while their social problems are basically the same. If there is a crisis of civic identity in the US as called to attention by Prof. Robert Bellah and his colleagues recently,[1] this is not only American, but with a tendency to become global; and it is not just a social crisis, but as much personal spiritual crises. Actually, one would find these dual crises featuring our times at the close of this century.

After fifty years of Cold War, all the major countries of the world have accumulated huge piles of domestic problems. They can hardly be resolved by fine-tuning fixings but call for structural changes. Any such reform will inevitably involve a redistribution of power and benefits. While almost all the major countries in the world are now undergoing fundamental economic, social reforms, no wonder, they also lead to the shattering of established value concepts and value systems and people everywhere are asking: "how are we to live in the next century?" So, the stage is set for a rethinking of ethical values in a global context.

II. A Global Ethic — Past and Present

Such rethinking will inevitably throw us back to our own cultural heritages. If a sense of individual identity was the main feature of human consciousness in the first "Axial Period" (in Karl Jaspers' sense of the term), it came in China differently from the Western experience. The world of thought in ancient China had always centered around the theme of humanity and its world. The Confucianists saw the path of humanity's spiritual perfection through its fulfillment of social obligations while the Taoists saw the way of humanity and society from a cosmic approach. The Confucianists tried to see the human's total immersion into the society as the consummation of human moral values, while the Taoists called for humanity's total immersion into nature as the meaning of human life. Comparing with the Axial consciousness of the West, they are equally self-reflective, analytic, critical consciousness, yet their contents are different. Maybe we can say that the Axial consciousness of the Chinese was not severed from their preaxial consciousness. They were a continuum in the inquiry of truth, goodness and beauty among which goodness comprised the focal point for the Confucianists.

What is goodness? The Confucianists considered the distinction between what is righteous and what is beneficial to be of the utmost importance in moral teaching. It was in essence the distinction between serving the public or serving the self. Serving the public is goodness; serving the self as necessitated by self-preservation without damaging public interest is also considered as good. However, serving self-interest at the expense of public interest is definitely evil.

Confucius emphasized *ren* (humanity or human-heartedness) in his entire system of thought. When asked what that means, Confucius answered, "Humanity consists in loving others." (*Analects*, XII, 22) What does "loving others" mean? Confucius' answers were: "Desiring to sustain oneself, sustain others; and desiring to develop oneself, develop others. To be able from one's own self to draw a parallel for the treatment of others, that may be called the way to practice *ren*. " (*Analects*, VI, 28). This was also called *chung*, or "conscientiousness to others." And the negative aspect of it is "Do not do to others what you do not wish yourself." (*Analects*, XII, 2) This was called by Confucius *shu* or "altruism." These two aspects put together was named "the way of conscientiousness to others and altruism" which are the contents of "loving others," or, in other words, *ren*. While teaching people to treat others as oneself, we sense that Confucius was trying to teach about the equality of human beings. It implies a common essence of human beings and the unity of humankind. Therefore, the self-consciousness of the individual is simultaneously the consciousness of humankind.

In the system of thought among the philosophical Taoists, the most important is unquestionably the concept of *Tao* (way). It is the unity of *you* (being) and *wu* (non-being). "Being" denotes the myriad things in the universe. "Non-being" can be understood as a formless and nameless incipient germ from which all myriad things were generated. Being the progenitor of all things, *Tao* is also the "way" underlying all the changes of the myriad things. This way becomes also the way or the norm that regulates the human world. Hence, in the eyes of Lao-tze:

> When *Tao* is lost, only then does the doctrine of virtues arise. When virtue is lost, only then does the doctrine of humanity arise. When humanity is lost, only then the doctrine of righteousness arise. When righteousness is lost, only then the doctrine of propriety arise. Now, propriety is a superficial expression of loyalty and faithfulness and the beginning of disorder. (*Tao Te Ching* ch. 38)

One of the unique features of the philosophical Taoists is their perception of the unity of ethics and ontology. In other words, their ethics is one that brings personal and social ethics into one with the essence and way of the universe. The Confucian ethics is a self-consciousness that integrates the individual and humanity while the Taoist ethics is the self-consciousness that integrates the self and the universe. These two trends of thought are equally deeply rooted in the Chinese world of thought. Their convergence becomes the spirit of Chinese culture.

When one applies such a perception of ethics to our lives in the contemporary world, he would easily notice that the world since Industrial Revolution has been marked by economism, materialism and individualism. Economism sends people to economic growth in disregard of ecological balance. Individualism becomes "ME-ism" in social life. And materialism exalts material comfort and pleasure-seeking as the cherished value. Their grave social, moral, environmental and even economic consequences are becoming more and more visible. In the last twenty-five years, physical scientists, sociologists, historians and philosophers as well as some economists are becoming more and more alarmed by this trend and its imminent dangers for the whole of humankind and call for a reorientation. The United Nations system has formulated a system of social indicators of development which comprises not only GNP per capita, but also food composition, housing conditions, energy consumption, health conditions, education, average life expectancy, etc. This system is undoubtedly much better than Prof. Simon Kuznets' system of calculating the economic strength of nations on the basis of GNP. However, the philosophy underlying this system is still economic determinism, the degree of material affluence determines the level of social development, human beings are judged by "things." Quantity takes the place of quality.

Any concern for a global ethic will, I think, have to begin by asking about the present state of existence of the globe, and inevitably come to the question of how to evaluate the development of human societies. This is a prerequisite for any query into what is goodness and what is evil in our present-day world. After worldwide praxis in the twentieth century, do we have any new light to shed upon our intellectual inquiry? Here, I venture to raise four kinds of relations for any assessment of human societies to supplement our understandings in the past two and half centuries:

(1) Our concern is lasting development of human societies. It is only when ecological health, social interest in its totality as well as opportunities for individuals to develop their talents freely and enjoy the fruits of their labor fairly are taken care of in a balanced way that a society will be able to grow perpetually.

(2) Economic growth is the basis of societal development, but not its consummation. GNP per capita easily covers up social polarity. Economic indicators do not necessarily reveal the state of the society. Social indicators do not necessarily reveal the quality of life and the quality of human beings in a society. We need to explore and define new concepts of development.

(3) Having examined the experience of the last three centuries, we would note that it is not easy to maintain a balanced development between the society on the one hand and the individual on the other. The East Asian societies tend to emphasize more social stability while the Western societies tend to emphasize more individual freedom. Either of the two can go

to extremes raising grave problems and therefore will not be able to last long.

(4) With regard to the relation between humanity and nature, and the relation between "humans" and "things" in our society, the trend in our present century is emphasizing the human "conquest" of nature. We seldom recognize the degree of dependency of humans on nature. Hence, many important natural resources such as soil, water, ozone layer in the atmosphere, foliage, animal and plant species are seriously devastated in the course of economic development. It is only when we ourselves are now suffering due to our own misconceptions and misbehavior that these problems begin to draw the attention of the public. We need to develop a basic perception that we humans are a part of nature and are dependent on nature for our survival. To protect and develop natural environs is to protect and develop human life; any devastation of natural environs is a crime against society and the entire humankind. At a societal level, any development is for the well-being of human beings. Any dehumanization in any realm of social life is working against the ultimate goal of human development.

These four relations may serve to demonstrate some of the most important findings in twentieth century human development. It is not my intention to claim that they have exhausted our experience. Rather what I mean to say is that when we try to discuss a global ethic, we would have to relate to the twentieth century human experience in its full scope. The Human Rights Declaration of the United Nations in 1948 is a useful point of reference. However, the world has learned much since then to be incorporated into our thinking today.

III. A Universal Declaration?

At present, development theories are being reexamined among thinking people. A global ethic would be relevant to peoples in the world only when two-thirds of humankind in the developing world discover that this "global ethic" is related to their vital concerns. What are their vital concerns? A peaceful world so that they may develop for a more rapid improvement of people's material and spiritual well-being. To safeguard peace and development, national sovereignty and national identity is considered the primary pre-requisites. Any intervention under whatever name from the external world is looked upon with suspicious eyes. The strong resentment of the former colonial peoples against Western colonialism is usually ignored or underestimated by the well-meaning people in the West. Prof. Samuel Huntington in his essay "The Clash of Civilizations?" observed: that

> Western ideas of individualism, liberalism, constitutionalism, human rights, equality, liberty . . . often have very little resonance in Islamic, Confucian, Japanese, Hindu, Buddhist or Orthodox cultures. Western efforts to propagate such ideas produce instead a reaction against "human right imperialism" and a reaffirmation of indigenous values . . . The very notion that there could be a "universal civilization" is a Western idea, directly at odds with the particularism of most Asian societies.[2]

Prof. Huntington did not go on to explain the reasons of it. Anyone familiar with the history of colonialism will remember how the colonialists made systematic efforts to uproot the indigenous cultures of the colonial peoples and replace them with that of the colonial masters from the West.

While begging to differ from Prof. Huntington's pessimistic conclusion of cultural conflicts leading eventually to World War III, I tend to think that what he had observed is by and large valid. There is another important observation by Prof. Huntington, that is, each of the two superpowers (United States as well as the former Soviet Union) "defined its identity in terms of its ideology."[3] This explains why the value system of the West (as well as that of the former Soviet Union) has been used as a political weapon and been seriously polluted by Cold War politics, which has unfortunately impaired its respectability. This further aggravates the suspicion of many in the developing world toward any form of "cultural universalism," religious or secular, based on Western values. Peoples having suffered colonialism usually keep long memories. There seems to be no better way than admitting the historical facts and assuming the historical responsibilities. This seems to be the experience of the United States on the issue of the Blacks and it should be equally useful at the international level. Time is needed to cure the historical wounds.

This is not a total passiveness. In the Chinese and Hindu cultural heritages, we discern a perception of the common essence of human beings and hence the unity of humankind. In my reading, among peoples with millennia-long civilizations, there has always been an acknowledgment of universal humanhood, and also a receptiveness to different cultures. This readiness for cultural exchange is one of the basic conditions that enabled these ancient civilizations to continue living and growing until this day. The grain will grow, but helping it to grow by pulling it up would be counterproductive. Therefore, in summary, I venture to suggest that:

First, global development experience must be our point of departure in the inquiry for a Global Ethic.

Second, vigorous dialogues for the sake of mutual understanding *is* the ethics of the Global Ethic.

Third, any realistic analysis of the world situation today will probably show that the time for "A Universal Declaration of a Global Ethic" is yet to come, and I confess that I don't know when it will.

Admitting this ignorance might, hopefully, enable the Holy Spirit to move more freely in the discussion - which could be, in my humble opinion, even more meaningful and fruitful than aiming at the drafting of "A Universal Declaration" now.

Footnotes

1 Robert Bellah, et al., "Individualism and the Crisis of Civil Membership," *The Christian Century*, May 8, 1996, pp. 510 ff.

2 Samuel Huntington, "The Clash of Civilizations," *Foreign Affairs* (Summer, 1993), pp. 40-41.

3 Ibid., p. 23.

Reflections on Approaches to a Universal Ethics from a Contemporary Neo-Confucian Perspective

Shu-hsien Liu

I PARTICIPATED IN THE first MEETING, organized by UNESCO Universal Ethics Project held in Paris in March, 1997, to consider the feasibility of drafting a Declaration for Universal Ethics. After engaging in serious debates among the participants some of us expressed the willingness to go on with the project. Notwithstanding reservations from various perspectives, I am still in favor of the attempt. I feel obliged to state the reasons why I support the project from a contemporary Neo-Confucian perspective.

First of all, I totally agree with Hans Küng that even though the Universal Declaration of Human Rights is a powerful document, it is not enough, as it deals only with the external aspects. There is the urgent need to draft a Declaration of a Global Ethic which addresses our commitment to an internal change of attitude. Even though I did not attend the World Parliament of Religions held in Chicago in 1993, I was greatly encouraged to hear that a "Declaration toward a Global Ethic drafted by Hans Küng had been endorsed by a number of religious organizations and individuals.

In my judgment, the only viable option is to take a pragmatic as well as minimalist approach. In 1964, when as a junior fellow I participated in the Fourth East and West Philosophers' Conference held in Hawaii, Richard Mckeon told me of his experience in drafting the Declaration of Human Rights: It was simply impossible to reach any agreement if a philosophical foundation had to be worked out for the drafting of the document; instead, through the collective wisdom of the participants, a list of human rights was quickly drawn up, and now we have our famous document. Certainly it is not perfect, as it has been challenged from a multicultural perspective more recently and is said to be too Western-oriented. Nevertheless, there is no denying that it has universal significance. Some of the items may not be liked by some of the countries, but it is still a powerful document because it has been endorsed by so many countries throughout the world. Now can we hope to do something similar by drafting a Declaration of Universal Ethics? A good beginning has been made.

First I would like to start by eliminating those so-called pragmatic and minimalist approaches which I consider to be inappropriate for our project. A pragmatic approach cannot mean that we may totally disregard our commitment to truth for the sake of expediency, for one's ultimate concern must not be pushed aside for other proximate concerns. On the contrary, it is precisely because of our commitment to the Way which compels us to adopt a pragmatic attitude so that our ideals have a better chance to be actualized in the world. A minimalist approach cannot mean that we may totally suppress the differences of the various traditions by looking for a common denominator with largest extension but least intention. Either we will never find such a thing or it will be a skeleton with too little muscle to be of any use at all. For example, if a universal ethics is bent to such an extent that it accommodates all and cannot even condemn the killing of innocent people, then it is a useless document. Thus we are aiming at producing a Declaration of Universal Ethics which includes principles broad enough to be compatible with all ultimate concerns with a strong moral commitment and specific enough to condemn most immoral and inhuman behavior as seen by a reasonable person with whatever cultural and religious background.

Such may appear to be an impossible ideal. But Hans Küng persuaded me otherwise. In February, 1989, I accepted an invitation to participate in the Symposium on World Religions and Human Rights held in Paris under the sponsorship of UNESCO. The format of the symposium was very interesting. Hans Küng presented his views on the theme from a Christian perspective. His lecture was entitled: "No World Peace without Peace among Religions." Then scholars from other religious traditions were asked to give responses to his views from the perspectives of Islam, Judaism, Confucianism, Buddhism, and Hinduism.[1] Küng's presentation is thought-provoking. The important problem he tries hard to deal with is precisely this: On the one hand religions aspire toward Absolute Truth, on the other hand there is the need for peaceful coexistence among them; if a balance cannot be found between these two, then conflicts are unavoidable. Küng suggests that for us to overcome our bias, the best strategy is for each to raise a soul-searching critique of one's own tradition. After criticizing the Christian tradition in a penetrating way, Küng suggested that true humanity, or the *humanum*, is the universal ecumenical criterion we are looking for. There is no need to destroy the plurality of religions, and there is no need to give up hope to find an ecumenical criterion of truth in the *humanum*.

As a scholar with a Confucian background, I have no trouble in accepting the main thrust of his article. Moreover, the distance between the Christian tradition and the Confucian tradition appears to be much less than I had thought existed between the two traditions. Each tradition is expected to find its own approach to universal ethics and look for possible rapprochement with other traditions. In so doing, the differences between various traditions are not ignored for expediency. Such an approach is certainly welcome in an age in which multiculturalism is a powerful trend; but it also urges various traditions to go beyond their traditional confines and not to be chained by their age-old biases. I think this is a new approach which aims at striking a balance between East and West, and even North and South, as well as tradition and modernity. The presupposition is that traditions do change, and they ought to change for the better. And it is certainly instructive for each tradition to review its own transforming process, as it can teach us valuable lessons at the present time.

One of the pressing problems of our own time is how to find the right balance between the universal and the particular, unity and plurality, and steer clear of the threats from Scylla and Charybdis, or between absolutism and relativism. In the Chinese, especially the Confucian, tradition we can find a great many resources to deal with the problem. Confucius was said to have made the following observation: "If you look at them [things] from the point of view of their differences, then there is liver and gall, Ch'u and Yüeh. But if you look at them from the point of view of their sameness, then the ten thousand things are all one."[2] There is always the perspective of difference as well as the perspective of sameness. The problem is how to strike a balance between the two.

Because Confucianism was just one of the so-called hundred schools in the late Chou period, it naturally transmitted a perspective different from others. Although Confucius never said what the Way is that runs through his doctrines, it is not difficult to figure out that his ultimate concern is *jen*—variously translated into English as benevolence, human-heartedness, humanity, or the *humanum* if one cares to use Küng's terminology—as he said,

> Wealth and honor are what every man desires. But if they have been obtained in violation of moral principles, they must not be kept. Poverty and humble station are what every man dislikes. But if they can be avoided only in violation of moral principles, they must not be avoided. If a superior man departs from humanity, how can he fulfil that name? A superior man never abandons humanity even for the lapse of a single meal. In moments of haste, he acts according to it. In times of difficulty or confusion, he acts according to it.[3]

Although Confucius has very definite ideas about a superior man (*chün-tzu*), he does not ask for conformity, as he said, "The superior man is conciliatory [*ho*] but does not identify [*tung*] himself with others; the inferior man identifies with others but is not conciliatory."[4] Clearly Confucius does not approve the closed mentality of people who blindly conform themselves to the beliefs of a given group. On the contrary, he holds an open mentality, as he declares that, "In education there should be no class distinction."[5] And he is said to have taught four things: "culture (*wen*), conduct, loyalty, and faithfulness."[6] Consequently his disciples have been able to distinguish themselves in different things, such as morality, language, politics, and literature.

Confucius travelled to many states to promote his ideal of a government of humanity without much success. His follower Mencius faced rather similar fate. It would have been beyond their wildest dream that Confucianism was adopted as the state orthodoxy of the empire in 126 C.E. in the Han dynasty. Since then the Confucian virtues of loyalty and filial piety have been widely spread, and Confucian classics have been greatly honored and studied by the posterity. But a politicized Confucianism had to pay a dear price. As the relations between ruler and subject, father and son, and husband and wife were transformed into a seemingly immutable pattern of domination, namely, the "three bonds," which stressed the authority of the ruler, the father, and the husband over the minister, the son, and the wife, respectively, the moral autonomy of Confucius and the critical spirit of Mencius simply disappeared. Since then the so-called "Confucian state" was really a highly complex combination of the Confucian ideals of humanity and righteousness displayed outside and the legalist practice of law and political maneuver under the table.

The political system developed in the Han period was largely maintained until the dynasty days were over. But Buddhism found its way into China in the late Han, and became the dominant trend of thought in the T'ang, dynasty (618-907). Owing to the stimulus from Buddhism, Neo-Confucianism developed sophisticated philosophies in response to the Buddhist challenge in the Sung dynasty (960-1279), and may be said to have brought about a Chinese Renaissance, as it launched the second golden period in Chinese philosophy after the so-called hundred schools in contention earlier in the late Chou period. The Neo-Confucian philosophers were no longer satisfied with the practice of *li* (propriety); they believed that the foundation of such practice is *li* (principle), a concept not quite developed in the ancient time. They probably borrowed the term from Hua-yen Buddhism, but gave it totally new meanings.

One of the important contributions of Neo-Confucian philosophers is their idea of *li-i-fen-shu* (Principle Is One, But Manifestations Are Many).[7] When Confucian thinkers talk about universal love, the implication is different from that understood by Buddhists or Moists. Moists believe that one should love without distinction but still practice must start with the parents. Confucian thinkers criticize them as having two foundations because of their lack of necessary differentiations. From the Confucian perspective, one must first love one's parents, then extend this love to others. Hence the principle is one, but the duties are different. Chu Hsi (1130-1200), commonly recognized as the greatest Neo-Confucian philosopher in the Southern Sung period, further developed the idea to have rich metaphysical and cosmological implications. His favorite metaphor was that the same moon casts different reflections in tens of thousands of streams. This is a creative universe. Ultimately there is the Principle of Creativity (*sheng*), as elaborated in the *Book of Changes*; when it is internalized in human beings as their nature, as taught by the *Doctrine of the Mean*, it is humanity. Here we find a correlation between the macrocosm and the microcosm; hence the union of Heaven and humanity (*T'ien-jen-ho-i*). Throughout the universe there is but one Principle, but it is manifested in different things; hence there are also different principles in a secondary sense. This is how Neo-Confucian philosophers proposed to deal with the problem of the universal and particular, or unity and plurality. I sincerely believe that giving new interpretations to the idea of *li-i-fen-shu* would have great significance for the present time. I will further elaborate on this issue from now on.

In any case, guided by the spirit behind the idea, differences in themselves are not a problem. When the Great Ultimate (*T'ai-chi*) is manifested in yin and yang, or Creativity is manifested in creations, there are bound to be differences. For example, there are difference between Confucius and Mencius, but still the same spirit runs through the doctrines of both. The spirit can be further extended to other traditions as well. In the late Ming dynasty (1368-1644), there were three great traditions: Confucianism, Taoism, and Buddhism, as the latter was totally absorbed into Chinese culture. They were compared to the lotus flowers, leaves and roots. The three were said to have come out of the same family. Of course, some scholars still guarded jealously the purity of their own traditions, but there was bound to be a fusion of horizons. Consequently there has been a remarkable lack of religious wars in Chinese history. A person may enjoy the beauty of nature in the morning as a Taoist, work hard and carry out duties during day as a Confucian, and lament the sorrows of life in the evening as a Buddhist.

Neo-Confucianism died out as a philosophical movement in the early Ch'ing dynasty (1644-1912), but its influence in shaping the Chinese mentality cannot be ignored, as Chu Hsi's "Commentaries on the Confucian Classics" were adopted as the basis for civil service examinations since the Yüan dynasty. In the last couple of hundred years, under the impact from the modern West, the Chinese, especially the Confucian tradition, seemed to totally collapse. In the twentieth century, Confucianism was no longer the main stream of Chinese thought.[8] At one time, there was a powerful trend urging wholesale Westernization, which was then eclipsed by the Marxist-Leninist-Maoist trend, which is still the official ideology of the People's Republic of China. Confucianism was thought to be something that can be found only in museums.[9] But there were a few contemporary Neo-Confucian thinkers who refused to follow the tide and vowed to revive the spirit of Confucian philosophy.[10] They were largely being ignored until the success stories of Japan and the four mini-dragons, all of whom happened to share a Confucian background. Once again Confucianism attracted the attention of the world in recent years.[11] After the end of the Cultural Revolution, Contemporary Neo-Confucianism even became a focus of study on Mainland China. This is the situation we are facing today.

There is no doubt that the West is leading the way in the present era. If we were in the early twentieth century, most probably we would endorse some of the Western values such as democracy, freedom and human rights as well as science, technology and commercialism as something universal, and try our best to play a catch-up game. But after the two World Wars, the Korean War, and the Vietnamese War, the West, including the richest and most powerful nation in the world, the USA, has lost its self-confidence and turned to make searching criticisms of its own culture. Its overemphasis on competitiveness and quantitative measures has eroded the foundation of society, and its colonialism and domination policy overseas have created crimes and harmful consequences that caused havoc on the earth unparalleled in human history. In short, not only is the West not the kind of world savior it portrayed itself to be, but it has occupied the position of the leadership without the necessary qualifications.[12] Today the whole world is concerned about the conservation of our environment and the maintenance of peace throughout the world. We must look for other alternatives if we hope to live harmoniously together in the ever shrinking global village.

A review of the famous "Manifesto for a Re-appraisal of Sinology and Reconstruction of the Chinese Culture," signed by four Contemporary Neo-Confucian scholars and published on New Year's day 1958, is instructive for our purposes.[13] They refused to see Chinese culture from the archaeologist's, the missionary's, or the politician's perspectives, and urged Western intellectuals to seek an understanding of it with a sympathetic and respectful attitude, to try to dig deep into the spiritual roots of that culture. They urged the West to learn from Chinese thought the following five elements:

(1) The spirit to assert what is here and now and to let everything go [that nature might take its own course];
(2) All round and all embracing understanding or wisdom;
(3) A feeling of warmth and compassion;
(4) The wisdom of how to perpetuate its culture;
(5) The attitude that the whole world is like one family.[14]

It seemed audacious for a few refugee Chinese scholars to give counsel to the powerful West. No wonder that at the time of its publication the document was totally ignored. However, after forty years, Contemporary Neo-Confucianism has become a popular subject for study both in mainland China and in the scholarly world of Western sinology.[15] And the counsels given appear to make a lot of sense to intellectuals today worldwide, as these elements are indeed things that have been treasured by the Chinese tradition while they were relatively neglected in the West. Granted that there is always a wide gap between ideals and facts, and in fact such wisdom has not been actualized very often in the long course of Chinese history. However, when we reread the document, we are struck that these scholars did not just hold an apologetic attitude and lament the past glory of the Chinese tradition. They sincerely believed that these elements are urgently needed for the survival of the human species, and hoped that the West could adopt such wisdom as it plays the role of world leader.

It is instructive to review these scholars' searching criticisms of their own tradition. Even though they would not compromise their ultimate commitment to creativity and humanity, they found that in order to actualize their ideals it would be necessary to take a roundabout way by absorbing the Western values of science and democracy into Chinese culture. As a matter of fact, the Chinese have valued their common sense so much that they refused to separate form from content. Consequently they have never been able to develop systems of formal logic and pure mathematics as in the West. For this they have had to pay a dear price, as Joseph Needham's massive study shows that even though the Chinese have made innumerable contributions to the world of science, they have not been able to pass the threshold of modern science and lagged far behind the West in the last several hundred years.[16] But there is no trouble for the Chinese to learn from the West, as has been proven by the fact that so far five physicists of Chinese descent have already won Nobel prize in physics, notwithstanding the fact that modern science was first initiated in Europe. There is no need to dwell on science, as most scholars would agree that it has universally recognized criteria, but the situation is very different as far as democracy is concerned. It will become the focus of our attention from now on, as it has bearing on the issues of human rights and universal ethics that are fiercely debated at the present time.

The Chinese tradition took politics as an extension of ethics. The ideal was "sageliness within and kingliness without" (*nei-sheng-wai-wang*).[17] Ironically, however, Chinese history did not produce any sage-emperors since the Han dynasty. Instead, Ming and Ch'ing rulers became more and more autocratic, and the ideal of a government of humanity was turned into rather empty rhetoric. The Contemporary Neo-Confucian thinkers find that by taking a roundabout way to adopt the Western democratic system of government with a check-balance mechanism to limit the power of the ruler it is easier to achieve the ideal of a government of the people, for the people, and by the people, which is actually not much different from the traditional ideal of a government of humanity. Thus, parallel to science, even though the democratic system of government was not initiated in China but in the West, there does not seem to be any intrinsic reason why the Chinese cannot learn from the West to adopt a system that could help China to actualize its political ideals as set forth in the Confucian classics. Likewise, with its emphasis on human dignity, there also should not be any trouble in endorsing the idea of human rights emphasized in the West.

There is no denying that China was forced to change its ways simply for survival reasons. But from a Neo-Confucian perspective, when Western culture is studied in depth, some of its values have universal significance and should be adopted on our own initiative for our own good. Therefore Neo-Confucians are definitely not ultraconservatives who reject all Western values. They embrace the ideals of democracy and science just as those who call for the modernization of Chinese culture. The difference lies in that they reject wholesale Westernization and vow to keep their ultimate commitment to creativity and humanity, and treasure the traditional ideals of the mean and harmony. They believe that Chinese culture can contribute to the world by giving totally new interpretations to the ideas of *T'ien-jen-ho-i* (Heaven and Humanity in Union) and *li-i-fen-shu* (One Principle, Many Manifestations) in the wake of the encounter with the modern West.

Some may question the Neo-Confucian standpoint today as it seems rather naive to embrace the Western values of democracy and science without serious reservations. The expansion of science and technology without any restraints have already caused worldwide problems, and the sale of democracy has appeared to be a ploy by the ugly Americans to exercise hegemony over non-Western nations in the world by forcing certain culturally bound political systems on states without the proper cultural background to make them work in a foreign soil. Actually these notions are based on a misunderstanding of the Neo-Confucian position. The Neo-Confucian thinkers would never follow blindly the lead of the West. With their ultimate commitment to creativity and humanity, they would never put the values of science and technology ahead of humanistic values, and they would fight against the domination of the capitalist countries. It is the West which has a tendency to separate existence from value and declared at one time that science is neutral in ethics. But new sciences like ecology take the quality of life into consideration and are much closer to the worldviews of the Orientals. However, underdeveloped and developing countries must be allowed a certain room for development and chances for modernization in order to shorten the distance between them and the developed countries.

Democracy is a much more complicated problem. The Neo-Confucian thinkers certainly have no intention of imposing a foreign system on their own country. It is quite correct for them to say that the democratic system of government is compatible with their ideal of a government of humanity. After the encounter with the West they realize that absolute power induces absolute corruption. Mere moral imperatives are not enough. Some kind of mechanism must be set up so that the abuse of power under the rule of despots can be avoided and a peaceful transfer of power can be guaranteed in democracy, even though it is not a panacea to solve all our problems. Moreover, the practice of democracy can take different forms. For example, American democracy is different from British democracy. There is no reason why we cannot find a form of democracy suitable for our own soil, and there is no timetable for the implementation of the ideal. Likewise, the idea of human rights is certainly compatible with the traditional emphasis on human dignity, but there is no reason why we have to accept the kind of individualism which served as the background for the emergence of the idea of human rights in the West. In fact, liberalism is challenged by communitarianism in North America nowadays. An over-emphasis on the individual would have harmful consequences for human beings must have a sense of belonging to a community, which has been ignored by the liberalist tradition. This means that a new interpretation of human rights can be developed so as to be quite congruent with the traditional worldviews of the Chinese people. The days of "East is East and West is West" are over. This is an age in which East is approaching West and vice versa. From this new perspective, the West can no longer monopolize science and democracy, or freedom and human rights, and the non-Western countries can find their own ways to implement these ideals.

Surely the Neo-Confucian thinkers fully realize that there must be certain core values in democracy and human rights which cannot be circumvented, as principle is one and manifestations are many. When they insist on finding their own ways to approach democracy and human rights, they are not just paying lip service to these things. Rather, they are absorbing these values as their own, instead of just blindly following the lead of the West's imposing something foreign on Chinese culture. There are certainly reasons for Western intellectuals to come up with critical reflections on the values and ideas of the Enlightenment, and we can certainly learn from their reflections, but we must make our own judgement to accept or reject such values and ideas, not just follow the fashion of the day in the West. I do not deny that in some respects the Neo-Confucian Declaration is a dated document. Their expressions were tinged with Kant and Hegel, but what is important is the spirit underlying the document. It is thoroughly open. That is why the next generation of Neo-Confucian scholars may find a greater rapprochement with hermeneutics or critical theory. They are free to draw from various resources of the West so long as they are able to keep an identity of their own.[18]

Contemporary Neo-Confucian scholars are very conscious of their own independence from political authorities. Hence, they keep their distance from the official positions of the governments. From their perspective, they would have great sympathy for some Contemporary Western trends of criticizing sharply the dictates of a rigid Reason or super-authority of any source. They saw enough harm done by the autocratic governments of the Ming and Ch'ing dynasties. Hence, more emphasis should be put on the side of *fen-shu*, which would encourage people to seek individual expression. The horrors of the Cultural Revolution in Mainland China show what devastating effects can be produced by the combination of the unchecked will of a superleader and the violent actions of the irrational masses following the calls of Chairman Mao, devoid of any critical spirit. From the Neo-Confucian perspective, however, current tendencies that put too much emphasis on pluralism or even relativism could also cause serious problems. If common ground could not be found and each ethnic, cultural, or religious group were to insist on its own ways without being willing to make any compromises, then conflicts could ruin the order of the society. The Bosnia situation should have taught us valuable lessons. By the critique of a rigid Reason or an overarching external authority, we are not aiming at replacing it with something irrational, but rather something even more reasonable. Thus our commitment to *li-i* must not be neglected, even though no one can claim to know the definite contents of the one principle or give definitive expressions to it. It is rather a regulative principle, as seen by Cassirer.[19] Following the lead of such insights, we realize that for a universal ethics project to be successful, it must care for both the perspective of difference and that of unity.

Perhaps tackling the problem from a comparative approach would help to clarify the issues. Recently, I have learned a lot as I helped my wife translate Huston Smith's *The World's Religions* into Chinese.[20] Some of his observations have a direct bearing on our discussions of difference, unity, and universal ethics. In the last chapter of his book he wrote that,

> as soon as it moves beyond vague generalities, every religion has some version of the Golden Rule . . . . The religions differ in what they consider essential and what negotiable . . . . In the nineteenth century Alexander Campbell tried to unite Protestants on grounds of their common acceptance of the Bible as the model for faith and

organization. To his surprise he discovered that denominational leaders were not prepared to concede that the uniting principle he proposed was more important than their distinctive tenets; his movement ended by adding another denomination—the Disciples of Christ (Christian Church)—to the Protestant roster. On a world scale Baha'u'llah's mission came to the same end. Baha'i, which originated in the hope of rallying the major religions around the beliefs they held in common, has settled into being another religion among many.[21]

This observation shows clearly that it is impractical to suppress the differences. For example, as a Confucian scholar I do not see how I can accept the Christian belief of Original Sin or the Hindu belief in the caste system. There is actually no need for us to seek unity in our beliefs, as manifestations are many. Each person is embedded in his or her culture and the language one uses forms a part of one's world. There is no way for one to completely transcend one's own *prejudice*, or better still, one's own preconception. Here we find the insight of Gadamer's hermeneutics profound.[22] And yet paradoxically, our language and culture also have a tendency to transcend their present horizon and move toward a fusion of horizons. There is no reason why we should close ourselves within the narrow confines of our own world and hold an hostile attitude against other languages, cultures, or religions.

When we try to find unity among religions, perhaps it is not correct to say, "in God we unite," for some religions like Buddhism do not believe in God. But Huston Smith finds that the word "God" has been used in different senses, as he observed.

Its meaning is not single, much less simple. Two meanings must be distinguished for its place in Buddhism to be understood.

One meaning of God is that of a personal being who created the universe by deliberate design. Defined in this sense *nirvana* is not God . . . .

There is a second meaning of God, however, which (to distinguish it from the first) had been called the Godhead. The idea of personality is not part of this concept, which appears in mystical traditions throughout the world. Impressed by similarities between *nirvana* and the Godhead, Edward Conze has compiled from Buddhist texts a series of attributes that apply to both . . . .

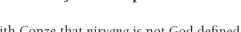

We may conclude with Conze that *nirvana* is not God defined as personal creator, but that it stands sufficiently close to the concept of God as Godhead to warrant the name in that sense.[23]

If we are not looking for substantial unity between Christianity and Buddhism, but rather a kind of functional unity as suggested by Cassirer,[24] then we can find many similarities among differences. When religion is understood as "ultimate concern," there is an unmistakable religious import in Confucian philosophy.[25] One of the important contributions of the Contemporary Neo-Confucian philosophers lies precisely in pointing out that Confucianism should never be understood as merely teaching a secular ethics. Dialogues between various religious traditions, or even between theists and atheists, are much more frequent than in previous times. The time is ripe for us to exchange ideas on our ultimate concerns as well as proximate concerns on all levels. And I am glad that UNESCO is providing opportunities for an exchange ideas on the universal ethics project.

In some ways it is easier for us to exchange ideas on ethical issues than religious issues, as religious faiths point to the transcendent for which we do not have adequate language to express ourselves on that level. It was declared in the opening paragraph of the *Lao Tzu* that "The Tao (Way) that can be told of is not the eternal Tao; The name that can be named is not the eternal name."[26] The wisdom conveyed in these statements is still very much applicable today. So long as we are modest enough to recognize that it is impossible for us to say anything definitive about the ultimate, we will be able to hold an open attitude toward other manifestations and at the same time work hard on our own manifestations that can find only limited applications in given time and space.

But ethics is a different matter. Ethical principles are needed to regulate our lives. Let us look at Huston Smith's observations on the Ten Commandments:

> What the Ten Commandments prescribe . . . are the minimum standards that make collective life possible . . . . Regarding force, they say in effect: You can bicker and fight, but killing within the ingroup will not be permitted, for it instigates blood feuds that shred community. Therefore *thou shalt not murder.* Similarly with sex. You can be a rounder, flirtatious, even promiscuous, and though we do not commend such behavior, we will not get the law after you. But at one

point we draw the line: Sexual indulgence of married persons out-side the nuptial bond will not be allowed, for it rouses passions the community cannot tolerate. Therefore *thou shalt not commit adul-tery*. As for possessions, you may make your pile as large as you please and be shrewd and cunning in the enterprise. One thing though, you may not do, and that is pilfer directly off someone else's pile, for this outrages the sense of fair play and builds animosities that become ungovernable. Therefore *thou shalt not steal*. Finally, regarding the spoken word, you may dissemble and equivocate, but there is one time when we require that you tell the truth, the whole truth, and nothing but the truth. If a dispute reaches such proportions as to be brought before a tribunal, on such occasions the judges must know what happened. If you lie then, while under oath to tell the truth, the penalty will be severe. *Thou shalt not bear false witness*.

The importance of the Ten Commandments in their ethical di-mensions lies not in their uniqueness but in their universality, not in their finality but in their foundational priority. They do not speak the final word on the topics they touch; they speak the words that must be spoken if other words are to follow. This is why, over three thousand years after Mount Sinai, they continue as the 'moral esperanto' of the world.[27]

Even though Huston Smith speaks in the Western context, and the formulation of the commandments could be different as Manifes-tations Are Many, I agree to the basic thrust of his thought. Ethical rules are not like scientific discoveries, they last much longer in time, and the spirit underlying them finds resonance in other traditions, as Principle Is One, even though no one can claim to have the last word on the subject. Thus we are not looking for certain vague generalities by induction. All we need is to work out a document that points to a direction each tradition feels comfortable to follow through on its own initiative. Again, let me quote Huston Smith:

> In the realm of ethics the Decalogue pretty much tells the cross-cul-tural story. We should avoid murder, thieving, lying, and adultery. These are the minimum guidelines . . . but they are not nothing, as we realize if we reflect on how much better the world would be if they were universally honored.[28]

Now to return to our present project, as a Confucian scholar, I do believe there is the need for a declaration of universal ethics which would complement the declaration of human rights. This is a substantive document, not just an agreement on procedural matters for communication purposes. It should have binding effects on the parties who subscribe to the declaration and can be used to condemn irrational, inhuman activities. Otherwise it would be a useless piece of paper. I do not mind that the document is first drafted in English, as it is the only international language for the time being that most people can use to communicate with one another. I also do not mind that it is formulated in Western concepts, so long as it has sufficient input from other traditions, and the product is seen as a manifestation pointing toward something beyond itself and leaves enough room for various groups and individuals to develop their own interpretations to their own satisfaction. I do not like to be bogged down by mere words or logical quibbles. If we can keep ourselves to the essentials, I suppose we would come out all right. Hans Küng has shown that this can be done for he drafted a global ethic which was subjected to criticisms by various groups, and still was subscribed to by most of the religious leaders present during the Parliament of World's Religions held in Chicago in 1993.[29]

Leonard Swidler is another outstanding scholar who besides Hans Küng is vigorously promoting the Global Ethic Project. As seen elsewhere in this volume, he too has prepared a carefully thought-out draft of a Universal Declaration of a Global Ethic. I am happy to work together from a Confucian perspective on this Project to create drafts of a Declaration of a Global Ethic which will be the bases for discussion and gradually be integrated and shaped so that it eventually can be signed by all, religious and non-religious alike.

At first sight the items listed in these documents may appear to be banal, but what affects us most are usually not exotic things, but that which we must deal with day in and day out in our lives. I hope in the above I have given sufficient reasons why a Confucian scholar such as myself is committed to support this meaningful project as I see it.

Footnotes

1 Hans Küng, and Karl-Josef Kuschel, eds., *A Global Ethic: The Declaration of Parliament of World's Religions* (New York: Continuum, 1993)

2 Burton Watson, trans., *Chuang Tzu: Basic Writings* (New York: Columbia University Press, 1964), p. 65. As Chuang Tzu loves to tell fables and stories, there is no guarantee that Confucius actually said these words.

3 Wing-tsit Chan trans. and ed., *A Source Book in Chinese Philosophy* (Princeton: Princeton University Press, 1963), p. 26.

4 5 Ibid., p. 41.

5 Ibid., p. 44.

6 Ibid., p. 32.

7 Cf. ibid., pp. 499f.

8 See the entry I contributed on Chinese Philosophy in the *Cambridge Dictionary of Philosophy,* published in 1995.

9 See Joseph R. Levenson, *Confucian China and Its Modern Fate: A Trilogy* (Berkeley: University of California Press, 1968), vol. 3.

10 See Shu-hsien Liu, "Postwar Neo-Confucian Philosophy: Its Development and Issues," *Religious Issues and Interreligious Dialogues*, ed. by Charles Wei-hsun Fu and Gerhard E. Spiegler (New York: Greenwood Press, 1989), pp. 277-302.

11 u Wei-ming, ed., *Confucian Tradition in East Asian Modernity: Moral Education and Economic Culture in Japan and the Four Mini-Dragons* (Cambridge, MA: Harvard University Press, 1996).

12 See Joseph Needham, *Within the Four Seas: The Dialogue of East and West* (London: George Allen & Unwin, 1969).

13 "A Manifesto for a Reappraisal of Sinology and Reconstruction of Chinese Culture" in Carsun Chang, *The Development of Neo-Confucian Thought*, 2 vols. (New York: Bookman Associates, 1957-1962), 2:455-483.

14 Ibid., 2:461.

15 See Lin Tongqi, Henry Rosemont, Jr., and Roger Ames, "Chinese Philosophy: A Philosophical Essay on the `State-of-the-Art'" The *Journal of Asian Studies*, 54, 3 (August, 1995), 727-758.

16 See Joseph Needham, *Science and Civilization in China* (Cambridge: Cambridge University Press, 1954-). Many volumes have been published since then.

17 Shu-hsien Liu, "On the Confucian Ideal of `Sageliness Within and Kingliness Without'," *Proceedings of the International Symposium on Confucianism and the Modern World* (1988), pp. 401-422.

18 Shu-hsien Liu, "On New Frontiers of Contemporary Neo-Confucian Philosophy," *Journal of Chinese Philosophy*, 23, 1 (March, 1996), 39-58.

19 Ernst Cassirer, *Determinism and Indeterminism in Modern Physics* (New Haven: Yale University Press, 1956), pp. 52f., 62f. I have borrowed Cassirer's insight to give a new interpretation of some of the ideas in traditional Chinese philosophy. See Shu-hsien Liu, "Toward a New Relation Between Humanity and Nature: Reconstructing *T'ien-jen-ho-i*," *Zygon*, 24, 4 (December. 1989), 457-468.

20 The book will be published by New Century Pub. Co. in 1998 in Taipei.

21 Huston Smith, *The World's Religions: Our Great Wisdom Traditions* (San Francisco: Harper, 1991). p. 385.

22 Hans-Georg Gadamer, *Truth and Method* (London: Sheed and Ward, 1975). pp. 238-240.

23 Smith, *The World's Religions*, pp. 114-115.

24 Ernst Cassirer, *An Essay on Man* (New Haven: Yale University Press, 1944), p. 222.

25 Shu-hsien Liu, "The Religious Import of Confucian Philosophy: Its Traditional Outlook and Contemporary Significance." *Philosophy East and West*, 21, 2 (April. 1971), 157-175.

26 Chan, *Source Book*, p. 139.

27 Smith, *The World's Religions*, pp. 287f.

28 Ibid., p. 387.

29 See note 1.

A HINDU IN DIALOGUE
WITH LEONARD SWIDLER

KANA MITRA

THE ENTERPRISE OF FORMULATING a declara-
tion of an ethic which is universally recognized as reflecting the diverse "understandings of the ultimate meaning of life, and how to live
accordingly" is challenging. I congratulate all who are accepting this
challenge—and especially Leonard Swidler, who, after formulating such
a document, always looks for contributions and critiques from diverse
people, and then offers further reflection and clarification.

The "globe" is, and always has been, one and interconnected, although consciousness about this oneness and interconnectedness, for
a large number of people, is rather recent. This "one" globe consists of
diverse beings. It is a unity with diversity. Among the diverse beings of
the globe, only humans think and believe in various "meanings of life,
and live accordingly," as far as we know. In different parts of the globe
there have been, and still are, different types of people. Although there
are more resemblances in the thinking of people regionally, there are
also diverse ways of thinking within these regions. Plurality is a characteristic of the globe. This characteristic has caused, and is still caus-
ing, many problems in the world. However, if in order to deal with the

problems we eliminate diversity, we will impoverish the world in the same way as if we would allow the extinction of a specific species, such as the bald eagle. Therefore, when a document for a Global Ethic is formulated, there is a need for caution, and a concern for the preservation of diversity.

Looking at the history of humankind as a whole, as well as humans of different regions, many paradigm shifts in human consciousness can indeed be noted, and many able scholars have very aptly described them (Hans Küng, Ewert Cousins, Leonard Swidler). In the twenty-first century, "global consciousness" is the prominent characteristic of the new paradigm of human consciousness, which Cousins describes as ushering in a "Second Axial Period," and Swidler describes as the dawning of the "Age of Dialogue." From Cousin's description of the different "Axial Periods" it becomes evident that "global consciousness" cannot be the characteristic of any one region of the world. Just as in the "First Axial Period" the same consciousness of individualism emerged differently in various regions of the world—in China as Confucianism, in Greece as Socratic philosophy, in India as *Atmavada*—in the same way in the "Second Axial Period" the same "global consciousness" is emerging differently in various regions of the world. For example, in the West as Christendom transformed by secularization and technology into Western Civilization; in the East as Zen, Neo-Vedanta and Neo-Confucianism. Otherwise, it would not be the "Second Axial Period." Likewise, what Leonard Swidler describes as the "Age of Dialogue" presupposes diversity, and thus the "global consciousness" which leads to dialogue, (sometimes it can be a result of dialogue) is a consciousness of diversity as well.

Leonard Swidler describes how Western Civilization emerged via many revolutions in understanding. Of particular importance is the role of the subject, or knower, in what is known. He mentions in a footnote that the importance of the perspective of the knower in what is known was referred to by Indian thinkers two millennia ago, but these reflections were not of importance to the development of Western thought. However, the globe was physically interconnected in the past as it is in the present.

There had been interchanges in ancient times via conquests and trades, such as Alexander's conquest and the Silk Route, though of course it was not as instantaneous as it is now. If, however, we scrutinize the writings of the thinkers who were influential during the eighteenth-century European Enlightenment, such as Voltaire, we can note that he was not only aware of Confucius, but was very appreciative of him. The world was connected all along! However, for the purpose of our discussion here, attributing credit or discredit to any one region of the world is not of importance, because all agree about the importance of diversity and enrichment of each by and for each other.

To emphasize perspectivalism again, what seems to be an "age of discovery and prosperity" from the perspective of Europe, appears to be an "age of demise and extinction" from the perspective of Native Americans. The secular scientific studies, as mentioned by Swidler, enable us to understand the dominated, the disenfranchised, the marginalized as well as the dominating, the powerful, and the central. The secular perspective thus also has its role to play. (Charles Long)

The religious perspectives likewise have their roles to play and are not to be subsumed under the secular perspective. It is under the predominance of secular thought, which transformed Christendom into Western Civilization, that many international institutions, such as the United Nations, have been organized and the Universal Declaration of Human Rights (1948) was formulated. This Secular Humanism was necessarily the foundation of that document. However, despite its legal status it could not alone attain the goal of peace and justice, although many groups, such as "Amnesty International" and others were empowered by the Declaration and organized a worldwide system of vigilance on the violations of human rights. Today most of the religions of the world do not have any legal power, but they still attract many persons by their invitation to the "power of transformation."

Yet, for many individuals and groups, a particular religion still provides a sense of identity. However, when the sense of identity from religious affiliation becomes colored by socio-political and economic conditions, and the relationship of dominance/subordination among individuals and groups, religions have and do become sources of disputes and violence. Just as secular thought cannot be neglected simply because it can, and at times did, generate absolute skepticism and cynicism and a sense of "anything goes," similarly the contributions of religions cannot be neglected simply because of their potential, sometimes realized, for sectarianism and violence.

The transformative power of religions can be noted in a very prominent way especially among the mystics of all the major world religions. The experience of transcendence transform them into holy and holistic personalities. They perceive reality holistically and hence act with compassion. Thus, in the life of the mystics we note the virtues that the "Universal Declaration of a Global Ethic" tries to inculcate, viz., recognizing all humans and nonhumans as valuable and relating to them with dignity. The mystics often also act with love. We have examples such as the stories of Gautama the Buddha giving some of his own flesh to a hungry hawk and St. Francis of Assisi talking and communing with "brother bird" and "sister fish." Of course, their holistic consciousness seems to be different from the holistic experience of astronauts when they look at the earth from their space crafts, although for some astronauts this vision of "globe" did lead to a transformation of "global consciousness."

The point is: "global" or expanded consciousness seems to be the key for a kind of human transformation which enables humans to recognize that self-love and love of others, well-being of each and well-being of all are interrelated. Thus, there is not any real conflict between the Declaration of Human Rights and the ethical precepts advocated by the different religions, although in the former the emphasis is on Rights and in the latter on Duties and Responsibilities. They compliment each other. Unfortunately, the traditional religions, wherein the emphasis is on responsibilities, have often misconstrued self-expansion and renunciation into self-abnegation and asceticism. Consequently, religious people too often fall in the trap of restrained consciousness, rather than stride into the freedom of an expanded one.

When thinkers have attempted to base ethical behavior on rationality alone, they encountered problems that are difficult to resolve intellectually. That is why Kant had to write his *Critique Of Practical Reason* after writing the *Critique of Pure Reason* and insisted that ethical precepts are "categorical imperatives." Thus, he formulated the precept: "Act only on that principle which you can at the same time universalize"—which is quite similar to the "Golden Rule." Just as intellectuals have pointed out that there are hardly any principles of action which can be absolutely universalized without any regard for circumstances, similarly all principles of action *can* be universalized if particular circumstances are taken into consideration.

The same intellectual criticisms can be raised about the Golden Rule which Swidler proposes as a "Fundamental Rule of Global Ethic." The different religions formulate their ethical precepts by way of their beliefs in transcendence. The important point to note, however, is that although the doctrines or beliefs about transcendence in the different religions vary, the ethical precepts are very similar. Swidler in his "Excursus on the Golden Rule" demonstrated this very aptly. Even concrete and specific rules such as non-killing or responsibility about life are present in all religions, although the rationale for them is different in the various religions. In Judaism "You shall not kill!" is God's command; in Buddhism it is essential for Nirvana. The problem is not that there is no common ethic among the different religions and ideologies, but that people do not follow the ethical precepts of their own religions and ideologies.

Religions, as pointed out by Swidler, are characterized by the four "C's". But they can also be looked at as ways of transformation from limited consciousness to expanded consciousness, or what are now called spiritualities. Many consider this aspect of religion to be the "core" of religion and "ethics" to be essential part of spiritual transformation. "Giving" is a common ethical precept in most religions. It may be hard to justify this precept intellectually, but once one "gives" because it is a "duty," one is then likely to experience the joy of giving and an expansion of consciousness. Many such experiences are reported by missionaries and service-oriented people. Eventually, one gives because of love and not out of a sense of duty or responsibility.

The different religions and ideologies have different perspectives regarding the ways of transformation, dependent on their belief systems. From the perspective of each, its own system is likely to appear to be the most adequate, and arguments or so-called empirical evidences can not settle the matter. When dialogue occurs and one is exposed to a different point of view than one's own, new insights may be generated which lead to shifting and arranging of data differently than when there is no exposure at all. Thus exposure to diversity leads to dynamism and vitality that keeps the religions and ideologies alive. When any religion or ideology tries to maintain itself by raising walls around it so that influences of the "other" cannot affect it, its demise is sure to occur. The collapse of the "Iron Curtain" and the Berlin Wall can be cited as examples. Each religion or ideology will survive if they are dynamic—and each will maintain its distinctiveness and not end in monolithic oneness.

What is distinctive about Hinduism is its ideology of unity in plurality. The Hinduism of the sixth century B.C.E. and the Hinduism of the twentieth century C.E. are very different because of its exposure to many religions and ideologies—however, the recognition of diversity and plurality still remains its characteristic mark. Of course, one cannot say that there are no sectarian Hindus. Among the different groups of Hindus, some worshippers of Vishnu make Shakti subordinate to Vishnu; similarly, some Shakti worshippers make Vishnu subordinate to Shakti. Further, many Hindus have an attitude of superiority regarding their own religion and subsume all other religions under their own way of thinking. However, Hindu mystics of an expanded consciousness displayed openness to all influences—for example, Ramakrishna Paramahamsa. Moreover, according to the various forms of Hindu thought, ethical cultivation is essential in order to gain a proper insight into the ideologies that are presented in the religious texts.

The *Yoga Sutra* of Patanjali can be considered a summary of Hindu spiritual exercise. This text outlines the seven steps of the spiritual exercises. Of them the first two are ethical culture. The first step, *yama*, means the observance of five virtues: nonviolence, non-lying or truth, non-stealing, continence, non-dependence on other's charity or self-reliance. The second step, *niyama*, suggests: cleanliness of body and mind, contentment or not complaining, discipline, study, and surrender to God. All these precepts are in agreement with the Golden Rule and do not disagree with Swidler's proposed Declaration. Not to kill is of course respect for life and non-stealing respect for right to property. Not to lie is related with treating each other with dignity. Continence is respect for one's own self and others and not to accept charity is also dignity for one's self. The virtues suggested in the *niyama* are more for the individual's cultivation of strength of character that leads to the expansion of consciousness, and therefore do not violate the precepts suggested by Swidler, but simply go beyond them.

In Hindu society there are many violations of the dignity of humans—for example, the *dalits* or subjugated ones (Untouchables), oppressed women, etc. These violations are sometimes justified by some scriptures. However, the Hindu spiritual paths do not suggest blind adherence to texts, but a verification of them by *yukti*, or rationality, and *anubhuti*, or personal spiritual intuitive experience. Many spiritual leaders, because of their transformation of consciousness, have decried the subjugation of any humans by other humans. Hindus, insofar as they believe in the possibility of the transformation of consciousness from narrowness to expansion, can join their voice to Hans Küng, Ewert Cousins and Leonard Swidler and celebrate ushering in of a "New Paradigm," the "Second Axial Period" and the "Age of Dialogue."

A Buddhist Perspective
on a Global Ethic Declaration

Chung Ok Lee

Buddhist Utopia

The Pure Land is a Buddhist Utopia. The
Pure Land is in the Western Paradise, a Buddha realm with the perfect
condition for practicing the Dharma and gaining enlightenment.[1] This
Pure Land can be built in the world through a constant practice and
cultivation of spirituality. The aim of Won Buddhism is to build a Pure
Land on earth. So-Tae-San, the founder of Won Buddhism, emphasized that we must realize that the Pure Land is our own True Nature.
So-Tae-San highlighted that, "Our purpose is to discover Amitabha in
our own minds and return to the paradise of our own Buddha nature."[2]

So-Tae-San's vision of a modern Utopia was *Ir-Won-Ju-Ye*: One
World Community. Based on the Buddhist truth of total interconnectedness and interdependence, he explained that all beings in the universe are of one essential nature and all Dharma are from one fundamental source. He recognized that a universal and even cosmic interdependence would bring people of all continents, all races and all religions together to face a common future. *Ir-Won-Ju-Ye* provides moral
principles for peaceful coexistence in the world, promoting justice,
love and compassion among all the members of the earth community.

His successor, Master Chung-San, elaborated on One World Community with *Sam-Dong Yoon Ri*, the triple global ethic. The first ethic is, "within One Fence and with One Principle." To enlightened eyes, all religions and all forms of life are based on one essential truth; in accord with this philosophy, we need to seek harmony among religions of the world. Following this ethic, Won Buddhism actively participates in interreligious understanding and cooperation. The second global ethic is, "One family within One House." Humanity is one family, and the world is the house we all share. We inherit the world from our ancestors. We live in it sharing its resources, its joy and its suffering. We pass it on to future generations. We must use our sense of One Family to stop hatred, to prevent injustice and to create love and compassion. In modern Utopia, enlightened ones will have this sense of One Family within One House. The third ethic is, "As Co-Workers in One work place." We have many different tasks and skills. But our ultimate task should be to build the House of truth, to make a home for love and justice. The aim of all social, political and religious enterprises should be the construction of a peaceful world. In this time of global transition, we must open our minds and hearts to building such a global community.

Won Buddhism offers a way to build the Pure Land, a modern Utopia, through integration of the spiritual and the material. One of the guiding principles for multi-integration in this new world, which So-Tae-San stated in 1916, is: "As material civilization develops, cultivate spiritual civilization accordingly." Inner spiritual enlightenment will verify, enrich and sustain external material concerns. To build modern Utopias, Won Buddhism suggests that spiritual evolution must accompany the ever expanding political, economic, technological and scientific revolutions. It is possible to change our lives for the better world of Utopia only through moral, ethical and spiritual transformation—the keys to unlocking the door of human interconnectedness and interdependence.

Necessity of Establishing a Global Ethic

The first step towards building a modern Utopia is establishing a global ethic, one which would foster shared values and principles to shape humanity's future. This global ethic must draw on all religious and

philosophical sources. A renewed spirituality must counter materialism by balancing and transcending it. For a future Utopia, we must
make life more democratic, more secure, and more sustainable than it
is today.

We now live in a global neighborhood and we must consider ourselves global citizens. "People may dislike their neighbors, they may
distrust or fear them, and they may even try to ignore or avoid them.
But they cannot escape from the effects of sharing space with them.
When the neighborhood is the planet, moving to get away from bad
neighbors is not an option."[3] A global ethic can engender the kind of
cooperation required in an interdependent world where sharp differences and disagreements still divide people.

To build a Utopia, a global ethic must introduce visions of a positive future in the troubled present. We know the nature of the massive
problems the human race will have to face in the coming years. We
know that only a collective effort of people, government, civil society
and the media is likely to be able to channel into a benign and constructive direction the forces that are already shaping the future. The
crisis we face today demands that humankind elevate its sense of consciousness. Unless we choose and apply new values and a global ethic
for our survival, the condition of the world will continue to deterio-
rate. We can attain this sense of conscience through greater harmony
in our lives and application of spiritual values. When we are able to do
so, thereby relating and integrating ethics with our activities and world,
humanity can move into the future and toward building a modern Utopia peacefully, cooperatively and successfully.

General Principle of a Global Ethic

From the Buddhist perspective, a world ethic should be mindful of and
benefit all members of the earth community. To secure the well-being
of our shared home and future generations, we have a responsibility to
restore peace and justice in order to build a modern Utopia. We are all
inter-connected and inter-dependent beings, essential to the functioning of the whole. The Earth is an interdependent community of life;
thus, we have to awaken to the idea of universal interdependence. "Be
aware and express your gratitude for life all around you. Respect and
appreciate life." A world full of gratitude is a paradise; one full of resentment, a hell.

Basic Principles

From the Buddhist viewpoint, it is important for individuals to culti-vate their minds, know intrinsic right and good, and restore inborn wisdom and inner peace for the benefit of all. The basic moral prin-ciples for this cultivation are summarized in the following precepts:

1. Although the mind-heart[4] has inner peace, it is distracted by the external world; let us restore inner peace through medita-tion and peaceful action.
2. Although the mind-heart has intrinsic wisdom, it becomes fool-ish due to material value; let us renew inborn wisdom.
3. Although the mind-heart has intrinsic right, it is covered by extrinsic social value; let us uncover intrinsic right.
4. Let us dispel disbelief, greed, laziness and illusion by means of faith, courage, sincerity and an inquiring mind.
5. Let us change resentment into gratitude.
6. Let us cultivate confidence and independence.
7. Let us change resistance to learning into willingness to learn.
8. Let us change resistance to teaching into willingness to teach.
9. Let us overcome our selfishness in order to serve the universal good.

Responsibilities Concerning Mind-Cultivation

Buddhists believe that all of us are born with a Buddha Nature and that we are all potential Buddhas. Through the mind-cultivation, we can channel our Positive Energy, and bring forth our inherent good. At the same time, however, the human mind-heart has a capacity for destruc-tive cruelty. It is therefore the source of all good and evil.[5]

To cultivate our mind-heart we must meditate. Through medita-tion we not only remove our own causes of suffering , but also attain enlightenment for the greatest benefit to others. Mind-cultivation is an essential step to the creation of a modern Utopia. It leads us to a love and compassion for all, and fuels the process of spiritual rejuvenation.

Responsibilities Concerning the Earth Community

Science has taught us that for every action, there is an equal and oppo-site reaction. In Buddhism, this relationship is interpreted as the Principle of Cause and Effect. For every activity in which we partake, humanity faces the outcome; a most basic example of this fact is the declining condition of the environment.

We must adopt a new way of living in order to pursue sustainable development and safeguard the global community. It is essential that we reform our wasteful lifestyles and create legislation to protect earth. In this way we can protect the interests of future generations.

Respect for life is vital to the well being of any society. The sanctity of life is a concept shared by people of all religions and spiritual traditions, as well as by secular humanists. Each diverse form of life has its own intrinsic value. All forms of life embody beauty so that they inspire human consciousness with wonder, joy and creativity.

Humans have a special responsibility to preserve life and its integrity. Our concern for the earth community should be expressed in action, in our personal, professional and political lives, as well as in our fundamental principles. We must have the wisdom and willingness to re-establish a better relationship among humans and between the earth and its people, humans and other living beings.

Responsibilities Concerning Justice

Justice is an essential human value. Justice is indispensable for peace and progress, as its absence gives rise to suffering. Justice demands that each person be able to obtain the basic necessities of life in a world of great disparities between rich and poor, between powerful and powerless. Justice demands recognition of universal principles and the application of *True Law*. Global solidarity is love of all Life and all Creation and justice is a natural effect. Currently we have ample wealth on earth, but do not have a sense of consciousness great enough to share and distribute it. A broader commitment to justice is essential to finding effective methods of reducing disparities and bringing about a more balanced dissemination of the world's resources.

Responsibilities Concerning Liberty

All human beings are born equal in their right to human dignity and are entitled to certain basic liberties. People want to define and express their own identity, to choose their own religion, to earn a livelihood, to be free from persecution and oppression, and to receive information. Liberty enables people to both broaden and choose the paths of their lives.

People around the world have become more aware of the possible threats to their liberty, threats which may arise from undemocratic governments, or financial, racial and gender inequality. We have a common responsibility to act against attempts to violate the right to liberty.

Responsibilities Concerning Gender Equality

There should not be discrimination between men and women, as in the past, but men and women should be treated well in accordance with what they do. The importance of gender equality and the right and responsibility of women to explore their full potential as complete persons equal to men must be recognized. The ability to support oneself as a woman is a moral discipline, and those who have attained this independence should not deny its cultivation in others. We have an obligation not only to encourage but to create this opportunity.

Women's involvement has awakened women's, as well as men's, political, social and religious consciousness. Many women are discovering their own independent identities and developing a more holistic view of the world; they are also seeking a more balanced values paradigm. Women's liberty is therefore helping to redefine the relationship between males and females in terms of social, economic, political and spiritual parity. Women's processes towards freedom will have a lasting, positive impact on future societies.

A Global Ethic for Gender Equality

Traditionally, society taught females that subordination and endurance are womanly virtues for which they should strive. Women were thus subtly persuaded into silence. Today, the continuing silence of the world community in the face of gender inequality has been deafening. There has been an overwhelming and a continuing silence about women, of women, by women and toward women.

Women's potential for inner silence, however, can be a positive force, a pulsating, healing power. Contemplative silence and the silence of compassionate listening are very positive. Silence in meditation can be the power that heals the wounds that other silences inflict, and the power that leads to the discovery of the divinity within, the Buddha Nature in every one of us. Through silent meditation, we discover ourselves and learn to use our own wisdom, our own Truth and our own inner strength.

Despite the progress of the recent years, women have yet to achieve social, political, religious and educational equality. The Fourth World Conference on Women in Beijing made the world's people more aware of the situation of women than they had been previously. It shared information about women throughout the world. It was an educational and thought provoking process. But still, opportunities for women are few. Women are poorly represented in ranks of power, policy and decision-making: Women make up less than five percent of the world's heads of States, heads of major corporations and top positions in international organizations.[6]

Boutros Boutros Ghali, Secretary General of the UN, expressed that the Platform for Action adopted in Beijing is not only the result of diplomatic negotiation but also the result of the strong and organized power of the women's movement.[7] The Platform for Action is the pivotal call for the empowerment of women to become equal partners with men. Our task now is the implementation and monitoring of the Platform for Action in every day life. We must continue to broaden women's opportunities for education, health, and professional careers.

The world's religions advocate the ethical and spiritual qualities of love, hope, peace, justice, and wisdom. Religion provides the vision for humanity and can and should act as a constructive force to create a peaceful global village. Religious views in the past, however, focused on male-dominant perspectives. Our understanding of life is underdeveloped and distorted because these explanations have excluded half of the human race. Only through the full inclusion of women's views and experiences of life and spirituality will we gain a fuller understanding of human behavior, development and religious experiences.

Women were assigned in general to subordinate positions within religious orders and had little hope of ever assuming leadership roles. This inequality continues today. We must adopt, therefore, a global ethic for gender equality in order to create a more unified social structure where men and women have an equal voice. For this change to transpire, women first must establish their identities as individuals. Thus, we must renew our commitment to nurturing ourselves to attain enlightenment for the benefit of all human beings. Only through this approach can we find the journey home to our Buddha Nature. Along the way, we will uplift, nourish, and foster the structures of family and society.

A Global Ethic for the United Nations

Half a century ago, leaders from fifty nations gathered in San Francisco to form a global organization. While the earth was still suffering from humanity's Second World War, these representatives persisted in their cause for a unified body to promote world peace and security. In founding the Untied Nations, these diverse representatives collaborated for our shared future, and committed themselves to the ideals of the UN Charter. This charter is the blue print for a modern Utopia. Yet, while the World Organization has made efforts to ameliorate circumstances on earth, the condition of the world continues to decline.

Although the global situation is growing worse, a better world is still conceivable. There is an urgent need and a timely opportunity to provide a spiritual and ethical vision for world peace and development. At this momentous time, all religious people must embark together on a mission of world peace and develop a global ethic which assists the world organization to be more effective and function with respect to the ideals of the Charter.

The Charter of the United Nations has its basis in spiritual values. The United Nations is an essential world organization which embodies our hopes for a more just and humane future. The most prominent role of the United Nations has been its active involvement in promoting world peace through political means. The results, however, have been limited. Against this backdrop, there has been a recent upsurge of support for the active involvement of the spiritual leaders. The second Secretary-General of the UN, Dag Hammarskjold, stated near the end of his term, "I see no hope for permanent world peace. We have tried and failed miserably. Unless the world has a spiritual rebirth, civilization is doomed."[8] This message should alert us to the urgent need for action.

The third Secretary-General of the UN, U Thant, reminded us that "an ideal man, an ideal woman, is one who is endowed with four attributes, four qualities: physical, intellectual, moral and spiritual qualities. . . . Above all I would attach the greatest importance to spiritual values, spiritual qualities. . . . With this approach, with this philosophy, with this concept alone, we will be able to fashion the kind of society we want, the society which was envisioned by the founding fathers of the United Nations."9 This philosophy is the one that we are advocating in our quest for global harmony. We must combine our different but equally important resources in order to foster our world community. Unless this spirit of cooperation flourishes, our world community will ceaselessly experience the brunt of war, environmental disaster, and moral deterioration.

In 1948, the United Nations adopted the Universal Declaration of Human Rights, sketching the inalienable rights with which all of us are born. Since then, the UN has agreed on a body of human rights covenants, protocols and declarations further defining our collective economic, social, cultural, political and civil rights, and creating systems to protect them. The UN Secretary-General Boutros Boutros Ghali articulated the underlying philosophy of Human Rights: "The human rights that we proclaim and seek to safeguard can be brought about only if we transcend ourselves, only if we make a conscious effort to find our common essence beyond our apparent divisions, our temporary differences, our ideological and cultural barriers." 10

It is painfully apparent that human rights continue to be violated worldwide, often on a massive scale. It is tragic that violence in the name of religion persists. At this urgent time, the world religions must work together and through collective efforts create a modern Utopia. Religious leaders must take the initiative in making a concerted effort to provide the spiritual guidance for all members of this world family.

We are living in an age of enlightenment where people question the moral and spiritual aspects of global issues and concerns. It is a time of global transition when it is acceptable even in the secular political atmosphere of the United Nations to express the moral and spiritual dimension of worldwide issues and concerns. Religious representatives at the United Nations are in a unique position to merge together the spiritual and moral values in their religious traditions with global issues to effect a positive change. Moral values are becoming increasingly applicable, as evidenced in the Programme of Action for the Social Summit, which states: "We, Heads of States and Government, are committed to a political, economic, ethical and spiritual vision for social development that is based on human dignity, human right, equality, respect, peace, democracy, mutual responsibility and cooperation and full respect for the various religious and ethical values and cultural background of people."[11]

The world religions and the United Nations should renew their commitments to peace and, more importantly, to translating their shared commitments into practical and effective actions by developing a global ethic of common rights and shared responsibilities. A global ethic would provide the moral foundation for constructing an effective system for the United Nations.

Buddhist Principles for a Shared World Ethic

A global ethic should encourage people to find intrinsic good in every human being. Every religious community, society, and government should function as co-workers to assist individuals and their fellow citizens to seek an ethic of intrinsic right and an ethic of intrinsic good. Second, a global ethic must strengthen the earth community. One of the fundamental teachings of Buddhism is called "Co-Dependence of Causality." Buddhists look at the world as interdependent and link human beings to sentient beings and to nature on our planet. The Great Master So-Tae-San emphasized this linkage of interdependency by calling it "Grace." It is the Grace of Heaven and Earth, Parents (past, present, and future), Brethren (which means all living beings) and the perfect Law.[12] This view presents the full interpretation of the old Buddhist truth of Co-dependence of Origination. We cannot survive without the assistance of other human beings and non human partners. We have to awaken to a universal inter-dependence of life.

We create our world by our attitudes and perceptions. Our inner state of mind is then projected onto the outer world. We therefore must deal with our own inner conflicts, divisions, struggles and egocentrism before they threaten to engulf the world in which we live. We must recognize the power of prayer and the need for spiritual healing to overcome our human frailties.

When people rediscover their inherent spiritual natures, they will naturally acquire more tolerance and respect for their fellow human beings. Thus, a return to spirituality will foster the spirit of cooperation and friendship that, sadly, is lacking in our world; it will foster a spirituality which is vital to the achievement of our goal of living harmoniously and productively together. We must begin on this monumental task by working together to discover and accomplish our common goals. We must serve as examples of the cooperation that we wish to foster in others. In this urgent mission, we are co-workers in one work place, and the world is our work place.

The need for spiritual guidance is evident as we reflect on how our civilization has succumbed, from time to time, to the human frailties of ambition and selfishness. We have seen that heinous acts are often committed under the veil of public mandate when in fact they are the wishes of the few in power, be it economic, political, military, or even religious. Other times, atrocities are committed out of a mistaken fear of the unknown. Regardless of the cause, these acts against humanity must not be allowed to continue. We as spiritual guardians, working with other world leaders, must take the lead in helping others back onto the path of spirituality. It is our task and our duty to curb and eventually eliminate violence in our world family. Essential to the accomplishment of this task is the cultivation of people's spiritual nature. Through spirituality, people will gain courage to eliminate the greed and egocentrism that choke our spiritual life.

As the twenty-first century approaches, we must go forward in our fervent efforts to foster cooperation in our world community. We are living in an increasingly inter-cultural and inter-religious world. It is imperative that we learn to cooperate and co-exist peacefully, respecting each other's beliefs and value systems while remaining true to our own.

We must convince others that the embodiment of true religious living and a modern Utopia is obtainable only through the relentless pursuit of peaceful coexistence. We must take a strong interest in global affairs and work together to alleviate and resolve problems and conflicts. In the upcoming millennium, religious leaders must fulfill their calling to unify the human race into one human family. To begin to accomplish this seemingly impossible task, religious leaders must first be united; then we can provide the moral and spiritual guidance for others to do likewise. We must look toward the future with hope in our hearts as we pledge our commitment to this goal. We need to put our hearts and souls into this noble mission both for our sake and for the sake of future generations. Through cooperation and mutual respect, we can and will build a new world of peace and harmony.

Conclusion

Now is the time to translate our words into actions. In this age of overwhelming material and technological advancement, we face the very real risk of a dwindling tide of spirituality. We must seize this opportunity to channel the tide back toward spirituality. Spirituality is becoming more and more difficult to teach. Those who try to suppress spirituality say that it hinders economic and scientific development. Science has developed technology that can connect the whole world, but only ethical values and spirituality can instill in us the wisdom to choose how to use the technology. We must maintain a balance and harmony between the material and the spiritual, and teach this balance to the world. The present global problems cannot be solved by an excessive dependency upon science and economics. We need spirituality in action. Therefore, all religious people must join in faithful practice to cultivate spiritual civilization. We have to work together to reincorporate spirituality back in our daily lives and endeavors. Our wonderful heritage of spirituality must not be lost in the rising flood of modern material and technological advancement. Through a global ethic endowed with spirituality, we may build a better world of modern Utopia.

Footnotes

1 Emma Layman, *Buddhism in America* (Chicago: Nelson and Hall, 1976), pp. 34-53.

2 So-Tae-San, *The Scripture of Won Buddhism*, trans. by Pal Khn Chon (Iri, Korea: Won Kwang University Press, 1988), p.43

3 The Commission on Global Governance, *Our Global Neighborhood* (Oxford University Press: Oxford, 1995), p. 44.

4 In the Korean language, one character means both mind *and* heart.

5 Ibid., 307.

6 United Nations, *The World's Women 1970-1990: Trends and Statistics* (New York: United Nations, 1991), p.6.

7 *The Earth Times* (The Earth Times Foundation: New York), VIII:16 (September 28, 1995), p.16.

8 Robert Muller, *My Testament to the UN* (World Happiness and Cooperation: Anacortes, WA, 1992), p.175.

9 Ibid., p.175.

10 The United Nations, *World Conference on Human Rights: The Vienna Declaration and Programme of Action June 1993*, 7.

11 The United Nations, *Report of the World Summit for Social Development* (A/CONF.166/9, April 9, 1995), p.9.

12 *The Scripture of Won Buddhism*, pp.8-88.

A ZEN APPROACH TO A GLOBAL ETHIC

BRIAN (DAIZEN) A. VICTORIA

Introduction

I WOULD LIKE TO BEGIN this discussion of Zen's approach to a Global Ethic with a statement of the obvious, i.e., Zen is a sect of Buddhism and as such should not be expected to have a "viewpoint" on any topic that does not conform to, or lies outside of, the basic tenets of Buddhism.

As obvious as this statement may be, it is necessary to state it at the outset because Zen is all too often presented as being not only irrational and illogical, but bizarre and incomprehensible as well. The Zen experience is often equated with complete absorption in the present moment, regardless of the activity involved. As John McRae of Cornell University has pointed out, "The word 'Zen' has entered the American vocabulary as a shorthand equivalent for an attitude of mindless dedication to any endeavor whatsoever."[1]

That Zen has nothing to do with "mindless dedication to any endeavor whatsoever" can easily be seen by numerous statements of the great masters of the Zen tradition. Thirteenth century Zen Master Dogen (1200-53), for example, wrote the following with regard to the type of life a Buddhist follower should lead:

There have been those who, seeking no reward, willingly gave their help to others. Supplying a ferry and building a bridge are both acts of giving, as are earning a living and producing goods . . . The foolish believe that their own interests will suffer if they put the benefit of others first. They are wrong, however. Benevolence is all-encompassing, equally benefiting oneself and others.[2]

In encouraging concern for the well-being of others, Dogen is doing no more than giving concrete expression to the "Bodhisattva ideal" as incorporated in the Mahayana school of Buddhism. In this school, of which Zen is a part, Bodhisattvas are those who have vowed not to realize enlightenment for themselves before, and unless, all sentient beings have done so.

In Buddhist art one often comes across a depiction of a hunter's pit in the bottom of which lies a trapped and emasculated lioness and her two cubs. Realizing that these animals are in danger of dying of starvation, a passing Bodhisattva quickly flings himself (or herself!) into the pit as a meal for the starving trio. In so doing, the popular view that "dumb animals" exist only to serve the needs of us supposed "smart creatures" is turned on its head. Even more importantly, Zen, as much as any other sect of Buddhism, looks to acts like this one to express, at least symbolically, its concern for the well-being of all sentient beings.

The Raft is Not the Shore

Having established Zen's credentials as a part of Buddhism does not mean that this sect lacks its own emphases or even special doctrines. Traditionally, Zen's core doctrinal foundation has been expressed by the following four line stanza:

A special transmission outside of the sutras,
Not founded upon words or letters.
Pointing directly at [one's] mind,
One sees into [one's true] nature and realizes Buddhahood.

While scholars today debate the origin and rationale behind the emergence of this stanza, it continues to express the essence of the Zen experience. As the Vietnamese Zen monk, Thich Nhat Hanh has pointed out, this experience is rooted firmly in the teachings of Buddhism's founder, Buddha Shakyamuni, who is reported to have said, "My doctrine is only a raft helping to bring you over to the other shore [of enlightenment], not ultimate reality; you shouldn't worship it."[3] In fact, for Buddhists to be attached to any doctrine, even a Buddhist doctrine, is to betray the spirit of Buddhism.

Is there anything to be learned from this insight in the context of promulgating a Global Ethic? I would suggest there is, namely, that the "words and letters" of the global ethic as contained in this book are just that — only words and letters — guiding means to be sure, but most definitely not "absolute truth" in and of themselves. Ironically, it is modern Zen history in Japan which proves this very point, that is to say, proves just how susceptible even "good words" steeped in "altruistic intentions" are to misuse, or abuse, at the hands of those who would use them to promote their own, often violent, ideologies.

Militarist Zen

As early as the Russo-Japanese War of 1904-5, Shaku Soen (1859-1919), abbot and head of the Engaku-ji branch of the Rinzai Zen sect, had this to say:

> In this world of particulars, the noblest and greatest thing one can achieve is to combat evil and bring it into complete subjection. The moral principle which guided the Buddha throughout his twelve years of preparation and in his forty eight years of religious wanderings, and which pervades his whole doctrine, however varied it may be when practically applied, is nothing else than the subjugation of evil .... War is an evil and a great one, indeed. But war against evils must be unflinchingly prosecuted till we attain the final aim. In the present hostilities, into which Japan has entered with great reluctance, she pursues no egotistic purpose, but seeks the subjugation of evils hostile to civilization, peace, and enlightenment. She deliberated long before she took up arms, as she was aware of the magnitude and gravity of the undertaking. But the firm conviction of the justice of her cause has endowed her with an indomitable courage, and she is determined to carry the struggle to the bitter end.[4]

Soen was not, of course, the only Buddhist leader to justify war from what purported to be a Buddhist viewpoint. Inoue Enryo one of the most noted scholars of Buddhism of the Meiji period, had this to say even before the Russo-Japanese War began:

> Buddhism is a teaching of compassion, a teaching for living human beings. Therefore, fighting on behalf of living humans beings is in accord with the spirit of compassion. In the event hostilities break out between Japan and Russia, it is only natural that Buddhists should fight willingly, for what is this if not repaying the debt of gratitude we owe the Buddha?
>
> It goes without saying that this is a war to protect the state and sustain our fellow countrymen. Beyond that, however, it is the conduct of a Bodhisattva seeking to save untold millions of living souls throughout China and Korea from the jaws of death. Therefore Russia is not only the enemy of our country, it is also the enemy of the Buddha.
>
> In Russia state and religion are one, and there is no religious freedom. Thus, religion is used as a chain in order to unify the [Russian] people. Therefore, when they [the Russian people] see Orientals, they are told that the latter are the bitter enemies of their religion. It is for this reason that on the one hand this is a war of politics and on the other hand it is a war of religion. . . . If theirs is the army of God, then ours is the army of the Buddha.[5]

Though it hardly bears repeating, this "army of the Buddha" which "pursu[ed] no egotistic purpose" did indeed "carry the struggle to the bitter end." The bitterest end, however, was reserved for the Korean people who, as a result of Japan's victory over Russia in 1905, were turned over to Japan for colonization. Hoping to protect its own Asian colony of the Philippines from Japanese encroachment, even the United States endorsed this move through the then secret Taft-Katsura agreement.

As distorted and warped as the above expressions of Buddhism are, they were only early indications of the support Japan's religious leaders would give to Japan's ever expanding, imperial ambitions. In a statement little known in the West, the famous scholar of Zen, D.T. Suzuki, showed that as a young man he, too, was not immune from the siren call of a narrowly formulated nationalism. He wrote:

> If a lawless country comes and obstructs our commerce, or tramples on our rights, this is something that would truly interrupt the progress

of all of humanity. In the name of religion our country could not submit to this. Thus, we would have no choice but to take up arms, not for the purpose of slaying the enemy, nor for the purpose of pillaging cities, let alone for the purpose of acquiring wealth. Instead, we would simply punish the people of the country representing injustice in order that justice might prevail. How is it possible that we could seek anything for ourselves? . . .

At the time of the commencement of hostilities with a foreign country, then marines fight on the sea and soldiers fight in the fields, swords flashing and cannon smoke belching, moving this way and that. In so doing, our soldiers regard their own lives as being as light as goose feathers while their devotion to duty is as heavy as Mt. Taishan [in China]. Should they fall on the battlefield they have no regrets. This is what is called "religion during a [national] emergency." This religion doesn't necessarily have to be described by [the words] "Buddha" or "God." Rather, if one simply discharges one's duty according to one's position [in society], what action could there be that is not religious in nature?[6]

Suzuki's belief that actions on the battlefield, as much as on the domestic front, were fundamentally "religious in nature" was in accord with the view of Japan's Buddhist leaders that they were engaged in a "holy war." Thus, the inevitable deaths accompanying the nation's war effort were equated with the self-sacrificing acts of a Bodhisattva engaged in "establishing eternal peace in East Asia." These very sentiments were expressed in the following proclamation by the leaders of the pan-Buddhist organization, Myowa-kai, issued on 28 July 1937 at the beginning of Japan's full-scale invasion of China. The proclamation read in part:

In order to establish eternal peace in East Asia, arousing the great benevolence and compassion of Buddhism, we are sometimes accepting and sometimes forceful. We now have no choice but to exercise the benevolent forcefulness of "killing one in order that many may live." This is something which Mahayana Buddhism approves of only with the greatest of seriousness. . . .

We believe it is time to make a major change to the course of human history which has been centered on Caucasians and inequality among humanity. To realize the true happiness of a peaceful humanity and construct a new civilization, it is necessary to change the false path into the true path within the advance of world history. Rooted in this sublime view of history, the mission and responsibility of Mahayana Buddhists is to bring into being true friendship between Japan and China.[7]

According to statistics subsequently compiled by the Chinese government, this "true friendship between Japan and China," brought to it with the support of Japan's Mahayana Buddhists, cost it a total of thirty five million dead. This figure does not include, of course, the deaths of hundreds of thousands of other conquered Asian peoples or opposing Allied soldiers, let alone the millions of dead among the Japanese people themselves. All of this was done in the name of "the great benevolence and compassion of Buddhism" in order to "establish eternal peace in East Asia"!

In evaluating the above, it is tempting to see this as either some kind of uniquely Japanese aberration of Buddhism or, alternatively, as an "ethical flaw" in Buddhist doctrine itself. Either, or even both, of these interpretations might be possible were Buddhism the only one of the world's great religions to have ever affirmed the concept of a "holy war."

The historical reality is, of course, that all of the world's major religions have, at some time in their long histories, been part of what are variously called "holy wars," *jihad*, "just wars," etc. It is, for example, only in retrospect that the Christian "Crusades" from the eleventh through thirteenth centuries are recognized as having fallen short, far short, of the teachings of Jesus of Nazareth. Closer to our own times, it must not be forgotten that the leaders of both the Protestant and Roman Catholic churches on the European continent remained silent, on the whole, in the face of Hitler's Holocaust against Jews and other "inferior persons and races." Even more recently, in the ongoing war between Iran and Iraq of the 1980s, both of these self-proclaimed Islamic countries claimed to be engaged in a religious *jihad* against the other. "For God and Country/In the name of Allah, the Merciful" *et al.*, are battle cries that continue to reverberate throughout the world, seemingly without end.

Though contemporary Christians no longer participate (to their credit) in Crusade-like "holy wars," numerous Christian leaders continue to provide allegedly religious justification for that mass-slaughter of one's fellow human beings that is modern warfare. To give but one recent example, there is the following statement made in August 1995 by Major Gary Perry, a Methodist chaplain in the U.S. Air Force stationed at Yokota AFB near Tokyo. When asked about the relationship between the Christian teaching prohibiting killing and the U.S. military, he replied:

> I interpret killing as a willful taking of life for personal gain, or because of hate or convenience. I view the military as an institution that when going to war, takes life to save people. . . . I believe it's sometimes necessary to kill in order to preserve life. Of course, I would always encourage actions short of that.[8]

As the U.S. Cavalry is known to have engaged in the massacre of various Native American tribes on numerous occasions as recently as a hundred years ago, one wonders what Maj. Perry would have thought about this "institution that when going to war, takes life to save people." One would like to ask him, "*Who* was being killed in order to preserve *whose* life?" Or as Daniel Berrigan has put it so eloquently:

> Everybody has always killed the bad guys. Nobody kills the good guys. The Church is tainted in this way as well. The Church plays the same cards; it likes the taste of imperial power too. This is the most profound kind of betrayal I can think of. Terrible! Jews and Christians and Buddhists and all kinds of people who come from a good place, who come from revolutionary beginnings and are descended from heroes and saints. This can all be lost, you know. We can give it all up. And we do. Religion becomes another resource for the same old death game.[9]

Clearly, none of those involved in the creation of Universal Declaration of a Global Ethic wish to see it become yet "another resource for the same old death-game." But how can this be prevented? What is to be done?

"Look at Your Feet!"

The Zen "answer" to the above question is as deceptively simple as it is difficult to practice. It is expressed in Sino-Japanese as "kan kyakka," i.e., "look at [what's going on right under] your feet!" "So what's so difficult about that?" one might ask. As the popular saying tells us, however, "the devil is in the details." That is to say, in the case of the Global Ethic it would be made almost meaningless if each of us is unable, or better said, unwilling, to incorporate its ideals into our daily lives. For example, when taking a shower, do we wet ourselves and then save precious water by turning off the shower head while we lather up, or do we think, "Hey, I'm paying for this, so I'll use just as much water as I want in any way I see fit! Don't talk to me about saving water when there's not even a water shortage in my area!"

With regard to the issue of "water conservation," Soto Zen tradition states that when Zen Master Dogen first founded the temple of Eihei-ji in approximately 1245 C.E., he went daily to a nearby mountain stream to perform his morning ablutions. There he would scoop up a dipper full of water and then pour a third of it back into the stream before using the remainder. Even today, monks at Eihei-ji, like those at other Zen temples, regularly place a few grains of cooked rice from their midday meals on a small wooden tray. Once collected, the rice is then put out for all the creatures of the forest to eat. Through acts like these, symbolic though they be, conservation is seen in the Zen tradition as going hand in hand with concern for the well-being of all.

The world has, of course, made much material progress, especially in technology, since Dogen's day. At present, most of us living in the "developed" world simply turn on our faucets to get what appears to be an endless supply of fresh, safe, drinking water. In addition, though power is no longer generally regarded as being endlessly available, it is still seen as being widely available (for a price) from a variety of sources. At the same time, we know that each of these power sources brings with it environmental costs ranging from increased air pollution up through the dangers arising from global warming and atomic catastrophe.

One part, if not a major part, of the answer to the power dilemma is increased energy conservation, coupled, of course, with enhanced environmentally friendly energy production (through solar, wind, wave, geothermal power, etc.) With regard to energy conservation, we need to ask ourselves whether we do such simple things as turn off our computers before leaving school or office for home, or do we think to ourselves: "Hey, I don't want to wait around for the computer to reboot in the morning when I come in, so I'll save a minute or so by leaving the computer on all night. After all, the company/school can afford it!"

As for concrete expressions of the Buddhist concern for all sentient beings, when we go out to a public park, or even take a walk on a public sidewalk, do we stop to pick up the trash we come across and dispose of it properly, knowing that if we fail to do so the next heavy rain will sweep it into the storm sewer and add just that much more pollution to nearby rivers or the ocean? Do we think to ourselves, "Wherever I go, I want to leave that place just a little cleaner and in better condition than when I came as a way to show my appreciation for the pleasure it gave me and so that the next person will enjoy it just that much more?" Or do we think, "Hey, I didn't make this mess, so don't expect me to get my hands dirty cleaning it up. I've got enough to do just cleaning up my own messes. Anyway, somebody must be getting paid to clean up around here!"

By now, some readers may be thinking that we should be discussing a "global" ethic here, i.e., the "big picture." Yet, if there is a grain of truth in the phrase, "Charity begins at home," then being concerned about the concrete implementation of the Global Ethic within one's immediate environment, within one's daily life, within one's relationships at home and at work, must become a priority. The only person we can "change" with any degree of certainty is ourselves! And each of us, not least of all the smokers and dieters among us, knows just how hard that is!

One of Japan's modern-day architects was famous for the attention he paid to architectural detail that, to the casual lay observer, was most likely never to be noticed. When asked about this, he said, "I don't do this for the benefit of the casual observer, but for myself. If I force myself to pay close attention to the parts of the building that can't be easily seen, the parts that can be seen will take care of themselves." This attitude is very much in accord with the Zen spirit.

Granting this, it must also be admitted that Zen Buddhism, more specifically Zen masters, have all too often used the phrase "kan kyakka" as a kind of brake on examining larger social issues, especially those that might threaten the established (and often unjust) social order. That is to say, such masters were wont to tell their disciples that the latter were unqualified to speak out on the larger issues until they had fully incorporated the Zen spirit into the details of their own daily lives. By the time this happened, often many years later, the fervor that is the prerogative of youth had often disappeared, avoiding any potentially dangerous conflict with the authorities of the day (and thereby preserving the masters in their own positions of importance).

Zen masters, like all those who would adhere to a truly Global Ethic, must come to realize that in the present age of instant electronic communication, the whole world (including space itself) is "at their feet." Today's Middle East war is literally tomorrow's gasoline shortage in mid-America or Japan. One country's air pollution is another country's forest destroying acid rain. One continent's medical crisis quickly becomes the world's medical epidemic. "Enlightened self-interest" alone tells us that we must be concerned with the welfare of not only other human beings on this planet but of the planet itself. When religious compassion and concern for the weak and the poor are added to the mix, the Global Ethic cries out for implementation.

The sceptic may be thinking, "If 'looking at your feet,' didn't prevent the Japanese Zen school from fervently supporting Japanese militarism, what guarantee is there that it will be any more successful in promulgating the Global Ethic?" The answer, of course, is that there is no guarantee. All religion has always depended on the degree of "faith," the level of "awareness" of the believer for its success (and failure). In this the outcome is never guaranteed. Rather, it is left to each generation, to each individual, to plunge into the existential maelstrom to acquire authentic faith. If this degree of uncertainty seems too "uncertain," we need only contemplate the alternative.

The alternative, of course, is what we have seen occurring over and over again, i.e., every individual, group, nation, even "hemisphere," is out for itself, out to make the "quick buck," out to rape the planet of its resources for their immediate benefit and "screw" future generations! The sceptic will say, "Hey, that's what is going to happen anyway. It always has and it always will, Global Ethic or no Global Ethic. 'Do-gooders' should stick to handing out food parcels to the poor!"

As mentioned above, there is no guarantee that the Global Ethic will succeed, with or without the endorsement of the world's religions. Increasing global unrest, accompanied by wars to acquire ever scarcer resources, may well be our collective fate. However, the sceptic fails to understand two important points. The first of these is that without a Global Ethic, i.e., without a collective commitment to "a better, saner, more caring way," then surely we humans will sooner or later destroy ourselves as we make "spaceship earth" uninhabitable for humankind.

Secondly, and most importantly, the religious quest has never depended for its existence on "measurable results." Instead, it is driven by an inner, subjective need to seek "wholeness" and "meaning" at the level of the individual. In the case of Zen, Zen Master Dogen explained it as follows:

> To study the Way is to study the self.
> To study the self is to forget the self.
> To forget the self is to be enlightened by all things.
> To be enlightened by all things is to remove the barriers
>   between one's self and others.[10]

The Global Ethic may fail, though those of us who support it pray that it won't. But succeed or fail, it does offer those of us who participate in it the opportunity to "remove the barriers" that separate us from our fellow human beings, our "brothers and sisters" on this planet. And in a very real, if yet mystical, sense, it offers us the chance to remove the barriers which separate us from the myriads of animate and inanimate beings that comprise this planet, nay, comprise the cosmos itself.

It is this joy of "at oneness," of "wholeness," that awaits the participant in changing the "words and letters" of the Global Ethic printed in this book into a force for positive social change at both individual and collective, micro- and macro-levels. Success or failure of the global ethic at the macro-level cannot destroy the joy of wholeness at the individual or micro-level. But just imagine the joy to be had at seeing ever larger numbers of people, representing diverse creeds and religious traditions, developing links of mutual respect and collective concern for each other and for this planet.

The publication of this Universal Declaration of a Global Ethic marks, if you will, a symbolic "invitation to the ball." But as we all know, it takes "two to tango." The dance cannot begin without you (and, equally, without me), i.e., without each one of "*us*." May we have the pleasure. . . ?

———————————

P.S. Should you decide to come (and even if you don't!), please do remember "to watch those feet!"

P.P.S. Before "rushing on" to the next article, may I invite the reader to reflect for a moment (or longer!) on the following statement by Thich Nhat Hanh, one of today's great Zen masters in the Vietnamese tradition:

> I like to walk alone on country paths, rice plants and wild grasses on both sides, putting each foot down on the earth in mindfulness, knowing that I walk on the wondrous earth. In such moments, existence is a miraculous and mysterious reality. People usually consider walking on water or in thin air a miracle. But I think the real miracle is not to walk either on water or in thin air, but to walk on earth. Every day we are engaged in a miracle which we don't even recognize: a blue sky, white clouds, green leaves, the black, curious eyes of a child - our own two eyes. All is a miracle.[11]

Footnotes

[1] John McRae, "American Scholars In Dialogue With Our Mentors," *1990 Anthology Of Fo Kuang Shan International Buddhist Conference*, p. 536.

[2] Translation appears in Yuho Yokoi with Daizen Victoria, *Zen Master Dogen* (New York: Weatherhill, 1976), p. 62.

[3] Daniel Berrigan and Thich Nhat Hanh, *The Raft Is Not the Shore* (Boston: Beacon Press, 1975), p. 107.

[4] Soyen Shaku, *Zen for Americans* (LaSalle, IL: Open Court, 1974), p. 97.

[5] Enryo Inoue, *Enryo Kowa-shu* (Tokyo: Komeisha, 1904), pp. 299-302.

[6] D. T. Suzuki, "Shin Shukyoron" [A Treatise on New Religion] as contained in Vol. 23, *Suzuki Daisetsu Zenshu* (Tokyo: Iwanami Shoten, 1969), pp. 139-40.

[7] Yujiro Hayashiya and Mei Shimakage, *Bukkyo no Senso-kan* (Tokyo: Daito Shuppansha, 1937), p. 4.

[8] Interview in the August 18, 1995 edition of the *Fuji Flyer* (Yokota Air Force Base, Tokyo), p. 4.

[9] Daniel Berrigan and Thich Nhat Hanh, *The Raft Is Not the Shore*, p. 34.

[10] Translation appears in Yuho Yokoi with Daizen Victoria, *Zen Master Dogen*, p. 5.

[11] Thich Nhat Hanh, *The Miracle of Mindfulness* (Boston: Beacon Press, 1975-76), p. 12.

TOWARD A UNIVERSAL DECLARATION OF A GLOBAL ETHIC: A CATHOLIC PERSPECTIVE

INGRID SHAFER

THE FOLLOWING REFLECTIONS are intended to apply not only to Leonard Swidler's and Hans Küng's contributions to the task of developing a global ethic but to the enterprise as such, which should eventually involve individuals and groups from all over the world. Viewed as complementary efforts, the Küng and Swidler approaches provide an object lesson of the manner in which such an ambitious project could proceed (and succeed). With his historical and methodological focus, Swidler sets the stage and provides an open-ended, dialogical framework not only for himself but for countless others who might wish to be part of this effort of the earth-community. The two internally connected Küng declarations, on the other hand, are the carefully developed prototype of what concerned citizens throughout the world should be doing from the perspective of their own grass roots. These documents are especially important because they not only represent one man's vision, but that one man's vision revised and expanded in dialogue with the delegates to the Parliament of the World's Religions and members of the InterAction Council. Hence the Küng double declaration is not merely one among many individual statements waiting to be reconciled, but a mini-version of "the" Global Ethic yet to be developed.

It is not at all surprising that Hans Küng and Leonard Swidler, the two pioneers of the international and ecumenical movement toward drafting a global ethic, are Catholic[1] scholars, committed to the vision of Church enunciated by the Second Vatican Council.[2] Neither is it surprising that they are not at the moment particularly popular with the Curia. During the current pontificate many of the more liberating ideals put forth during the Council are being quietly domesticated and even reversed. However, in a dynamic Church this reaction was to be anticipated and is bound to generate its own countermovement in due time. In the words of the director of a pastoral ministry program in a conservative diocese, "the Genie is out of the bottle and they won't be able to stuff it back in." After all, even apparently revolutionary and novel teachings of the Second Vatican Council had their tent poles securely anchored in the vast, many-colored Catholic canopy. This Catholic canopy had permitted a great deal of diversity within the Church prior to the siege mentality generated in reaction to the Reformation and even in the centuries of the "Garrison Church" continued to support a wide variety of national approaches to "being Catholic." This world-wide diversity (distinguishing Japanese, Irish, Polish, Italian, French, and German Catholics, for example) became part of the "American experiment" as immigrants from all over the globe arrived in this country. It can still be seen in the neighborhoods of major cities throughout the U.S. and is living proof that unity and diversity can complement and enrich one another.

As many of the most significant Council documents, the very notion of a global ethic is deeply embedded in that Christian strand which inspired Cardinal Nicolas of Cusa's (1401-1464) appreciation for religious diversity[3] and gave birth to Catholicism's "changeling child,"[4] the European Enlightenment. Despite the animosity of many "Enlightened Rulers" toward the institutional Church, there is no doubt that the call for liberty, brotherhood, equality, and respect for diversity represents the very best Christianity has to offer and is infinitely closer to the message of Jesus than the crusading intolerance that burned witches, Jews, and heretics, ignited the assorted religious wars of the 17th century, and prepared the seedbed for the Holocaust.[5] Overall, the Enlightenment is an extraordinarily important and in most ways very beneficial movement, but one which is both complex and ambivalent. On the one hand, it liberated many of its disciples from childish ignorance, superstition, and intolerance—in the words of Immanuel Kant, from "selfimposed minority"[6]—but on the other hand it also tended to vilify its intellectual parent and offer caricatures of enemies to be immolated on the altar of rationality and Western thought in general. The progenitor of both the Enlightenment and Vatican II is that strand of the Christian braid which combines the notion of the Stoic cosmopolis with emphasis on the Incarnation, the kingdom of God on Earth, the sacramentality of the world, the linking of reason and faith, the primacy of conscience, service, community, the Golden Rule, following Jesus through acts of kindness, loving one's enemies, the liberation of the powerless, and the essential equality as human beings of men and women, sovereigns and subjects.

As Leonard Swidler points out, the Church "is in a position similar to that of the parent and the teacher. In fact, the Church is often referred to as 'Holy Mother Church,' and one of the most vital functions of the Church is to fulfill its mission to proclaim the Gospel, to be a teacher of the nations, to exercise magisterium.If this is true, then at least one of the major goals of the Church must also be that of the parent and the teacher—the development of maturity in those for whom it has concern."[7] In other words, it is the task of the teacher to help students to hone their critical skills and creative powers, to become autonomous, and to think for themselves. Good parents do not confine toddlers to the play pen and teenagers to safely fenced yards.

Of course, we have to keep in mind that this is not the only definition of proper parenting. There are those who would insist that parents should permanently think for their children, protecting them from the evil that lurks within their psyche and threatens them from outside. This attitude is also part of the Catholic tradition and would tend to oppose the democratic approach to developing a global ethic proposed by Swidler and Küng. Swidler continues, "Fortunately, with Vatican II Catholics began to find ways for increasing numbers of the faithful to act as free, responsible adults in the Church."[8] It is precisely this faith in humanity that authoritarian Catholics find so disturbing.

Those newly empowered adults became increasingly aware of their calling in the course of that Council. Pope John XXIII had convoked this universal synod—the largest and first ever truly global ecumenical council—and became its beacon. But the Council might still have turned into little more than 2500 bishops agreeing on the agenda and routinely rubber-stamping documents sent down from above—prepared in advance and circulated by various Commissions—if it had not been for Achille Cardinal Lienart's courageous wake-up call at the very beginning of the first working session. The French Cardinal, seconded by Joseph Cardinal Frings of Cologne, challenged the assembled fathers to take personal control of the proceedings and claim the Council authentically for themselves—to elect representatives from national groups, to write their own documents, to forge coalitions and learn to dialogue—in sum, to work ground-up from the episcopal grass roots and give the democratic process a chance.[9]

Hence, at the Council's very inception implicitly there was already the call which would transform the self-image of the Church as constituted not solely or even primarily by the Roman pontiff and magisterium, but as incarnated initially in the voting bishops and ultimately in the *sensus fidelium* of all the People of God—including but not limited to ordained bishops, priests, and pope. The realization that "We are the Church" was born, and from then on Catholics everywhere began to feel responsible for their church not as meek and unreflective assenting automata, "bumps in the pews," but as active collaborators called to build the Pilgrim Church. This was a Church, many among the faithful were beginning to realize, which was unchanging only in the sense that it was itself a process of growth and renewal, called from the very beginning to reflection and continuous reform in the Spirit of Dialogue, Compassion, and Love.

On September 28, 1964, during the discussion of the *Declaration on Relgious Liberty*, the Pope's personal theologian, Bishop Carlo Colombo said bluntly, "If there is no dialogue among men, they will not find integral truth."[10] The age of intellectual and spiritual despotism was coming to an end. Fesquet summarizes the Council's accomplishment as "we may say that Vatican II has shaken the conviction widely held by Catholics that doctrine is unchangeable. The whole course of the Council has proven the contrary; everything that is not strictly an article of faith is subject to changes according to the wellknown adage, *Ecclesia semper reformanda* ("The eternally to be reformed Church")."[11]

This radical turn, of course, was opposed by a minority of Council participants (eventually leading to the departure and excommunication of Archbishop Marcel Lefebvre) and has never been accepted by those fearful paternalistic partisans of the status quo who are passionately attached to Saint Augustine's not quite ex-Manichean two city cosmology and the Tridentine "Fortress Church" under perpetual siege. Clearly, those Catholics did not "hear" Pope John XXIII's message condemning the "prophets of gloom" as ultimately un-Catholic:

> We feel we must disagree with those prophets of gloom, who are always forecasting disaster, as though the end of the world were at hand. In the present order of things, Divine Providence is leading us to a new order of human relations which, by men's own efforts and even beyond their very expectations, are directed toward the fufillment of God's superior and inscrutable designs. And everything, even human differences, leads to the greater good of the Church.[12]

Human efforts! This attitude is worlds removed from that of Pius X who insisted less than 60 years earlier that:

> Our predecessor Pius IX wrote: "These enemies of divine revelation extol human progress to the skies, and with rash and sacrilegious daring would have it introduced into the Catholic religion as if this religion were not the work of God but of man, or some kind of philosophical discovery susceptible of perfection by human efforts." . . . [T]he doctrine of the Modernists offers nothing new. We find it condemned in the Syllabus of Pius IX, where it is enunciated in these terms: "Divine revelation is imperfect, and therefore subject to continual and indefinite progress, corresponding with the progress of human reason"; and condemned still more solemnly in the Vatican Council: "The doctrine of the faith which God has revealed has not been proposed to human intelligences to be perfected by them as if it were a philosophical system, but as a divine deposit entrusted to the Spouse of Christ to be faithfully guarded and infallibly interpreted. Hence also that sense of the sacred dogmas is to be perpetually retained which our Holy Mother the Church has once declared, nor is this sense ever to be abandoned on plea or pretext of a more profound comprehension of the truth."[13]

The current age is finally giving us an opportunity to transcend this kind of "either/or" antagonism and draw strength from another, non-adversarial, and even more ancient Christian tradition: the Catholic tendency to think in terms of the fluid, permeable boundaries of the incarnational "both/and" paradigm—the paradigm which can inspire and support a non-imperialistic global ethic based on respect for pluralism and grounded in the conviction, to cite Küng, "of the fundamental unity of the human family."

While my focus in this essay is on Vatican II, the Council did not engender its vision in a vacuum but out of a fundamental strand of the Catholic tradition, and it is that same strand which makes Catholicism such an appropriate progenitrix of a global ethic. Years before the notion of a global ethic emerged, Andrew Greeley, in a fascinating little monograph, *No Bigger than Necessary*, pointed to those aspects of Catholic social theory which would turn out to be crucial for the implementation of the Küng/Swidler paradigms of a global ethic—the principles of personalism, subsidiarity, and pluralism:

> *Rerum novarum* was essentially a defense of the rights of the working man combined with a vigorous condemnation of nineteenth-century socialism. Forty years after the encyclical *Quadragesimo anno* came closer to articulating a positive Catholic view of an organic society in particular by laying out the three cardinal principles of Catholic social theory: personalism, subsidiarity, and pluralism. Personalism insists that the goal of the society is to develop and enrich the individual human person; the state and society exist for the person and not vice versa. Subsidiarity insists that no organization should be bigger than necessary and that nothing should be done by a large and higher social unit than can be done effectively by a lower and smaller unit. Pluralism contends that a healthy society is characterized by a wide variety of intermediate groups freely flourishing between the individual and the state.[14]

In an utterly unexpected development, Vatican II abandoned centuries of navel-gazing and triumphalist insistence of the Catholic Church that there was only One Truth, the Catholic Truth, and only One Concern, otherworldly salvation, to be granted exclusively to those who followed the Catholic Truth. Instead, the Council acknowledged the value of pluralism, turned its attention to the role of the Church in the world, and called on Catholics everywhere to collaborate with others—including Protestants, atheists, and nonbelievers in general—to achieve global justice on earth. Reading the Vatican II documents, one finds it almost inconceivable that exactly a century earlier, in 1864,

Pope Pius IX had issued the notorious "Syllabus of Errors" which insisted that it was a serious error for a Catholic to argue that "the Roman Pontiff can and ought to reconcile and harmonize himself with progress, with liberalism, and with modern civilization."[15] Eventually, Pius IX tried to anathemize not only liberalism, but democracy, science, and any contact with non-Catholics.

The contrast with Vatican II is stunning. In their opening "Message to Humanity" the Council Fathers "look forward to a spiritual renewal from which will also flow a happy impulse on behalf of human values such as scientific discoveries, technological advances, and a wider diffusion of knowledge." They continue: "As we undertake our work, therefore, we would emphasize whatever concerns the dignity of man, whatever contributes to a genuine community of peoples." Finally, and most significantly, they "humbly and ardently call for all men to work along with us in building up a more just and brotherly city in this world."[16]

This is the spirit of Pope John XXIII, this great champion of human rights and human liberty. In *Pacem in terris* he calls the Universal Declaration of Human Rights "an act of the highest importance," adding that "the recognition and respect of those rights and respective liberties is proclaimed as a goal to be achieved by all peoples and all countries."[17] He considers the Declaration:

> an important step on the path towards the juridical-political organization of all the peoples of the world. For in it, in most solemn form, the dignity of a human person is acknowledged to all human beings; and as a consequence there is proclaimed, as a fundamental right, the right of every man freely to investigate the truth and to follow the norms of moral good and justice, and also the right to a life worthy of man's dignity, while other rights connected with those mentioned are likewise proclaimed.[18]

Greeley notes that:

> In *Mater et magistra* and *Pacem in terris*, Pope John brought to brilliant fruition the theorizing of the previous seven decades. *Mater et magistra* updated *Quadragesimo anno* and laid out a strong, positive defense of the integrity of the human person and the social rights and obligations of that person in the modern world. Much less than his predecessors was John disturbed by the world he saw around

him, and much more than any pope in recent memory was he capable of seeing the opportunity in the human quest for freedom, justice, and dignity, and the contributions the Catholic tradition could make to that quest. In *Pacem in terris* he turned to the world economic and political order and, in what may be the most successful of all papal encyclicals, applied to world problems the Catholic social theoretical perspective.[19]

Contrast these encyclicals with Pope Leo XIII's insistence in 1888 that the doctrine of human rights is:

> most hurtful both to individuals and to the State. For, once ascribe to human reason the only authority to decide what is true and what is good, and the real distinction between good and evil is destroyed; honor and dishonor differ not in their nature, but in the opinion and judgment of each one; pleasure is the measure of what is lawful; and, given a code of morality which can have little or no power to restrain or quiet the unruly propensities of man, a way is naturally opened to universal corruption[20]

As recently as 31 December 1930, Pius XI condemned the equality of women in *Casti conubii*: insisting on the "primacy of the husband with regard to the wife and children, the ready subjection of the wife and her willing obedience, ..."[21] He continued:

> The same false teachers who try to dim the luster of conjugal faith and purity do not scruple to do away the with the honorable and trusting obedience which the woman owes to the man. Many of them even go further an assert that such a subjection of one party to the other is unworthy of human dignity, that the rights of husband and wife are equal; wherefore, they boldly proclaim the emancipation of women has been or ought to be effected. . . . [T]hat is to say, the woman is to be freed at her own good pleasure from the burdensome duties properly belonging to a wife as companion and mother (We have already said that this is not an emancipation but a crime). . . [22]

In tune with Teilhard de Chardin's (1881-1955) cautiously optimistic vision of the Church as part of God's evolutionary process and Karl Rahner's (1904-1985) incarnational notion of the "sacramentality of the world," the Council documents remind us that there is much in the world that is good, that the perceived contradiction between Church and World is a false dichotomy, and that both Church and World can and should learn from the other. This is the approach taken by Swidler when he suggests the Golden Rule as the foundation for a Global Ethic:

> It could well start with—though not limit itself to—elements of the so-called "Golden Rule" . . . which for thousands of years has been affirmed in many religious and ethical traditions, as a fundamental principle upon which to base a global ethic: "What you do not wish done to yourself, do not do to others," or in positive terms, "What you wish done to yourself, do to others." This rule should be valid not only for one's own family, friends, community and nation, but also for all other individuals, families, communities, nations, the entire world, the cosmos.

Rahner's notion is an extension of St. Thomas' *analogia entis*, the "analogy of being," which reflects the traditional Catholic supposition that God is like what is best in the world, only infinitely more so, and that human reason is a God-given path to truth, albeit one to be supplemented by faith. This whole set of assumptions is rejected by the paradigmatic Protestant theologian Karl Barth (1886-1968) who focuses on the chasm that separates God's infinite goodness and the fallen state of humanity. He insists on the worthlessness of human reason and all secular cultural an intellectual achievements which he views as mired in sin.

Of course, since the Reformation has Catholic roots, this dualistic focus on original sin and the God-World dichotomy has been part of the Catholic tradition almost from the beginning as well, and was canonized for posterity by Paul and Augustine—in contrast to the Jew Jesus "who came that you may have life, and live more abundantly." Currently it tends to be characteristic of those extreme conservatives who reject Vatican II, along with members of several cult-like so-called "new movements," such as Opus Dei, the Legionnaires of Christ, Focolare, Communion and Liberation, and the Neocatechumenate,[23] all of which have global ambitions and are bound to either oppose or seek to insert their own agenda into any Global Ethic Declaration. During a post-Parliament of the World's Religions symposium on the Küng draft of the Global Ethic at the Lutheran School of Theology in Chicago, I had a long conversation with a committed member of Focolare and was initially very attracted by his emphasis on universal love. However, I was soon taken aback by what seemed like his veneration of Chiara Lubich, Focolare's founder, coupled with his wholesale rejection of the secular values of the contemporary word and a general "group-think" attitude. The longer I listened, the more I sensed similarities to a couple of gentle Hare Krishna monks who did their best to convert me in 1969.

Paradoxically, Pope John Paul II is an outspoken supporter of these movements and their agenda (while there are clearly distinctions between those groups, they all share sharp opposition to the world-affirming, and relatively tolerant vision of Vatican II). Since those movements, too, have global ambitions, the kind of Global Ethic envisioned by Küng and Swidler would be seen as competition. The very notion of religious or ideological pluralism and the call for a grassroots up, democratic approach to developing such an ethic has as its premise trust in humanity. It is anathema to those who consider all people by nature under the sway of Satan, extol the superiority of celibacy over the married state, distrust both human experience and reason, want to return to the pre-Vatican II authoritarian model of blind obedience to a leader (whether priest, bishop, pope or some charismatic founder), and cannot even envision authentic ecumenical dialogue which is not designed to proselytize. In fact, the most determined enemies of a global ethic in all religious traditions would be extreme fundamentalists who insist that their way is the best and only way and are literally incapable of genuine dialogue because they cannot grant others the right they presume for themselves—the right to be deeply committed to their own faith.

As for Catholics, we must acknowledge that the association of the notions of dialogue and evangelization may seem automatic to some Christians, even to those who view themselves as ecumenically inclined. Pope Paul VI dedicates most of the encyclical *Ecclesiam suam* (6 Aug. 1964) to the power of what he calls dialogue, but he clearly does not mean by the term fully what Leonard Swidler does. On the one hand, like Swidler, he insists that: "our own dialogue should be potentially universal, i.e., all-embracing and capable of including all, excepting only one who would either absolutely reject it or insincerely pretend to accept it,"[24] but on the other hand, he views dialogue clearly as path of evangelization:

Well do we know that "going, therefore, make disciples of all nations" [#41] is the last command of Christ to His Apostles. By the very term "apostles" these men define their inescapable mission. To this internal drive of charity which tends to become the external gift of charity we will give the name of dialogue, which has in these days come into common usage.

The Church should enter into dialogue with the world in which it exists and labors. The Church has something to say; the Church has a message to deliver; the Church has a communication to offer.[25]

Paul continues that this kind of dialogue "compels us to declare openly our conviction that there is but one true religion, the religion of Christianity. It is our hope that all who seek God and adore Him may come to acknowledge its truth."[26] However, he then takes the radical step toward a new era of ecumenism by adding that:

We do, nevertheless, recognize and respect the moral and spiritual values of the various non-Christian religions, and we desire to join with them in promoting and defending common ideals of religious liberty, human brotherhood, good culture, social welfare and civil order. For our part, we are ready to enter into discussion on these common ideals, and will not fail to take the initiative where our offer of discussion in genuine, mutual respect, would be well received.[27]

This approach differs sharply from the Neocatechumenal understanding. According to Kiko Arguello, the co-founder of the Neocatechumenate, "Man . . . is dominated by the serpent, by the devil, by death, by sin."[28] After listing the evils which ensnare humanity, such as the pursuit of wealth, fame, marriage, children, and sexuality, Arguello begins to echo Cornelius Jansen (1585-1638) whose pessimistic determinism was condemned as heretical in the 17th century. Jansen taught that the fulfilment of God's commandments is impossible without special grace and that the operation of grace is irresistible. Jansenism was distinguished by harshness and extreme moral rigorism and opposed to the Jesuit nuanced approach. In a similar spirit, Arguello insists:

Man cannot do good because he has separated himself from God, because he has sinned and because he has been rendered radically powerless and useless, under the sway of the devil. He is slave to the devil. The devil is his Lord. (That is why neither advice nor sermons of encouragement are any use. Man cannot do good). . . [You] are a servant of the devil that manipulates you as he wills, because he is much more powerful than you. You cannot fulfil the law, because the law tells you to love, not to resist evil, but you cannot: you do what the evil one wants.[29]

Both Pope Paul VI and Pope John Paul II have praised the Neocate-chumenate for its evangelizing efforts.However, it seems doubtful (one hopes) that either pope really knew/knows the extent to which dual-ism pervades the movement.[30] In a general audience for members of the Neocatechumenal Way on January 12, 1977, Paul VI said:

He who knows how to see, to read, into the heart of the masses, the heart of the world, sees that deep down there is discontent, there is restlessness, there is need of a true word, a good word, a word which tells the meaning of life!. . . We have the lantern, we have the lamp, we have the Word of the Gospel, which becomes the light of the world. The Lord told his apostles, *you are the light of the world.* Well, if we are the light of the world, we must go towards these people who are lost, who are so angry, so cruel, who have become so disorien-tated, so without principles, without lines of conduct which are good and human; we must go towards them and say: Look, this is the path, here is the way.[31]

He continued: "Many people are attracted to these Neocate-chumenal Communities, because they see that there is a sincerity, a truth in them, something alive and authentic, Christ living in the world. May this happen with our Apostolic Blessing."[32] Surely insisting that the human person is "slave to the devil" and that "the devil is his Lord" does not indicate the connection of goodness and humanity Paul pre-sumes and is not a way of being the light of the world.[33]

Over the years, Pope John Paul II has had many opportunities to investigate this movement, and it is disquieting, to say the least, that he gave this approach to evangelization his at least semi-official stamp of approval in a personal letter which states, "I recognize the Neocatechumenal Way as an internary [sic; this should, I presume, be "itinerary"] of Catholic formation, valid for today's society and times."[34] He also praises the movement for its missionary drive, conversions, and vocations to religious life and the priesthood. One wonders if the Pope is aware of the Neocatechumenal belief that attachment to one's children is idolatry, that human love kills, that youngsters are damaged by their parents' neurotic love, and that they should therefore be turned over to the movement where they can be raised in a closed environment and discouraged from thinking and choosing for themselves.[35] This clearly contradicts his focus on the family.

As we have already seen in some of the opposing papal pronouncements, it is important to realize that the Catholic Church is not now—and never has been—a monolith, that believers all the way up to the popes frequently disagree, and that consequently any Catholic commentary on the two present drafts of a Global Ethic will not be representative of the Church as a whole. This is the main reason—in addition to my deep admiration for John XXIII—that I have chosen to gauge the Global Ethic proposals by the documents of the Second Vatican Council and the central position given to the notion of dialogue with the "other" in those documents.

The key concept here is "dialogue and collaborate" rather than "disinfect and condemn." In fact, the *Declaration on Christian Education* positively acknowledges the pluralistic character of modern society, and praises state agencies for taking "into account the right of religious liberty, by helping families in such a way that in all schools the education of their children can be carried out according to the moral and religious convictions of each family."[36]

The *Pastoral Constitution in the Church in the Modern World* (*Gaudium et spes:* appropriately entitled "Joy and Hope"), according to Henri Fesquet[37] and Donald R. Campion, S.J.,[38] the most characteristic or the very crux of the Council documents, and one called for from the Council floor by an intervention of Léon-Joseph Cardinal Suenens,[39] points to the Church putting itself into the service of the human family.[40] Main themes of *Gaudium et spes* are precisely the kinds of *leitmotifs* that pervade both the Küng and Swidler "Global Ethic" drafts: the dignity of the human person, the community of humankind and nations of the earth, and the fostering of peace by seeking justice in the economic, social, and political spheres across the globe.[41] "Throughout the Constitution," we read in the introduction to the English translation, "there is a strongly personalist note and a concurrent optimism about the future of the human family if all communities can come to emphasize the importance not only of truth, justice, and love but also of freedom for a sound society of man."[42]

Gaudium et spes bridges and heals the pessimistic dualism that has for so long, and particularly since the Protestant Reformation, vitiated certain understandings of the Church. We note a humanistic thrust that evokes the Italian Renaissance exuberance of Pico della Mirandola's "Oration on the Dignity of Man" with its focus on humans formed in God's image: "Thus, far from thinking that works produced by man's own talent and energy are in opposition to God's power, and that the rational creature exists as a kind of rival to the Creator, Christians are convinced that the triumphs of the human race are a sign of God's greatness and the flowering of his own mysterious design."[43] The passage concludes: "Hence it is clear that men are not deterred by the Christian message from building up the world, or impelled to neglect the welfare of their fellows. They are, rather, more stringently bound to do these very things."[44] Vatican II reminds us that Catholics are called, in the words of Teilhard, "to build the earth."

What are the historic origins of this puzzling conjunction of opposing tracks in the Christian story which make it possible for people to consider themselves "good Catholics" while refusing to acknowledge a large portion of the Catholic heritage along with some of the most essential reforms initiated by Vatican II? The Western intellectual tradition interweaves a Greco-Roman strand with a Judeo-Christian strand. The former stresses moderation, rationality, humanistic learning, objectivity, as well as the superiority of men over women and spirit over matter. The latter separated into two further branches, the dominant "right-handed" ascetic-spiritual-judgmental branch of the Church Fathers and the subordinate "left-handed" humane-earthy-optimistic branch of the people. The Fathers envisioned God as primarily Ruler/Judge, the material world as evil, and people as fallen creatures in need of harsh discipline and stern guidance. The people envisioned God as loving Parent (at least in his feminine dimension as Mother Mary), the material world as neutral and potentially sacramental, and themselves as fallible but also blessed and capable of doing good. They readily baptized and absorbed pagan elements, turned gods and goddesses into saints, composed and enjoyed the songs of bards and troubadours, joined spiritual and erotic love, delighted in grail quest tales and bawdy scholars' songs, and managed to sneak many of their beliefs into official teachings through the back door. In particular, they venerated the ancient Great Mother in her Christian incarnation as the Virgin who would intercede with her Son to protect them from stern Yahweh's wrath.[45]

In Western Europe the various branches remained braided in vibrant (if occasionally belligerent) tension under the single Catholic tent until the 16th century. After the Reformation they separated. Protestants (particularly Calvinists) tended to adopt the fault-finding mode which focuses on original sin and human depravity—emphasizing divine transcendence. Members of the Catholic hierarchy, popes and bishops, generally also identified with the authoritarian fault-finding mode. On the other hand, parish priests and most lay people continued to prefer the compassionate mode—emphasizing divine immanence. Elite ideas were primarily formed by combining the Greco-Roman strand with some aspects of the acerbic Judeo-Christian branch. Since the guardians of ethical principles are generally members of the intellectual elite, our official concepts of moral standards tend to be drawn from Greco-Roman antiquity and the pessimistic, critical branch of the Judeo-Christian tradition (including its heresy: Marxism). Hence, it is not surprising that moral and aesthetic critics generally prefer a tragic or ironic vision which is at odds with the alternate Catholic tradition of hopefulness, but perfectly in tune with the contemporary high culture sense of post-modern social atomism, cosmic absurdity, cynicism, and condemnation of such supposedly all-pervasive Western sins as "the culture of death" (Pope John Paul II's catch-all phrase for assorted evils from birth control and abortion to full gender equality and homosexual acts) and "consumerism."

In fact, the battle and interplay of these two modes of religious imagination constitute the cultural matrix of the West, the Platonic-Augustinian dialectical strand (leading to such as Søren Kierkegaard and Karl Barth) and the Aristotelian-Thomistic analogical strand (leading to such as Teilhard de Chardin, Karl Rahner, and David Tracy).[46] Applying this paradigm, we can classify Christians into those who tend to reject and criticize versus those who tend to adopt and adapt; those who focus on divine transcendence versus those who focus on divine immanence; those who see the world fractured by original sin, versus those who see the world connected by original blessing; those for whom God is primarily a distant if righteous Father/ King/ Judge versus those for whom God is primarily a close and caring Father-Mother/ Friend/ Lover.[47]

The humanistic and democratic agenda propelled into the foreground by Vatican II for the Catholic Church can be easily translated into the general and supra-national set of basic human rights and responsibilities, in other words, a global ethic. Such church-specific demands as the call for the ordination of married men and women, democratization of the Church and reduction of papal authority, relative autonomy for national churches, regular ecumenical councils or synods, tolerance for theological dissent, and a flexible approach to sexual morality turn into an overall emphasis on respect for human persons and a willingness to "listen" to diverse local conditions—the "signs of the times." In this perspective, a democratized global Catholic Church can become a major force for liberating people everywhere, not only for the hereafter but by becoming part of a vital faith community, in the here and now, in their own religious or ideological tradition, whatever it may be.[48] Simultaneously, in a corresponding counter-movement, work on and eventual acceptance of a Global Ethic will strengthen the democratic tendencies in the Church. Ultimately, there is no more meaningful and pressing concern for Catholics at the edge of the third millennium of the Christian era than pursuing the vision of a world in which all of us, no matter how different, can imagine ourselves as siblings, united by some version of the ancient Golden Rule, working together toward peace and justice.[49]

Footnotes

1 After the 19th century era of economic and democratic upheavals with the concurrent awakening of social consciousness in the West and specifically since the pontificate of Leo XIII (1878-1903), popes have been issuing a series of official letters and encyclicals dealing with a wide range of what we would now consider "justice issues" or even issues related to an emergent global ethic. Those papal injunctions were clearly intended to be universal, since the church envisioned itself as the sole legitimate source of values and moral standards for all of humanity everywhere at all times. The popes tended to follow the example of Saint Thomas (1225-1274) who had addressed such practical issues as selling items for more than they were worth or charging interest by placing them in the context of, to use a contemporary category, "Catholic social theory." In contrast to the earlier post-Tridentine

documents with their otherworldly orientation, most of the official magisterial utterances of the past century are clearly concerned with life in this world and address a spectrum of concerns pertaining to human relationships, including church and state, individual and society, employers and employees, men and women, parents and children. They also demonstrate that Catholic social theory has changed significantly over the past century from authoritarian paternalism to genuine advocacy of human freedom and accountability. For an excellent summary of those developments, see Charles E. Curran's chapter on the "Changing Anthropological Bases" in *Moral Theology: A Continuing Journey* (Notre Dame, IN: University of Notre Dame Press, 1982), esp. pp. 175-208.

2 The Second Vatican Council (1962-1965), popularly called "Vatican II" is the last of a series of 21 ecumenical councils which have over the centuries determined the path of the Catholic Church, beginning with the Council of Nicea (325 CE). Vatican II represents a 180 degree turn away from the direction taken by the post-Reformation Council of Trent (1545-1563) and the First Vatican Council (1869-1870), both of which emphasized the hierarchical nature of the Church, papal authority, Catholicism as exclusive path to salvation, and absolute obedience of the laity. Among the most stunning declarations of Vatican II were the decrees on ecumenism (*Unitatio redintegratio*), religious freedom (*Dignitatis humanae*), and non-Christians (*Nostra aetate*). The latter states that "The Catholic Church rejects nothing which is true and holy in these religions" (Abbott, p. 662) and strongly repudiates at least a millennium of anti-Judaism: "[M]indful of her common patrimony with the Jews, and motivated by the gospel's spiritual love and by no political considerations, she deplores the hatred, persecutions, and displays of anti-Semitism directed against the Jews at any time and from any source." (Ibid., pp. 666-667). It seems inconceivable that it took the cosmic crime of the Holocaust to serve as a belated wake-up call to our Church founded by Yeshua the Jew.

3 Nicolas writes, "It happened after some days, perhaps as the fruit of an intense and sustained meditation, that a vision appeared to this ardently devoted Man. In this vision it was manifested that by means of a few sages versed in the variety of religions that exist throughout the world it could be possible to reach a certain peaceful concord. And it is through this concord that a lasting peace in religion may be attained and established by convenient and truthful means." Cited in Raimundo Panikkar, *The Intrareligious Dialogue* (New York: Paulist Press, 1978), p. ix.

4 Leonard Swidler, *Toward a Catholic Constitution* (New York: Crossroad, 1996), p. 9.

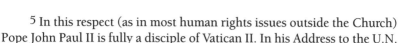

5 In this respect (as in most human rights issues outside the Church) Pope John Paul II is fully a disciple of Vatican II. In his Address to the U.N. he writes:

Our century has seen the ultimate consequences of Christian Jewish policies of bygone eras. Today, 40 years after the outbreak of World War II, I wish to recall the whole of the experiences by individuals and nations that were sustained by a generation that is largely still alive. I had occasion not long ago to reflect again on some of those experiences, in one of the places that are most distressing and over-flowing with contempt for man and his fundamental rights—the extermination camp of Oswiecim (Auschwitz), which I visited during my pilgrimage to Poland last June. . . .

You will forgive me, ladies and gentlemen, for evoking this memory. But I would be untrue to the history of this century, I would be dishonest with regard to the great cause of man, which we all wish to serve, if I should keep silent, I who come from the country on whose living body Oswiecim was at one time constructed. But my purpose in invoking this memory is above all to show what painful experiences and sufferings by millions of people gave rise to the Universal Declaration of Human Rights, which has been placed as the basic inspiration and cornerstone of the United Nations organization. This declaration was paid for by millions of our brothers and sisters at the cost of their suffering and sacrifice, brought about by the brutalization that darkened and made insensitive the human consciences of their oppressors and of those who carried out a real genocide. This price cannot have been paid in vain! The Universal Declaration of Human Rights—with its train of many declarations and conventions on highly important aspects of human rights, in favor of children, of women, of equality between races, and especially the two international covenants on economic; social and cultural rights and on civil and political rights—must remain the basic value in the United Nations with which the consciences of its members must be confronted and from which they must draw continual inspiration. (*Address to the United Nations General Assembly*, October 2, 1979)

One cannot help but contrast this papal statement with Pope Bendict XIV's encyclical on the Polish Jews. In *A quo primum* (14 June 1751) he praised the Polish bishops for prohibiting the principle of freedom of conscience and for having done "all they could to aid the Poles in their resistance to the Jews."(#1) He then expressed his deep concern over recent changes in Jewish-Christian relationship, specifically that the number of Jews had increased considerably, that they controlled businesses and estates,(#2) and that "It is now even commonplace for Christians and Jews to intermingle anywhere."(#3) He cites Innocent III, who "after saying that Jews were being received by Christians into their cities, warns that the method and condition of this reception should guard against their repaying the benefit with evildoing. `They on being admitted to our acquaintance in a spirit of mercy, repay us, the popular proverb says, as the mouse in the wallet, the snake in the lap and fire in the bosom usually repay their host.'" (#5)

While Benedict advocates that Christians should not kill Jews, he does so with a reference to Saint Bernard's insistence that the Jews should be spared, so they could be perpetually punished or converted: "Alive, however, they are eminent reminders for us of the Lord's suffering. On this account they are scattered through all lands in order that they may be witnesses to Our redemption while they pay the just penalties for so great a crime (epistle 363)." Bendecit adds another Bernard citation: "Doesn't the Church every day triumph more fully over the Jews in convicting or converting them than if once and for all she destroyed them with the edge of the sword . . . (epistle 365)."

6 "Ausgang des Menschen aus seiner selbstverschuldeten Unmündigkeit," in Immanuel Kant, *Was ist Aufklärung?* (Stuttgart: Reklam/Erhart Bahr, 1974) p. 9.

7 *Toward a Catholic Constitution*, p. 29.

8 Ibid.

9 Henri Fesquet, *The Drama of Vatican II: The Ecumenical Council June, 1962-December, 1965* (New York: Random House, 1967), pp. 21-22

10 Ibid., p. 355

11 Ibid.

12 Walter S. Abbot, S.J., ed., *The Documents of Vatican II* (New York: Herder and Herder, 1966) pp. 712-713.

13 [#14-15]] (Pius X, September 8, 1907 *Pascendi Dominici gregis*, 28). The Vatican Council mentioned is the First Vatican Council (1869-1870) and culminated in the doctrine of the Infallibility of the Roman Pontiff when he speaks *ex cathedra* on an issue of faith or morals.

14 Andrew Greeley, *No Bigger than Necessary* (New York: New American Library, 1977) Greeley continues:

> In the wake of *Quadragesimo anno* there was a flowering of Catholic social-action movements. in the United States. In the 1930s and 1940s there were Catholic labor schools, the Association of Catholic Trade Unionists, and in Chicago, the Catholic Council on Working Life. There were also groups such as the Catholic Interracial Council and the Catholic Conference on Religion and Race, the National Catho-

lic Rural Life Conference—each of which tried to articulate concrete social policies that were derived from the theoretical perspectives laid down in *Quadragesimo anno*. In addition, activist groups such as the Young Christian Workers and the Young Students and the Christian Family Movement enjoyed considerable vigor in the years between the end of World War II and the Second Vatican Council. . . . In other countries there were parallel developments.

15 *Pope Pius IX: Syllabus of Errors, 8 December 1864* 10.80 in Coleman J. Barry, O.S.B., ed., *Readings in Church History Volume III* (Westminster, Maryland: the Newman Press, 1965) pp. 70-74.

16 Abbott, pp. 5-6.

17 *Pacem in terris*, #143 (http://www.csn.net/advent/docs/jo23pt.htm).

18 Ibid., #144

19 *No Bigger than Necessary*, pp. 11-12.

20 *Libertas praesentissimum*, #16. As should be obvious by now, we can trace both notions that are opposed to a global ethic as envisioned by Küng and Swidler and ideas that support such an effort to the same pope at different times and/or in different pronouncements. *Rerum novarum* contains much of value to the development of a global ethic, but this does not soften Leo's authoritarian rigidity.

21 *Casti connubii*, p. 7.

22 Ibid., p. 21.

23 An excellent (and chilling) discussion of Focolare, Communion and Liberation, and the Neochatecumenate is presented by Gordon Urquhart in *The Pope's Armada* (London: Corgi Books, Transworld Publishers, 1996).

24 *Ecclesiam suam* #51 (http://www.csn.net/advent/docs/pa06es.htm)

25 Ibid., #64-65. Cf. #78-81:

As is clear, the relationships between the Church and the world can assume many mutually different aspects. Theoretically speaking, the Church could set its mind on reducing such relationships to a minimum, endeavoring to isolate itself from dealings with secular society; just as it could set itself the task of pointing out the evils that can be found in secular society, condemning them and declaring crusades against them, so also it could approach so close to secular society as to strive to exert a preponderant influence on it or even to exercise a theocratic power over it, and so on.

But it seems to us that the relationship of the Church to the world, without precluding other legitimate forms of expression, can be represented better in a dialogue, not, of course, a dialogue in a univocal sense, but rather a dialogue adapted to the nature of the interlocutor and to factual circumstances (the dialogue with a child differs from

that with an adult; that with a believer from that with an unbeliever)
. . . .

This type of relationship indicates a proposal of courteous esteem, of understanding and of goodness on the part of the one who inaugurates the dialogue; it excludes the *a priori* condemnation, the offensive and time-worn polemic and emptiness of useless conversation. If this approach does not aim at effecting the immediate conversion of the interlocutor, inasmuch as it respects both his dignity and his freedom, nevertheless it does aim at helping him, and tries to dispose him for a fuller sharing of sentiments and convictions.

Hence, the dialogue supposes that we possess a state of mind which we intend to communicate to others and to foster in all our neighbors: It is a state of mind of one who feels within himself the burden of the apostolic mandate, of one who realizes that he can no longer separate his own salvation from the endeavor to save others, of one who strives constantly to put the message of which he is custodian into the mainstream of human discourse.

The dialogue is, then, a method of accomplishing the apostolic mission. It is an example of the art of spiritual communication.

26 Ibid., #107

27 Ibid., #108

28 Cited in Urquhart, p. 456

29 Ibid.

30 The Neocatechumenate insists on not being called a movement but "the Way."

31 Paul VI: general audience, 12th January, 1977—text translated from the original recording by Vatican Radio (http://ourworld.compuserve.com/homepages/Sbenigni/popes.htm).

32 Ibid.

33 Cf. A website developed by members of the Diocese of Clifton, Bristol, England, to publicize and protest the takeover of their parish by the Neocatechumenate, includes a letter by Karen Anderson (http://ourworld.compuserve.com/homepages/Ronald_Haynes/nc-kla1.htm) who had gone through part of the Neocatechumenal formation. She wrote that self doubt was encouraged, that lack of self worth was promoted, that people were told that they are incapable of doing good—sin is eminent, that if one doesn't agree with the Neocatechumenate it probably is because Satan is closing one's ears, that even if one thinks life is rich and growthful—it is really empty, full of suffering and is meaningless, that if someone wants to take advantage of you, let him/her—you will show them God's love and forgiveness, and

finally, that we must try to do what God wants—but of course really we can't anyway because we're sinful.

34 Ibid., p. 210

35 Ibid., p. 336-337.

36 Abbott, *Declaration on Christian Education,* # 7, p. 645

37 Fesquet, p. xiii.

38 Donald R. Campion, S.J., "The Church Today," p. 183 in Abbott, pp. 183-198.

39 Ibid., p. 184

40 Ibid., p. 185.

41 Ibid., p. 186.

42 Ibid., p. 187.

43 *Pastoral Constitution on the Church in the Modern World* # 34 in Abbott, pp. 199-308.

44 Ibid.

45 In May of 1992 I saw an interesting late medieval example of this sort of imaginative, popular harmonizing. A 15th century fresco in the tiny 8th century church of St. Prokulus at Naturns in the Vinschgau region of Northern Italy shows an angry Yahweh shoot arrows at sinful humanity. The people below are huddled under the cloaks of Mary and Jesus; they are safe because the arrow-proof mantles deflect the missiles back toward heaven!

46 See David Tracy, *The Analogical Imagination: Christian Theology and the Culture of Pluralism* (1981. New York: Crossroad, 1986), esp. pp. 405-449, where Father Tracy distinguishes between dialectical theologians of the word with their radical negative dialectic (p. 415), and analogical theologians of the imagination who articulate similarity in difference (p. 408). It should be noted, however, that Tracy's definition of "dialectical" is Barthian rather then Hegelian.

Several years ago I published a more extensive discussion of the two types of Christian imagination in "Non-Adversarial Criticism, Cross-Cultural Conversation and Popular Literature," *Proteus* 6.1 (Spring 1989), 6-15. Also see my "Religion as Poetry: The Catholic Imagination According to Andrew Greeley" in *European Legacy: Toward New Paradigms* 1.4 (1996): 1515-1521.

47 For extensive discussion of these categories and they way the were used in actual survey research, see Andrew Greeley's work, especially the *Religious Imagination* (New York: Sadlier, 1981), *Religion a Secular Theory* (New York: The Free Press, 1982), *God in Popular Culture* (Chicago, Thomas More, 1988), *Religious Change in America* (Harvard University Press, 1989), the *Catholic Myth* (New York: Charles Scribner's, 1990), and *Religion as Poetry* (New Brunswick, NJ: Transaction, 1995).

48 Hence it is not surprising that Leonard Swidler is not only working toward a Global Ethic but is also the founder of the Association for the Rights of Catholics in the Church (originally established in 1980 as response to the condemnation by the Vatican of Hans Küng and others), a group seeking to develop a Catholic Constitution to ensure fairness and due process for all Catholics, regardless of status, age, and gender. Cf. Swidler, *Toward a Catholic Constitution.*

49For an alternate exploration of this vision with special focus on ecological issues, see my article "From the Senses to Sense: the Hermeneutics of Love," Zygon: *Journal of Religion and Science* 29.4 (December 1994): 579-602.

A DIALOGIC RESPONSE

LEONARD SWIDLER

Mutombo Nkulu N'Sengha

IT WAS MOST ENCOURAGING to read the positive essay on African openness to a Global Ethic. Mutombo Nkulu, of course, is not naive or
pollyanish about the African scene. The massacres of Rwanda stand in
the way of that error, as do the ongoing civil war and oppression in the
Sudan and Algeria, and other flashpoints. However, what offers hope
are the extraordinary positive developments. Mutombo names many,
but singles out two, namely, the issuance in 1981 of the "African Charter on Human and Peoples' Rights" and the ending of the Cold War in
1990. With the new government in South Africa, and a yet newer one
in the Congo (former Zaïre), besides new hope in Nigeria—the most
populous and influential countries of sub-Saharan Africa—and the beginnings of an economic upturn, freedom, democracy and human rights
are starting to become realities in ever increasing areas of Africa.

It is apparent from Mutombo's presentation that not only is much
of Africa open to a *Global* Ethic, but is fully capable of contributing
from its own rich traditions to such an Ethic. Indeed, Mutombo's essay
substantially begins to articulate that contribution. I hope that this
promising beginning will be pursued and taken up by other African
thinkers and scholars, so as to produce, in dialogue with each other

and the rest of the globe, African versions of a Global Ethic, which can ultimately be integrated into a truly Universal Declaration of a Global Ethic.

John Hick

John Hick's main point is also developed by Ingrid Shafer. She argues that it is no surprise that the Global Ethic Project flowed not only from Western and Christian culture, but even more specifically from the "Enlightenment" mode of Vatican II Catholicism. Having once been launched, however, it must move into its next phase if it is to succeed at all. Hence, I would, along with Hick, want to reinforce my prior expressed position, urging all groups, religious, ethical, ethnic, etc. to undertake writing their own draft of what they conceive the whole globe would find ethically acceptable. As Hick also urges, it is especially vital that those outside the Western and Christian worlds create their own drafts of a Global Ethic. Only thus can the Global Ethic Project achieve its goal: by becoming global in its very conceptual articulation so that it might then become global in its implementation.

Michael Kogan

No one could disagree with Michael Kogan's examples of centrifugal rather than centripetal actions of various groups in the contemporary world. He is also doubtless correct in pointing out that the consciousness of modernity prevails largely in those levels of society which are more highly educated—the elites he calls them. Of course there are many scores or even hundreds of millions of these so-called elites, though that is still less than ten percent of the world population of nearly six billion.

However, two important factors suggests that the unhappy facts Kogan point to do not undermine the claim that the world is entering in the Second Axial Period of the "Age of Global Dialogue." First, major changes in society are always precipitated by very small percentages of the population. Second, one cannot look for complete straight line development in a world as varied as ours, especially in short periods of time.

One might add that modernity is moving into every quarter of the globe and with it what Küng spoke of as a major paradigm shift, which is of such a magnitude that Cousins designated it the Second Axial Period and I pointed to its unique character such that is constitutes a radical shift from the beginning of human history, moving out of the "Age of Monologue" into the "Age of Global Dialogue." Talk of post-modernism is largely a chimera in that it points to various "hermeneutics of suspicion," starting with Feuerbach, Marx, Nietzsche, Durkheim, and Freud already in the nineteenth century. But these were not in opposition to the fundamental thrust of the eighteenth-century Enlightenment focus on reason. Rather, they are simply expansions and deepenings of the reach of reason.

Khalid Duran

Khalid Duran notes the fundamental sympathy of Islam with a project of a Global Ethic by recalling that Mohammed did not initially intend to form one more religion in a world already over-filled with them. Rather, he wanted to call *all* men and women back to the *Urmonotheismus* of Abraham—a unifying move similar to many before and since. Duran mentions the inadvertent "founders" of Sikhism and Baha'ism, Guru Nanak and Baha'u'llah. One could add such "Western" figures as the Jew Jesus as the inadvertent "founder" of Christianity, the Catholic Augustinian monk Martin Luther as inadvertent "founder" of Lutheranism, the Anglican divine John Wesley as inadvertent "founder" of Methodism, Alexander Campbell as inadvertent "founder" of the Disciples of Christ. They all initially wished to call their fellows back to their religious wellsprings and thereby foster religious unity— but ended by adding to the panoply of religions in the world.

Duran comments that though the initial goal of unity, along with renewal, was deflected in all these initiatives, it was never completely lost, and hence there will be a fundamental openness to a project of a global ethic. These examples also should reassure those who are concerned not to lose their specific religious identity that humankind will *never* merge into a single religion. That is why, as Duran accurately reports, interreligious, intercultural dialogue aims not at uniformity but unity in diversity—*e pluribus unum*—in which the immanent pluralism remains joined with the transcendent unity. This is precisely the point of a Global Ethic—an undergirding unity or consensus which likewise recognizes (and where appropriate even celebrates) differences, arrived at through *dialogue*.

Moojan Momen

One of the most encouraging aspects of the essay by the Baha'i scholar Moojan Momen is that he undertook at least to begin to write an essay showing the Baha'i support for various components of the Draft Declaration, citing both Baha'u'llah and other authoritative sources. Momen also rendered the Global Ethic Project another important service by engaging in an initial dialogue concerning the Proposed Draft itself. How else are we to make progress in articulating a Global Ethic that is acceptable to the vast majority of humans if we do not undertake the arduous work of such close textual dialogue? Hence, I wish to take his beginning effort in this regard seriously by making an initial response to at least some of his comments. Would that we were members of an interreligious Working Group focused on spelling out a Universal Declaration of a Global Ethic that I called for in my initial essay! Then this exchange would be but the promising beginning of what I am certain would be a fruitful dialogue. But let us at least begin and trust that ways will be found to continue and deepen this indispensable dialogue.

Having expressed my deep appreciation for Momen's over all and specific positive support for the Declaration, let me turn to some of the criticisms he mentions. He states that he discerns an assumption in the Draft Declaration that humans are inherently good, and offers as evidence the Declaration's words, "such an ethic presumes a readiness and intention on the part of people to act justly." In response I would suggest that this phrase does not assume the inherent goodness or evil of humans. Rather, it is simply pointing out that when we speak of ethic we are not speaking of law. The latter one can enforce, the former is by definition something interior, something that cannot be enforced. As such, an articulated ethic will function only if, and to the extent, there is a "readiness and intention on the part of people to act justly." What a Declaration of a Global Ethic does is to announce to the world that: I/we will act in accordance with the following principles of behavior—you can morally hold me/us to them.

Momen then goes on to argue that most religions "do not agree with this humanist viewpoint." Of course it is true that in all major religions there is a strong tradition that moves "away from materialism and towards spirituality." But it is also true that most religions maintain a balancing tradition which stresses the goodness of matter itself (in the Genesis 1 creation story the text says repeatedly that the matter

God created "was good," "was good" . . . "was very good." These different approaches to "why" one should or should not do something present even in the same religions is another strong argument why a particular religious rationale for the agreed upon ethical principles in the Global Ethic cannot be brought into the text—for the simple reason that consensus on the rationales is unattainable!

Momen argues that a conceptual framework for a Declaration of a Global Ethic is necessary, "either religious or secular"—which he claims is missing in the Draft Declaration. However, he apparently does not perceive at least part of an assumed conceptual framework, which he refers to as "humanist," but rejects it. He then insists on a religious conceptual framework for he requires that a Global Ethic be based on the transcendent—even though in the next breath he acknowledges that today to insist on theism would be to exclude the hundreds of millions of Buddhists of the world.

This is a crucial issue, and in response I would argue that the Draft Declaration does provide the essential elements of a rationale for the ethical principles affirmed, but they are deliberately and necessarily clothed in language and conceptualization that does not call upon the divine or transcendent, for any such language or conceptualization would automatically exclude hundreds of millions or billions not only in the "West" but also in the former Soviet Union and in China, Japan, etc. The rationale is "humanist" in the sense that our humanity is what all humans share in common; as soon as we move beyond this humanity-based language and conceptualization we fall into serious disagreement. Of course, humanist here does not, can not, mean an exclusion of the divine or transcendent; it merely means that one cannot insist upon it. Rather, whether one affirms the transcendent is the individual free choice of each human.

Another thought is prompted by Momen's reflection that each civilization is shaped by a religion at its heart. This has certainly been true—up to the present, for now we are entering into, not a time of a Chinese civilization, or an Islamic civilization, or a Christian civilization, or even a Western civilization. Rather, we are, *nolens volens*, entering a time of Global Civilization. In the past the religion Islam was the spiritual center of the Islamic civilization, Confucianism/Taoism of the Chinese civilization, etc., but what will be at the heart of the pluralistic global civilization? The only possible answer is, not any particular religion or ideology, including not a synthesized religion-ideol-ogy. Rather, the heart of the emerging pluralistic *Global Civilization* is *Interreligious, Intercultural Dialogue*—and that fact is reflected in the present Draft Declaration.

Lastly, Momen lifts up two key words of the Draft Declaration, "democracy" and "liberty," and wonders out loud about some extreme, rather destructive interpretations of those terms. I must confess to not find this kind of deliberate focusing on obvious distortions of terms a helpful exercise. It seems to be more debate-like than like dialogue; from the former usually comes only irritation, or at best amusement, whereas the latter will always move individuals and groups closer, and may well even resolve conceptual issues. In the face of such reflections one thinks of responses like: "Even the devil can quote the Bible for his purposes"; the corruption of the best becomes the worst (*corruptio optimae pessima*); the presence of the "crazies" on the fringe of an idea or movement, far from discrediting that idea or movement, is proof that it is about something terribly important.

As I wrote, this can only be the beginning of what I am certain will be a very long, ongoing dialogue about very important issues, and I am very grateful to Moojan Momen for the engagement.

Kana Mitra

One traditionally expects an open, tolerant attitude from Hindu think-ers and scholars. We find that in Kana Mitra's essay here. There is the emphasis on oneness in diversity. But there is more in Mitra's essay as well. She is aware of the elements of absolutism (the essay was written before the Hindu Nationalist Party took power in India and conducted nuclear explosions) and broadly oppressed groups, such as the Dalits (Untouchables) and women, within Hinduism, and is healthily criti-cal of them. Beyond that, as a Hindu, Mitra finds no insurmountable difficulty in collaborating with the rest of the globe, including India's former colonizer, the Christian West, in agreeing to a Global Ethic. The problem, she notes, is practicing the Ethic once it is agreed to!

Who can argue with noting this perennial human defect? How-ever, the raising of the consciousness of peoples around the world to the need for a Global Ethic, then the articulating of it on a broad, par-ticipatory basis, and finally the public committing of all religious and ethical communities to that Global Ethic will provide a very helpful rod to stiffen the moral spine of the religious and ethical communities to live up to their promises. It is precisely that to which this whole Global Ethic Project is dedicated.

Fu San Zhao

Reading the essay by Professor Fu San Zhao, makes the "congruence" of a Global Ethic and the two indigenous Chinese "religions," Confucianism and Taoism, abundantly apparent. The core of former is the notion of "ren," or humanness in all its fullness, both individual and communal. The heart of the second is the harmonizing of humanity and nature. Taken together, these two foci largely frame the contemporary program for a Global Ethic. Hence, I am very grateful for this explicitation of the Confucian and Taoist support for a Global Ethic.

I likewise wish to lift up and emphasize the final points Professor Zhao makes, for they are critical at this juncture if the project of a Global Ethic is to proceed fruitfully. The first of the final three points made is that the *dialogue* **is** the Global Ethic. This is perhaps a deliberate exaggeration, but there is nevertheless a core truth in it. A Global Ethic cannot be imposed from above in a pluralist situation. It can be discerned only through patient dialogue. And, once initially arrived at, it will forever expand through continuous dialogue, for the problems of how to act ethically will constantly face new challenges resulting from the always changing world.

Professor Zhao believes that we cannot yet formulate the Global Ethic, that it lies in the future. In a very real sense, I agree with him most profoundly: any articulation of a Global Ethic now—very much including the three printed in this volume—can only be incohative, tentative, serving as stimuli. Many, many groups need to articulate the basic principles of ethical behavior they believe everyone can agree to, share them with each other and make them available to eventually be integrated into what will become the universally agreed-to (through dialogue) Universal Declaration of a Global Ethic.

The third point made is really a variant of the above, namely, that the discussion of, the *dialogue* about, the Global Ethic is in itself profoundly valuable. It will bring the vital issues of fundamental ethics and dialogue themselves to the forefront of human consciousness on a global scale. As that happens, the momentum engendered will carry the project to undreamed of creative consequences.

Shu-Hsien Liu

Though I was familiar with the contemporary revival of Confucianism growing out of Taiwan—in which Professor Liu is a major contributor—it was most encouraging to learn more of the creativity and openness that pervades this movement. It is no wonder that Contemporary Neo-Confucian scholars like Liu are supportive of the Global Ethic Project. The essence of Contemporary Neo-Confucianism is the bringing of the core values of the ancient tradition into an open dialogue with the best values of modernity.

This dialogical approach, which is at the heart of the "Age of Global Dialogue," is one which has deep roots in Chinese religion and culture. There have been, of course, vigorous, at times even rancorous, differences among Chinese religious and philosophical schools of thought and practice. Still, China is known as the land of the three religions: Confucianism, Taoism, Buddhism. For centuries Chinese people thought it perfectly reasonable to understand themselves as full participants in two or more religions—something quite unimaginable for most Jews, Christians or Muslims. Consequently, there have been almost no religious wars in Chinese history, again, quite unlike the histories of Christianity and Islam, and modern Israel.

The lesson to be drawn from this aspect of Chinese history is not that all should become adherents of two or more religions, but that nonviolence and respect for the religiously and ideologically other is at the heart of what it means to be human, to be *ren*. To be human fundamentally means to be free, and to be free one must receive respect—implying, of course, that one must also give respect. One might at this point be thinking that the China of the past half century has been anything but nonviolent and respectful to those religiously and ideologically other; Marxism became the club with which to beat all things and persons religious and those ideologically different. To be sure—but Marxism, as the name clearly indicates, is a Western import, sprung from a German Jew.

Contemporary Neo-Confucianism, however, looked in a quite different direction when it stood on its own critically re-appropriated ancient tradition and opened itself to the contemporary West. It looked to the values of democracy and modern critical-thinking science. It found a convergence in its own valuing of *ren* and Western *demos*. There was seen to be a fusion of horizons between the relationship between heaven and humanity, *T'ien-ren-ho-i*, and the Judeo-Christian doctrine of humanity being the image of God, the *imago Dei*. Here, of course, is the foundation of a Global Ethic, which is reflected in the versions of the Golden Rule found in the Chinese and Judeo-Christian traditions, along with most other religious.

Chung Ok Lee

Chung Ok Lee reflects well the fusion of the ancient insights of Siddharta Gautama, the Buddha, with a fundamental acceptance of science and modernity wrought by the founder of the twentieth-century Korean Buddhist sect, Won Buddhism. There is no fleeing from modern material civilization—only its excesses. And who can fault that? Chung goes still further in abetting the formation of a Global Ethic by promoting the building of a "utopia," not unlike Teilhard de Chardin's image of "building the earth." In fact, Chung takes up the themes of the contemporary ecological movement and moves with it beyond the traditional Buddhist care for all sentient being (on the popular level practiced because all we humans may have been and/or will be one day nonhuman sentient beings); she insists that our Global Ethic must care for all the earth community, not just sentient beings.

In fact, all the fundamental contemporary values of modernity are embraced by Chung, giving the lie to the strange notion that the values of human liberty, social justice for all oppressed and marginalized, care for the entire environment, and equality for women are solely "Western" values, that somehow "Asian values" are different and don't include them. There no doubt are special contributions that Asian cultures make to the modern world, but the above named values are not alien to Asians, as some Asian political leaders have publicly claimed. Such tactics of "divide and conquer" are as old as Rome, and more so; they were more recently touted by the dictatorial communist leaderships of Eastern Europe and China, but such strategies of oppression were roundly rejected by their peoples as soon as given a chance.

Brian (Daizen) A. Victoria

It is especially heartening to read the reflections of a Zen Master who is also thoroughly self-critical in the area of ethics. I have seen those enamored of Zen Buddhism agonize over the apparently amoral attitude and behavior of Buddhist institutions in social, economic, military and political matters—just as I have seen contemporary Christians agonize. Perhaps because Christianity is the religion identified with the socially, economically, militarily and politically triumphant, it has become not uncommon for many Christians to become scathingly self-critical, but it has been much less so for those religions related to the not-triumphant nations and cultures: Confucianism, Islam, Buddhism, etc. Daizen Victoria contributes here to the redressing of that imbalance.

We also see in Zen as presented here the epitome of the saying that "all politics is local politics." Or again the motto: "think globally, act locally." We find there in Zen the ageless religious, human wisdom: "While it is not given to us to know whether or not in the end we will succeed with a virtuous action, it is not permitted to us not to attempt." Somehow this is what it means to be human, to be self-transcending. In the Judeo-Christian tradition that is what it means to be an image of God, to partake of the infinite; in the Buddhist tradition that is what it means to live in union with one's Buddhanature. This why it is vital that each group of humans attempt to create the Global Ethic in dialogue with each other.

Ingrid Shafer

Ingrid Shafer makes a very strong case for the congruence of the Global Ethic Project with what she sees as the best strand of the Catholic tradition, the one she associates with Jesus' loving, affirming mental mode and manner of acting. She finds the roots of support for a Global Ethic going all the way back to the beginning of the Bible with the creation stories' affirmation of the goodness of humanity and of all creation, including matter. Shafer, however, does not paint a one-sided picture of the Catholic tradition, but lays out those negative, body- and world-hating strands which have from the first century (though clearly not from that devout Jew, Jesus of Nazareth, but from the surrounding Hellenistic culture) infested Christianity down to the present day.

I believe that she very rightly sees a great leap forward for humankind in the eighteenth-century Enlightenment with its stress on human freedom, human rights, self-responsibility and reason—despite its shortcomings and partial myopia. Indeed, what human effort does not have its shortcomings? None can stand on it own shoulders; only its successors, and beneficiaries, can. Shafer likewise correctly sees the second huge leap forward for Catholics and all those affected by Catholics (given that there are one billion Catholics, and if they each affect significantly in some way two others, that three billion constitutes over one half of the present world population!) coming in Vatican Council II (1962-65) with its five-fold Copernican Turn: 1) to a historical, dynamic understanding of all reality, 2) to freedom as central to humanness, 3) to internal reform of the Catholic Church, 4) to *dialogue* with the "other", 5) to concern for this world.

Here is the potential foundation for the Global Ethic Project. So, Shafer is absolutely right to link the conceiving and launching of the Global Ethic Project with the "Enlightenment" of the Catholic Church at the Second Vatican Council. It is doubtless no accident that Hans Küng and I launched the Project in 1991 with our declaration in the first issue of the *Journal of Ecumenical Studies*[1], that since the 1950s we both have been closely associated with the Catholic Theological Faculty of the University of Tübingen, a wellspring of progressive Catholic thought since the Enlightenment, that Küng was intimately involved in the Second Vatican Council, that in its midst, in 1963, my wife Arlene and I founded the *Journal of Ecumenical Studies* (with Küng as an Associate Editor from the beginning), which was subsequently named the foremost *dialogue* publication of the world by the Directors of the ecumenical and interreligious dialogue institutes all around the globe. In all this she rightly sees *dialogue* as the core characteristic giving birth to the Global Ethic Project.

Conclusion

Let me close this volume by reiterating the plea expressed several times earlier by myself and many of the other dialogue partners here:

First, the Global Ethic Project must include the broadest possible of involvement of individuals, groups and communities around the world in the articulation of the Global Ethic.

Second, every conceivable group should in a spirit of dialogue focus on the study of the question of a Global Ethic and attempt to articulate what it believes to be the basic principles of ethics all human beings, regardless of their particular religious or ethical commitment, would be able to affirm. This version will have the special advantage of incorporating that group's specific contribution to the building of a Global Ethic.

Each group should then send in their version of a Global Ethic to:

> Professor Leonard Swidler
> Center for Global Ethics
> C/o *Journal of Ecumenical Studies*
> Temple University (022-38)
> 1114 W. Berks St., Philadelphia, PA 19122-6090
> Tel: 215-204-7251; Fax: 215-204-4569
> E-mail: dialogue@vm.temple.edu
> E-mail Forum: g-ethic@listserv.temple.edu
> Web: http://blue.temple.edu/~dialogue

The Center for Global Ethics—in collaboration with others, such as Hans Küng's Foundation for Global Ethics—will serve as a collection and collation center for the various versions of a Global Ethic developed around the world, and will collaborate with all other pertinent organizations to set up a representative commission to articulate, out of the richness of the documents sent in from around the world, an integrated version of a "Universal Declaration of a Global Ethic" and distribute it as widely as possible. It will utilize all available means to do this, including traditional publishing and distribution, as well as radio, television, internet, use in classrooms, churches, synagogues, mosques, temples, etc., civil organizations . . . . wherever our creative imaginations can take us.

Third, The Center for Global Ethics will collaborate with all pertinent organizations to devise an appropriate time, place and structure for the widest possible ratification of and public commitment to the finally accepted "Universal Declaration of a Global Ethic," as well as ways to monitor its implementation, and forums to continue the dialogue which will continually expand the Global Ethic on into the future.

Dear Reader, if you have come this far, then don't just sit there. Do something! Get your groups and organizations actively involved in this Global Ethic Project. Be in contact with us at the Center for Global Ethics, letting us know what you are undertaking, sharing your progress and problems—we will pass your news on to all the others involved around the world, particularly through our web site and our interactive e-mail forum (which you are urged to join by sending an e-mail message to: listserv@listserv.temple.edu and say: subscribe g-ethic).

Footnotes

1 Leonard Swidler and Hans Küng, "Editorial: Toward a Universal Declaration of a Global Ethos," *Journal of Ecumenical Studies*, 28, 1 (Winter, 1991), pp. 123-125. Another 24 world renowned religious scholars from various religious traditions added their signatures.

ABOUT THE AUTHORS

LEONARD SWIDLER (Catholic [American]), Professor of Catholic Thought and Interreligious Dialogue at Temple University, Co-Founder with his wife Professor Arlene Anderson Swidler, and Editor of the *Journal of Ecumenical Studies*, is the author/editor of sixty books, including *Bursting the Bonds. A Jewish-Christian Dialogue on Jesus and Paul* (Orbis, 1990), *After the Absolute. The Dialogical Future of Religious Reflection* (Fortress, 1990), and *Muslims in Dialogue* (Mellen, 1992). He is also the Co-Founder-Director of the Global Dialogue Institute.

HANS KÜNG (Catholic [Swiss]) has been at the forefront of interfaith dialogue for the last 30 years. He was director of the Institute of Ecumenical Research at the University of Tübingen. Since 1997 he has served as President of the new Foundation for Global Ethics. His best-selling books include *On Being a Christian, Does God Exist?, Christianity and the World Religions: Paths to Dialogue with Islam, Hinduism, and Buddhism* (with Joseph van Ess, Heinrich von Steitencron and Heinz Bechert), and *Global Responsibility: In Search of a New World Ethic*.

MUTOMBO NKULU N'SENGHA (Catholic [African]) was born and raised in the Democratic Republic of the Congo (formerly Zaire), studied at the Grand Seminaire Saint Paul (Lubumbashi) and the Jesuit Institut Superieur de Philosophie (Kinshasa) from 1978 to 1989, the Gregorian University, the Biblicum and the Instituto G. Lazzati e Caymari in Rome, 1989 to 1992, and completed his Ph.D. in religious studies at Temple University in 1998. He has been the Editor-in-Chief of *Forum Zarois*, a journal promoting democracy and human rights in Central Africa; he has taught at Haverford College, Montclair State University and at present is professor of African philosophy and religion in the Department of Afro-American Studies of Temple University. He has published several scholarly articles and is completing a book on an African theology of human rights.

JOHN HICK (Presbyterian [English]), winner of the 1991 Grawemeyer Award for the most significant new thinking in religion during the past five years, is a Fellow of the Institute for Advanced Research in the Hunanities at Birminghan University, UK, and Danforth Professor of the Philosophy of Religion, emeritus, at the Claremont Graduate School, California. He is the author of many books on theology and the philosophy or relition, including *An Interpretation of Religion; Faith and Knowledge; Problems of Religious Pluralism; Arguments for the Existence of God; Three Faiths—One God: A Jewish, Christian, Muslim Encounter;* and *God and the Universe of Faiths*.

MICHAEL S. KOGAN (Jewish [American]) has taught at Montclair State University, Upper Montclair, NJ, since 1973, and chairs its Department of Philosophy and Religious Studies. He chairs the Interfaith Committee of Essex and was a founding member of "The Rainbow Group" (Jewish and Christian theologians). His articles have appeared in *Faith and Thought*, the *National Dialogue Newsletter*, *Journal of Ecumenical Studies* , and a forthcoming anthology on the Abrahamic faiths from Catholic University Press.

KHALID DURAN (Muslim [Spanish]), has taught Islamic studies in Pakistan, Germany and the United States. He is the author of several books and many articles on Islam and interreligious dialogue, including *Islam und politischer Extremismus* (Deutsches Orient-Institute, 1985), and since 1995 is the Founder and Editor of the quarterly journal *TransStateIslam*.

MOOJAN MOMEN (Baha'i [Iranian]) is a graduate of the University of Cambridge. He is author of numerous books and academic articles in the fields of Islamic and Baha'i studies, including *An Introduction to Shi'i Islam* (Yale University Press) and *Hinduism and the Baha'i Faith*. (George Ronald).

FUSAN ZHAO (Anglican [Chinese]) was born, raised, educated and ordained an Anglican priest in China. He rose to the rank of Vice President of the Chinese Academy of Social Sciences in Beijing. As a scholar he specialized in the history of ideas. He publicly insisted in China that religion is not the opiate of the people, but a deposit of the spiritual experience and cultures of every people in the world. In the spring of 1989 he was doing research in Berlin and protested the armed suppression of students at Tian-an-men, June, 1989, and was subsequently condemned by the Chinese authorities. Since then he has been a scholar-in-exile in Germany, France and the United States.

SHU-HSIEN LIU (Confucian [Chinese]) received his Ph.D. in Philosophy from Southern Illinois University. He taught at Tunghai University in Taiwan and Southern Illinois University, and has been Professor and Chair of Chinese Philosophy at The Chinese University of Hong Kong since 1981. He has published many articles and books both in English and in Chinese, including books on Chu Hsi (3rd rev. and enlarged ed., 1995) and Huang Tsung-hsi (1986) in Chinese. His most recent publication in English is: *Understanding Confucian Philosophy: Classical and Sung-Ming* (Greenwood Press and Praeger Paperback, 1998).

KANA MITRA (Hindu [Indian]) received an MA in philosophy from Calcutta University in 1956 and a Ph.D. in religion from Temple University in 1980. She taught at Calcutta University for over ten years and more than two decades at several U.S. universities. She has published a number of scholarly articles and the book *Catholicism-Hinduism: A Vedantic Investigation of Raimundo Panikkar's Attempt at Bridge Building* (1987). She is an Associate Editor of the *Journal of Ecumenical Studies*.

CHUNG OK LEE, having received full ordination in 1981 in Korea, is an Associate Professor at the Graduate School of Won Buddhism at Won Kwang University in Korea, Main Representative of Won Buddhism International to the United Nations, and Head Minister of the Manhattan Won Buddhist Temple. She earned a Ph.D in Religious Education from New York University in 1996 and has been International President of the 1993 Parliament of World's Religions in Chicago, President of the Committee of Religious Non-Governmental Organizations at the United Nations, and Co-Chair of Values Caucus at the United Nations. Dr. Lee is both a peace activist and a scholar and has delivered keynote addresses in many international interreligious conferences.

PROFESSOR BRIAN A. VICTORIA (Zen Buddhist [American]) holds a M.A. in Buddhist Studies (Soto Zen), Komazawa University in Tokyo, and a Ph.D. from the Department of Religion of Temple University. He also holds a first degree black belt in the martial discipline of Aikido and is a priest in the Soto Zen tradition, having received Dharma transmission from the Ven. Asada Daisen, chief abbot of Jokuin Temple in Saitama Prefecture. His writings include an autobiographical work in Japanese entitled *Gaijin de ari, Zenbozu de ari* (As a Foreigner, As a Zen Priest), (San-ichi Shobo, 1971); *Zen Master Dogen*, co-authored with Prof. Yokoi Yuho of Aichi-gakuin University (John Weatherhill, 1976); a translation of *The Zen Life* by Sato Koji (John Weatherhill, 1972); and *Zen at War* (John Weatherhill, 1997). Non-violent opposition to U.S. involvement in the Vietnam War, coupled with support for political prisoners throughout Asia, led to his imprisonment in Japan and deportation from the Republic of China on Taiwan, the People's Republic of China, South Korea, South Vietnam, and Japan. At present, Dr. Victoria lectures in the Department of Asian Languages and Literatures, University of Auckland (Tamaki Campus), New Zealand.

INGRID H. SHAFER (Catholic [American]), is Professor of Philosophy and Religion and Mary Jo Ragan Professor of Inter-disciplinary Studies at the University of Science and Arts of Oklahoma where she has taught since 1968. A native of Innsbruck, Austria, she began her graduate studies at Vienna and Innsbruck. She holds Master's degrees in Literature and Human Relations, as well as a Ph.D. in Philosophy from the University of Oklahoma. Among her books are *Eros and the Womanliness of God* and *The Incarnate Imagination*.